SuSE

SuSE Linux

USER GUIDE

1. edition 2003

Please direct suggestions and comments to documentation@suse.de

Authors: Stefanie Haefner, Carsten Fischer, Viviane Glanz, Holger Hetterich, Johannes Meixner, Matthias Nagorny, Siegfried Olschner, Marcus Schäfer, Arvin Schnell, Adrian Schröter, Gabriele Strattner, Rebecca Walter
Translators: Daniel Pisano, Tino Tanner
Editors: Jörg Arndt, Antje Faber, Roland Haidl, Jana Jaeger, Edith Parzefall, Peter Reinhart, Thomas Rölz, Thomas Schraitle, Rebecca Walter
Layout: Manuela Piotrowski, Thomas Schraitle
Setting: LaTeX

This book has been printed on 100 % chlorine-free bleached paper.

Contents

Welcome

SuSE Linux is an easy-to-install Linux distribution. In the past few releases, the installation and configuration tool YaST has undergone serious development. Install with just a few clicks or choose to customize aspects of the installation to your specific needs. Both the quick install method and the customized method are explained in this manual. Also find information to help new Linux users get started.

Configuration is also easy with YaST. Aspects of configuration, such as hardware administration and Internet access, are the topic of the second part of the manual. It also discusses configuration of the desktop environments KDE and GNOME.

SuSE Linux includes a range of applications. Some of these are introduced in the third section. OpenOffice.org, which has replaced StarOffice as the standard office package in the distribution, is described extensively. Multimedia and graphics applications, such as those used for scanning and modifying images and playing sound files, are also introduced. Chapters discussing web browsers and e-mail programs can help you choose your ideal tools for the Internet.

SuSE also addresses your needs for more information and support in the final section. Find information about installation support and online help. Also get answers to frequently asked questions and, in the glossary, definitions of important terms.

Illustrations of the SuSE 8.2 Distributions

Personal Edition

The illustration for the Personal Edition shows a surface constructed by Werner Boy in 1901, which represents an immersion of the real projective plane in the three-dimensional real space. The image was calculated with the help of the `surf` application (see `http://surf.sourceforge.net`), using the following equation:

$$\begin{aligned}36zy^4 + 36x^2z^4 + 36x^4z - 243x^4y^2 - 243x^2y^4 + 36z^4y^2 + 72x^2zy^2 \\ -48\sqrt{2}z^3y^3 + 72\sqrt{2}y^2z^3x - 90y^4z^2 - 16y^2z^2 - 16z^2x^2 - 90z^2x^4 \\ -81y^6 - 24z^6 + 48z^5 - 32z^4 + 64/9z^3 - 81x^6 - 180y^2z^2x^2 \\ -24\sqrt{2}z^3x^3 + 48\sqrt{2}y^3z^2 - 144\sqrt{2}yz^2x^2 - 324\sqrt{2}y^4zx \\ -216\sqrt{2}y^2zx^3 + 108\sqrt{2}zx^5 + 144\sqrt{2}x^2z^3y &= 0\end{aligned}$$

Refer to `http://www.OliverLabs.net/suse/` for more information. The `surf` file used for drawing the image is available for download.

Professional Edition

The illustration for the Professional Edition is a quintic surface with four higher-order double points. To be able to draw the projective equation

$$\begin{aligned}(x+z)^2(y^3+w^3) + (y+w)^2(x^3+z^3) \\ +(8yzw + 8xzw + 8xyw + 8xyz)(y+w)(x+z) \\ +4y^2w^2(x+z) + 4x^2z^2(y+w) &= 0\end{aligned}$$

of the tetrahedron-symmetrical surface with the `surf` application (see `http://surf.sourceforge.net`), the tetrahedral coordinates

$$x' = z-1+\sqrt{2}x, \quad y' = z-1-\sqrt{2}x, \quad z' = -(z+1+\sqrt{2}y), \quad w' = -(z+1--\sqrt{2}y)$$

were used. Refer to `http://www.OliverLabs.net/suse/` for more information. The `surf` file used for drawing the image is available for download.

Typographical Conventions

The following typographic conventions are used in this book:

Example	Meaning
YaST	programs
`/etc/passwd`	files or directories
⟨*placeholder*⟩	replace the character string `placeholder` (including the angle brackets) with the actual value
`PATH`	an environment variable called `PATH`
`192.168.1.2`	the value of a variable
`ls`	commands
`user`	users
`earth:~ #` **`ls`**	enter the command `ls` in the shell of the user `root` in his home directory on the host "Earth"
`newbie@earth:~ >` **`ls`**	enter the command `ls` in the shell of the user `newbie` in his home directory on the host "Earth"
`C:\>` **`fdisk`**	at the DOS prompt, enter the command `fdisk`
(Alt)	press this key; keys to press sequentially are separated by spaces
(Ctrl) + (Alt) + (Del)	keys to press simultaneously are connected with a `'+'`
"Permission denied"	system messages
'System update'	menu item or button text 'System update'
☞*boot*	reference to an entry in the glossary in the appendix

Acknowledgments

Developers have contributed a great deal of voluntary work to Linux, cooperating on a world-wide basis to make the project thrive. We would like to thank them for their effort. Without them, this distribution would not exist. Additional thanks go to Frank Zappa and Pawar.

Special thanks, of course, to Linus Torvalds.

Have a lot of fun!

Your SuSE Team

Migrating to Linux

This chapter is intended mainly for people coming from other operating systems who are about to use Linux for the first time. The text is organized as a list of questions and answers to talk about the most important doubts and issues arising when first using Linux.

At the end of this manual, find a glossary explaining important concepts and a list of frequently asked questions about SuSE Linux. Both of them are a good complement to the present chapter.

The answers are based on a standard installation of SuSE Linux. If you have already customized your system, the answers still apply, but take into account the changed settings.

Important Requirements

- *How much hard disk space do I need? What will happen to my Windows?* Naturally, a Linux installation requires an amount of hard disk space. About 1.5 GB of free space is required for a standard installation. 400 MB may be sufficient for a minimum system. SuSE Linux can be installed as the only operating system on the computer. However, it can also share the hard disks with other operating systems. In this case, it needs at least one free partition.

  If you have installed Windows and there are several partitions (drive C: and other hard disk drives), theoretically you can install SuSE Linux on one of the additional partitions. If the partition in which to install Linux contains data, first save it to another partition.

  If your previous system consisted of a single partition that occupies the entire hard disk, SuSE Linux can easily and speedily resize it, provided it is a "FAT" file system (FAT or FAT32), which is the case with Windows 95, 98, and ME. If your Windows (NT, 2000, or XP) uses a partition with an NTFS file system, this partition cannot be resized by SuSE Linux.

  If Windows XP was preinstalled using the NTFS file system, but you have the installation CDs, you can reinstall Windows XP and select "FAT32" as file system for XP. This causes the hard disk to be formatted with the FAT file system, which can easily be resized during the Linux installation.

  Note

  A FAT32 partition must be smaller than 32 GB.

  Note

  Instructions for partitioning hard disks and resizing your Windows system are provided in *Resizing a Windows Partition* on page 27.

Working with Linux

- *Are there programs for Linux that I can use to read my old files created under Windows?*
  For the most part, you can continue to use your old files under Linux. Standard programs, such as OpenOffice.org and The GIMP, can handle most of the file formats you have used so far, whether they are for documents, pictures or other graphics, or video or audio data. SuSE Linux

comes with a suitable application for all of these and lets you work with your old files without difficulty.

- *Where can I get applications for Linux?*
  SuSE Linux comes with the programs and applications needed for daily work. Just click the SuSE menu at the bottom left of your KDE desktop to find out about them. Many programs are available.

- *Why can't I simply switch off my computer?*
  You should not simply switch a computer off. It is important to shut down properly. Shutting the computer down properly avoids data losses. Simply switching a running system off is like a knock-out. A second user may using your computer by way of a network connection. If you simply switch the system off, you will also endanger the data the other user has not yet saved. The same also applies to your data. However, if you log out and shut down properly, you can be sure that all data is saved.

- *How do I format a floppy disk for Linux?*
  The easiest way to do this is with the KDE floppy formatter. To start this tool, click the SuSE menu at the bottom left of your desktop then select 'System' →'Tools' →'KFloppy'. Choose between the FAT format (used for DOS and Windows) and Linux's own ext2 file system format. You could also use mtools. More information is available in *mtools* on page 310.

- *Where can I find a description of the included software and how can I get help for the many programs that come with SuSE Linux?*
  Click the SuSE help button. A window opens on your desktop from which to access the SuSE Help System and find answers to all your questions.

- *What is a virtual desktop?*
  You may run into a situation where you want to have so many windows open that things get a little disorganized. Under Linux, this problem can easily be avoided: Look at the panel to find the numbered icons of the available virtual desktops, which represent different spaces where you can open and arrange windows.

  Then switch between virtual desktops at any moment to access the windows.

- *Where is the file manager?*
  Try Konqueror, which is not only a file manager, but also a web browser, viewer application, and more. Konqueror is the KDE program of choice for anything related to file management.

Files, Folders, and Directories

- *What happened to drive C:?*
  Drives are storage media, such as a floppy disk, a CD-ROM, or a hard disk. You have probably come to know these under the names `A:`, `C:`, `D:`, and so on. Unlike Windows, however, Linux incorporates all drives directly into the system's directory structure. The result is that drives are not accessed using names like C:, but using folders (names of storage areas) to tell the user where data is located.

- *What is root?*
  The root directory is identified by a slash (`'/'`). The Linux file system normally holds a directory tree that starts at a / and is subdivided into many branches. These subdirectories have names like `home`, (a subdirectory for personal files of users) or `bin` (which contains binary files — mostly programs). The place where the entire directory tree originates is called the "root directory". From this point, access all the subdirectories. Theoretically, it would be possible to call the root directory by a name, but it is historically known as `/`. Each directory or folder will also have a slash in front of its name. Each such folder could, in turn, be used as the root of another, separate file system.

- *Where are things located in the file system?*
  Linux has a number of standard directories. The most important of them are explained below. For a more complete overview, see Figure 21.1 on page 303.

  `/home`
  : This is where the home directories of individual users are located. Your home directory contains all your data, personal configuration files, and anything else to which only you should have access. The majority of this data is readable for other users but can only be changed by the owner. This default setting can be changed at any time. To learn more about this, read *File System Permissions* on page 311.

  `/root`
  : The home directory of the administrator `root`.

  `/usr` (Unix System Resources)
  : Many programs are stored under this directory together with help files, documentation, and other important data.

/bin and /sbin (executable files)

These directories hold many programs closely related to the operating system itself, which are needed early in the boot procedure.

/opt (optional software)

Commercial software and very big packages not forming part of the system itself go into this directory. This includes things like KDE, Netscape, Mozilla, and some others.

/etc (configuration directory)

Files related to the system configuration are stored in this folder. This includes things like the setup information for your Internet access, the boot configuration, and the configuration of individual programs, such as backup routines.

/boot (directory for system boot files)

This is the place where any files and programs needed for booting are stored, such as the Linux kernel.

Others

In addition to that, there are other folders containing information about the system and the devices connected to it:

/lib and /usr/lib (libraries), /var (variable data), /proc (processes), /media (removable storage media like the floppy and CD-ROM), /dev (all connected devices, such as printers, hard disks, and the keyboard).

More information is available in *Files and Directories* on page 303.

Passwords, Users, and root

- *Why do I need a password?*

  The password is the key to your home directory. Unlike other operating systems, Linux is a true multiuser system: files and settings of different users are managed while keeping them separate and those different users can access the system at the same time. If you imagine that your machine had two keyboards and two screens, you could use it alongside another user without getting in each other's way.

  Linux distributes system resources between active users in an intelligent way, so if that other keyboard and screen were located in another room (because they are connected to the system through a network), you probably would not even notice that there is another user at work.

  Each user has a private directory — the home directory. The home directory is used for all personal data as well as for personal configuration settings of applications. Examples of this are the web browser's bookmark list and the address book of an e-mail program. For security reasons, the whole area is protected with a password. Full access to this personal data is only granted if this password is known.

- *Who is root?*
  Root is one of several users on your Linux system, a multiuser system. However, `root` is a very special user in that it is the most powerful one on your machine and consequently the one that requires the greatest degree of responsibility. Like a building manager for a building, `root` is responsible for the entire Linux system, making sure that it runs reliably, that the infrastructure works, that all programs are up to date, and that none of the "occupants" transgress the rights of others. Again like a building manager, root owns the master key for the entire Linux system, enabling this user to change things that are not possible for normal users. Also, `root` has access to the main directory / and all its subdirectories. For all these reasons, this user is called `root`.

  Caution

  Make it a rule to only log in as `root` on your system if this is really required for the job. Examples for this are the creation of a new user account or the installation of programs. In general, the system will explicitly prompt you to enter the root password (the master key) if a particular action requires it.

  Caution

- *Why can I read some files but cannot delete them?*
  You do not have the necessary permissions. After reading the password that you have entered, the system will not only know about your home directory, but also about the permissions you have as a user — the things you are allowed to do and those you are not. For instance, you have the permissions to read most of the files in `/etc`, but changing them would require the permissions of the system administrator. Directories with files affecting the security and stability of the system are read-only for normal users or are completely inaccessible to them.

  In your home directory, however, it is entirely up to you to decide which files should be hidden from other users or which are shared. To set this in Konqueror, right-click the file then select 'Properties'.

- *How can I add or remove users?*
  New users must be created by `root`. Always log in as `root` to perform tasks related to system administration, such as creating a new user. To

do so, start the YaST2 Control Center as a normal user, enter the `root` password, and click the key to select 'Security and Users'. To the right, you can see a number of options, including 'User Administration'. Select 'Create a New User'. The new user account can be created after you have filled out the fields (First name, Last name) and provided a password.

When entering a password, be sure to distinguish between uppercase and lowercase letters. A password should be at least five characters long and must not include special characters, such as accents. The characters #*,.;:._-+!$%&/ | ? are allowed, however, as are spaces and any of the digits from 0 to 9. Normally, you should make up a password consisting of about eight characters. To make certain the password has been entered correctly, it must be reentered in a second input field.

Let YaST2 create the user name for you then edit the field or create a user name yourself. A user name may only consist of lowercase letters (without umlauts), the three characters ._- and digits. The restrictions on user names are somewhat stronger than those on passwords.

To start working at the system, identify yourself by providing this user name and the password. This is commonly called the login procedure.

To delete a user, select 'Edit and Create Users'. In the dialog, select the corresponding user from the list and click 'Delete'.

Mounting, Shell, and Other Topics

- *How do I read my media (CDs, floppy disks, ZIP, etc.) with Linux?*
  In KDE, click the corresponding icon (CD, floppy disk, or ZIP) to open a window with the corresponding content. KDE actually runs `mount` in the background to bind the selected medium to your system. Because the medium is mounted, it needs to be unmounted before it can be ejected.

  Why is this necessary?
  This might seem a Linux oddity at first, but it is actually quite practical. To a Linux file system, it does not matter what kind of medium is mounted in used: whether it is a floppy, a DVD, a hard disk, or a ZIP disk. By mounting them, they are registered with the system. On a system available to many users, this is important, because several users and several programs can access the same directory at the same time.

  Imagine that someone came to your office and exchanged the drawers in your desk because he needed to work there for an hour. When you come back after a while, you cannot find that draft contract that must be ready before tomorrow — the drawer is not where is used to be. Therefore, under Linux any drives or media (the "drawers" of the file system) must be explicitly mounted and unmounted.

- *Working with the Shell*
  With Linux, there are always several ways to achieve a particular goal. This may be a bit confusing at first, but has many advantages. If a particular function fails or becomes unavailable for some reason, the same commands can be given to the computer by other means.

  For instance, if a program cannot be started with a mouse click from a menu, enter the program name with the keyboard and still launch the application. As another example, to see the contents of a directory, use the text command `ls`.

  Such commands are entered in a text console, a small, no-frills text window (also referred to as the "shell") that enables you to control almost every aspect of your computer. Experienced users often prefer the console. It makes it possible to combine different commands into one long command line, which then might act like a new, small program. This may have practical advantages over using the mouse, depending on what you want to achieve. Learn more about working with the shell in *Introduction to Bash* on page 302.

Quick Installation

In the best case, a few clicks are sufficient to install SuSE Linux on your computer. If no Linux system was installed on your computer previously, your hard disk is automatically partitioned, an installed Windows system (95, 98, or ME) is resized, a software selection is installed, and your hardware is configured automatically. If you do not like the suggestions of the system assistant YaST or have special requirements for your system, change the individual installation suggestions manually as described in *User-Defined Installation* on page 13.

Step One: The Start Screen

Turn on your computer and all connected hardware components and immediately insert CD 1 or the DVD in the respective drive. In the start screen, select an installation mode or boot an installed operating system. Following the successful installation, the CD only needs to be inserted in the drive occasionally to install additional software. As the CD can be forgotten in the drive, the option to boot the installed system is preselected. For installation, use the arrow keys to select 'Installation'. If your computer does not boot from CD 1 or the DVD, read *The Boot Screen* on page 15.

Step Two: Accept Suggestions

Then the SuSE system assistant YaST starts. First, select the language for your system. The language setting is automatically adopted for the keyboard layout. Then YaST checks your system. If you already installed a SuSE Linux version on your computer, the next dialog asks whether to install SuSE Linux from scratch or perform an update of your previous system.

If Linux was not installed on your computer previously or if you select 'New installation', YaST checks all your hardware and list the result in the "suggestion dialog", shown in Figure 2.1 on the facing page. This dialog also displays the partitioning suggestion (possibly Windows will be resized) and the selected installation type. If installing Linux for the first time, you should accept these suggestions, which are usually suitable. The following messages and suggestions are displayed after the system check:

Mode 'New installation' is the default value here.

Keyboard The keyboard layout defaults to the selected language. This can easily be changed.

Mouse The detected mouse type is listed here.

Partitioning Suggests a suitable partitioning. If Windows 9x or ME (FAT32 file system) exists on the hard disk, the resizing rate is indicated.

Software A default system with office applications is preset.

Booting Determines where SuSE Linux installs the boot manager. The Master Boot Record (MBR) of the first hard disk is the default setting.

Time Zone Depending on the selected language settings, the time zone of the respective country is selected. Check this setting as many languages are used in several countries.

Modify the YaST suggestions at any time by clicking the respective heading. The dialogs displayed enable detailed settings. The exact procedure is described in *YaST Takes Over* on page 17.After the changes, you are returned to the overview and can proceed with the installation using the modified values by clicking 'Accept'.

Caution

If the hardware was detected correctly, you do not need to change anything. Do not change the boot loader, partitioning, or hardware settings unless you know what you are doing.

Caution

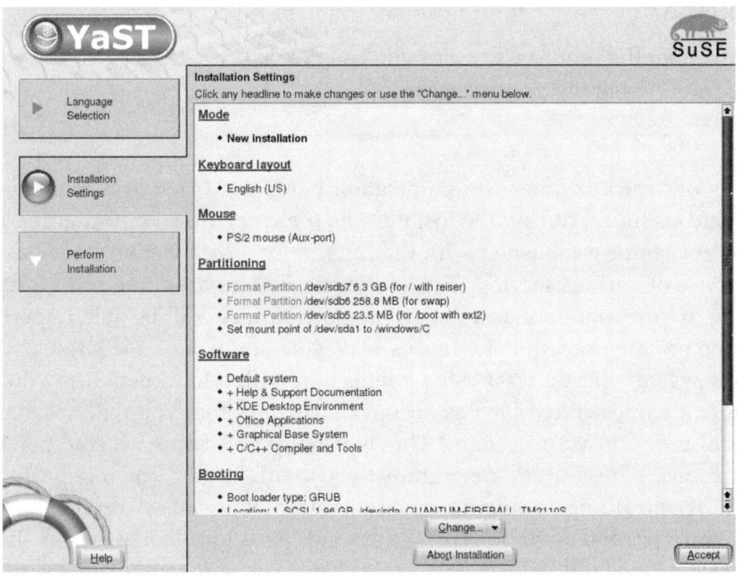

Figure 2.1: Suggestion Screen

Step Three: Installation

Start the installation with the current settings by clicking 'Yes' in the green window displayed by YaST. Depending on the performance of your computer, the complete installation of your system with about 350 program packages takes approximately fifteen minutes.

Configuration

Following the installation, specify some important settings before starting using SuSE Linux. Detailed instructions are available in *Finishing the Installation* on page 33. First, set a password for the system administrator (user ☞*root*).This special user is always configured by YaST and is needed for system maintenance tasks.

Caution

Remember the root password as you can only modify the system or install programs using the `root` identity.

Caution

If a network card or other communication hardware (such as a modem or ISDN card) is found during the installation, these can now be configured and a connection can be established with the Internet or a local network (LAN). This enables use of various services during the remaining part of the procedure. For example, if you configure an Internet connection, you will be able to perform an online update immediately. In this way, you can include the latest updates for your system. If you establish a connection with a local network, you can configure a name service such as NIS. YaST assumes that you will not manage any local users on your system. This is usually the case with commercial workstations, whose users are administered centrally (e.g., on a department server). If you do not configure a name service, you can set up local users intended for normal operations on the system. An additional overview displays the detected screen, graphics card, and other hardware components (printer, sound card, etc.). If necessary, change settings, such as the suggested screen resolution or the color depth. Refer to *Hardware Configuration* on page 40. Some of the dialogs for the configuration of the additional hardware are able to search for connected devices. However, these settings do not need to be specified at this stage. You can also skip this step and do it later on. After the completion of this last step, your newly installed system is booted and you can start using it.

User-Defined Installation

The previous chapter covered the quick installation procedure. This chapter provides detailed information about the settings you can modify by starting the relevant module from the suggestion window. This gives complete control over the installation.

Starting Your System from the CD-ROM

Insert the first SuSE Linux CD or the DVD into the drive. Then reboot the computer to start the installation program from the medium in the drive.

Possible Problems When Starting from the CD/DVD

If your computer does not boot from CD, there may be several causes:

- The CD-ROM drive is not able to read the boot image on the first CD. In this case, use CD 2 to boot the system. CD 2 contains a conventional 2.88 MB boot image, which can be read even by older drives.
- The boot sequence as set in the computer's BIOS is not correct. Information about changing the BIOS settings are provided in the documentation of your motherboard and in the following paragraphs.

  The BIOS is a small set of software routines to activate the basic functions of a computer. The BIOS is provided by motherboard manufacturers and is specially made to work with the features of the board.

  Normally, the BIOS setup can only be accessed at a specific time — when the machine is booting. During this initialization phase, the machine performs a number of diagnostic hardware tests. One of them is a memory check, recognizable from the memory counter. Try to catch this moment when the counter appears and look for a line telling you about the key that must be pressed to enter the BIOS setup. This line is usually below the counter or somewhere at the bottom. Usually the key to be pressed is either (Del), (F1), or (Esc). Press this key until the BIOS setup screen appears.

  To change the boot sequence in an AWARD BIOS, look for the 'BIOS FEATURES SETUP' entry. Other manufacturers may have a different name for this, such as 'ADVANCED CMOS SETUP'. When you have found the entry, select it and confirm with (↵).

  In the screen that has opened, look for a subentry called 'BOOT SEQUENCE'. The boot sequence will often be set to something like `C,A` or `A,C`. In the former case, the machine first searches the hard disk (C) then the floppy drive (A) to find a bootable medium. You should be able to change the settings by pressing (Page ↑) or (Page ↓) until the sequence is `A,CDROM,C`.

  You can leave the BIOS setup screen by pressing (Esc). To save the changes, select 'SAVE & EXIT SETUP' or press (F10). To confirm that your settings should be saved, press (Y).

If you have a SCSI CD-ROM drive, you need to change the setup of the SCSI BIOS. In the case of an Adaptec host adapter, for instance, the setup can be opened by pressing Ctrl + A. After that, select 'Disk Utilities', which displays the connected hardware components. Make a note of the SCSI ID for your CD-ROM drive. Exit the menu with Esc then open the 'Configure Adapter Settings' screen. Under 'Additional Options', select 'Boot Device Options' and press ↵. Enter the ID of the CD-ROM drive and press ↵ again. Then press Esc twice to return to the start screen of the SCSI BIOS. Exit this screen and confirm with 'Yes' to ☞*boot* again.

- Your CD-ROM drive may not be supported because it is an older model.

The Boot Screen

In the boot screen, select 'Installation'. The default selection, 'Boot Installed OS', is used to boot an already installed system. Move from item to item using the arrow keys. Confirm selection so YaST can load and start the installation.

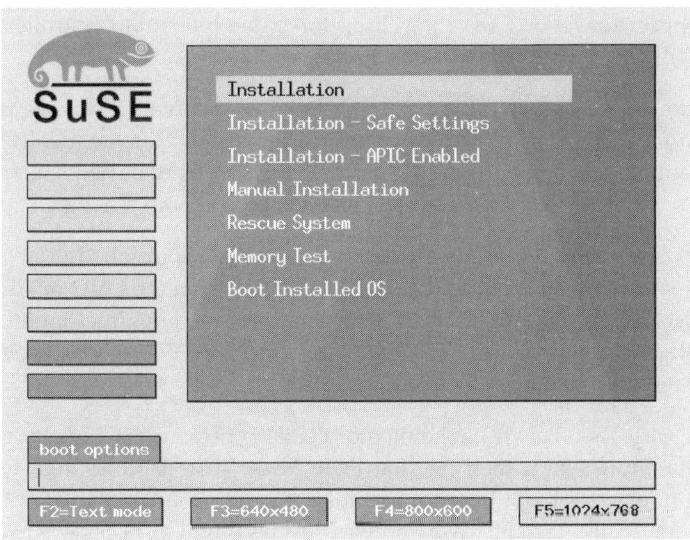

Figure 3.1: *The Boot Screen*

Problems during the installation are rare, but may occur with older hardware or hardware that is not well optimized with regard to certain functions. Often such difficulties are related to power management features or to disk drives not coping well with DMA modes. As the system cannot be scanned for such problems beforehand, they may sporadically interfere with the installation. If you cannot complete the installation because of such problems, reboot and select 'Installation — Safe Settings' from the boot screen. In this installation mode, some of the more modern hardware functions are skipped, which usually prevents the problems.

These are the individual options of the boot screen and the actions triggered by them:

- *Boot Installed OS*: Boots the system installed on the hard disk (the system normally booted when the machine is powered on).
- *Installation*: The "normal" installation mode. All modern hardware functions are enabled.
- *Installation — Safe Settings*: The DMA mode (for CD-ROM drives) and any unsafe power management functions are disabled. Experts can also use the command line to enter or change kernel parameters.
- *Installation — APIC Enabled*: This may be needed for newer machines with support for APIC (Advanced Programmable Interrupt Controller) if the normal installation mode fails.
- *Manual Installation*: If the automatic loading of drivers is causing problems with the installation, you can perform the installation "manually". In a manual installation, drivers must be loaded by hand as needed. However, this will not work if you use a USB keyboard on your machine.
- *Rescue System*: If you are unable to boot into your installed Linux system for some reason, you can boot the computer from the DVD or CD1 then select this item. This starts a "rescue system" — a minimal Linux system without any graphical user interface, which can be used by experts to access disk partitions to repair the errors.
- *Memory Test*: This tests the memory (RAM) of your machine by writing data chunks to it then reading them back. This is done repeatedly in an endless loop, because memory corruption often shows up very sporadically, so many read and write cycles might be necessary to detect it. If you suspect that your computer's memory might be defective, start this test and let it run for several hours. If no errors are detected after a longer time period, safely assume that the memory is intact. Terminate the test by rebooting.

A few seconds after starting the installation, SuSE Linux loads a minimal ☞*Linux system*, which takes control and performs the installation. A number of messages and copyright notices are displayed then, at the end of the loading process, the YaST installation program is started. After a few more seconds, the screen should display the graphical interface that will guide you through the installation.

YaST Takes Over

Now YaST starts for the installation of SuSE Linux. The YaST screens have a common format. All buttons, entry fields, and lists can be accessed with the mouse. If your mouse pointer does not move, the mouse has not been correctly detected. In this case, you must use the keyboard for navigation.

Selecting a Language

Select the language to use for SuSE Linux and YaST. English is the default setting for the international distribution. If your mouse does not work, navigate with the arrow keys until the desired language is selected. After this, press (Tab) until 'Next' is highlighted. Then press (↵) to confirm your language selection.

Installation Mode

If you already have another version of SuSE Linux installed on your computer, select whether to perform a 'New Installation' or to 'Update an Existing System'. There is also an option for booting an existing operating system. If you did not install SuSE Linux before, only a new installation is possible. After selecting an option, click 'Next' to continue. See Figure 3.3 on page 19.

This section only describes the steps after selecting 'New Installation'. Detailed instructions for a system update are available in *System Update* on page 51.

Installation Suggestions

After hardware detection, the suggestion window, shown in Figure 3.4 on page 20, displays some information about the hardware recognized and proposes a number of installation and partitioning options. When selecting any

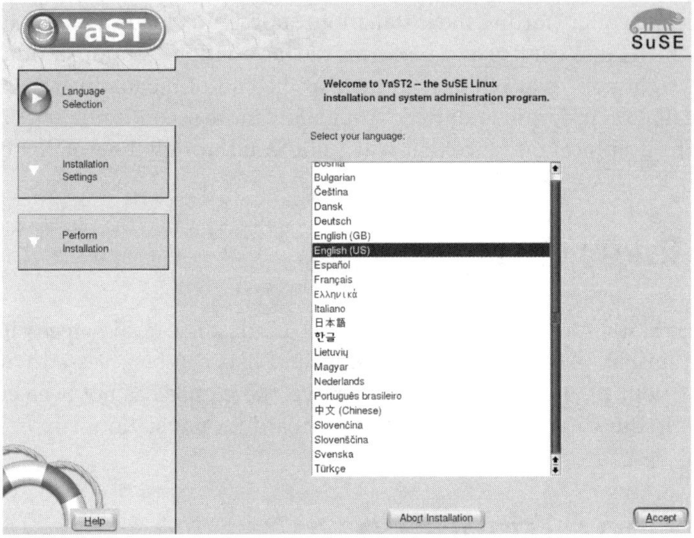

Figure 3.2: Selecting the Language

of these items and configuring them in the corresponding dialogs, you are always returned to the suggestion window, which is updated accordingly. The individual settings are discussed in the following sections.

Installation Mode

This offers the opportunity to change the installation type selected previously. If you already have a Linux system installed on your machine, you can use the option to boot into that system. This is useful if the system is damaged for some reason and cannot be booted from the hard disk.

Keyboard Layout

Select the keyboard layout. By default, the layout corresponds to the selected language. After changing the layout, test Y, Z, and special characters to make sure the selection is correct. When finished, select 'Next' to return to the suggestion window.

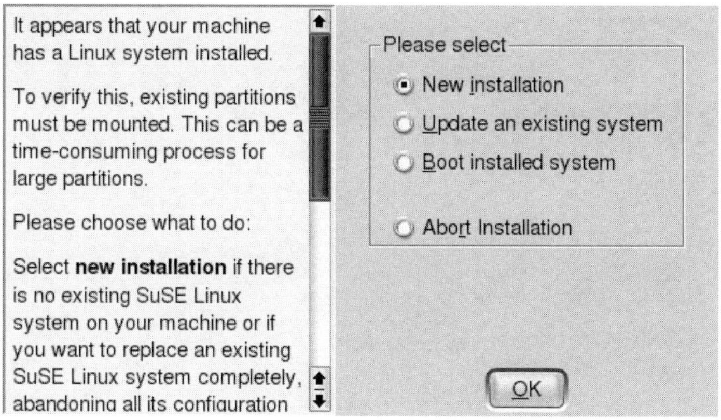

Figure 3.3: Selecting the Installation Mode

Mouse

If YaST did not detect your mouse automatically, press Tab in the suggestion window several times until 'Mouse' is selected. Then use Space to open the dialog in which to set the mouse type. This dialog is shown in Figure 3.5 on page 21.

To select the mouse type, use ↑ and ↓. Consult the mouse documentation for information about the mouse type. After selecting a mouse type, use the key combination Alt + T to test whether the device works correctly without selecting it permanently. If the mouse does not behave as expected, use the keyboard to select another type and test again. Use Tab and ↵ to make the current selection permanent.

Partitioning

In most cases, YaST proposes a reasonable partitioning scheme that can be accepted without change. If desired, modify this scheme to meet your needs or create a new one.

Partition Types

Every hard disk has a partition table with space for four entries. Each entry in the partition table can be a primary partition or an extended partition. Only *one*

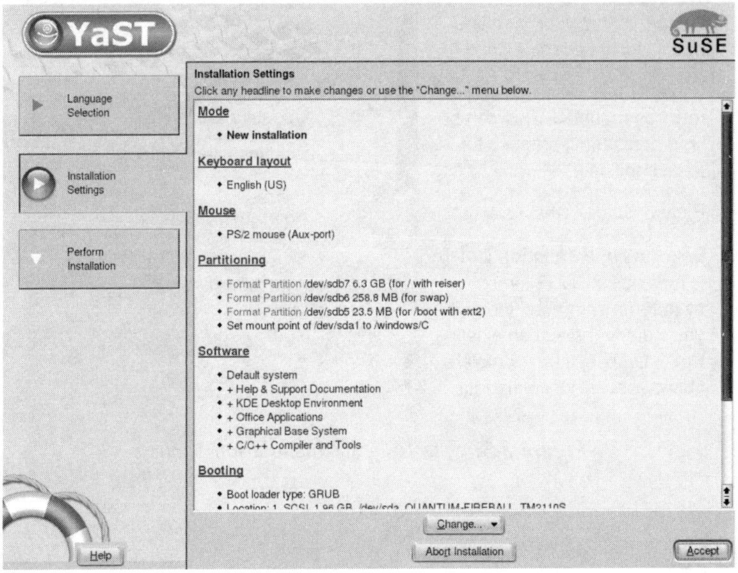

Figure 3.4: Suggestion Window

extended partition entry is allowed, however.

Primary partitions consist of a continuous range of cylinders (physical disk areas) assigned to a particular operating system. Using primary partitions, you could not set up more than four partitions per hard disk. More do not fit in the partition table.

This is why extended partitions are used. Extended partitions are also continuous ranges of disk cylinders, but an extended partition may itself be subdivided into *logical partitions*. Logical partitions do not require entries in the partition table. In other words, an extended partition is a container for logical partitions.

If you need more than four partitions, create an extended partition. This extended partition should span the entire remaining free cylinder range. Then create multiple logical partitions within the extended partition. The maximum number of logical partitions is fifteen on SCSI disks and 63 on (E)IDE disks.

It does not matter which type of partitions are used for Linux. Primary and logical partitions both work fine.

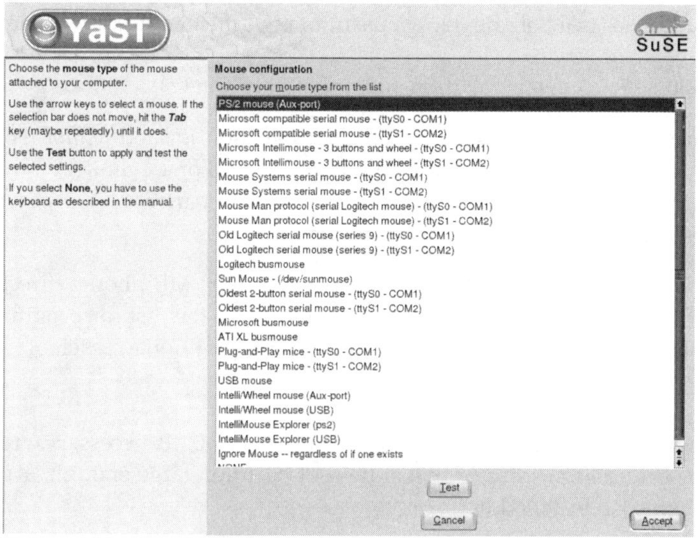

Figure 3.5: Selecting the Mouse Type

Required Disk Space

The amount of hard disk space needed depends on the intended use of the system. Less space limits what applications can be installed. The following hints give some guidelines for space requirements:

Minimal system: 180 MB. No graphical interface (X Window System) is installed, which means only console applications can be used. Also, only a very basic selection of software is installed.

Minimal system with graphical interface: 500 MB. This includes X and some applications.

Graphical system with modern applications: between 1 GB and 2 GB. This includes recent versions of graphical desktops, namely KDE and GNOME, and also provides sufficient space for the bigger application packages such as OpenOffice.org, Netscape, or Mozilla.

For downloading lots of movies and music with Linux: 2 GB

Both items: 3 GB

Burning CDs and the items listed above: 4 GB

These guidelines can help develop a partitioning scheme for your system:

Under 500 MB: A swap partition and a root partition (/).

Between 500 MB and 4 GB: A small boot partition located *within the first cylinders* of the hard disk (`/boot`, at least 8 MB or 1 cylinder) to hold the kernel and the boot loader. Also create a swap partition of approximately 256 MB then use the rest for the root partition (/).

For more than 4 GB: Boot (`/boot`), swap, root (250 MB), home directories (`/home`) with about 200 MB for each user, and the rest for programs and data (`/usr`). You may also reserve one extra partition for each of `/opt` and `/var`.

Some commercial programs install their data in `/opt`. If necessary, create a separate partition for `/opt` or make the root partition large enough. KDE and GNOME are also installed in `/opt`.

Tip

Things should be fine if your partitioning setup is similar to that proposed by YaST. This is usually a small partition for `/boot` at the beginning of the hard disk (about 10 MB, or 1 cylinder on a large hard disk), a swap partition (between 128 and 256 MB), and the rest for /.

Tip

Partitioning with YaST

When you select the partitioning item in the suggestion window for the first time, YaST displays a dialog listing the partition settings as currently proposed. Accept these current settings without change or change them before continuing.Alternatively, discard all the settings and start over from scratch.

Nothing in the partitioning setup is changed if you select 'Accept Suggested Partitioning Setup'. If you select 'Change Suggested Partitioning Setup', the 'Expert Partitioner' opens. It allows you to tweak the partition setup in every detail. This dialog is explained in *Expert Partitioning with YaST* on the facing page. The original setup as proposed by YaST is offered there as a starting point.

If you select 'Create custom partitioning setup', a dialog, like that in Figure 3.7 on page 24, opens in which to select a hard disk from those on your system. SuSE Linux will be installed on the disk selected in this dialog.

The next step is to determine whether the entire disk should be used ('Use entire hard disk') or whether to use any existing partitions, if available, for the

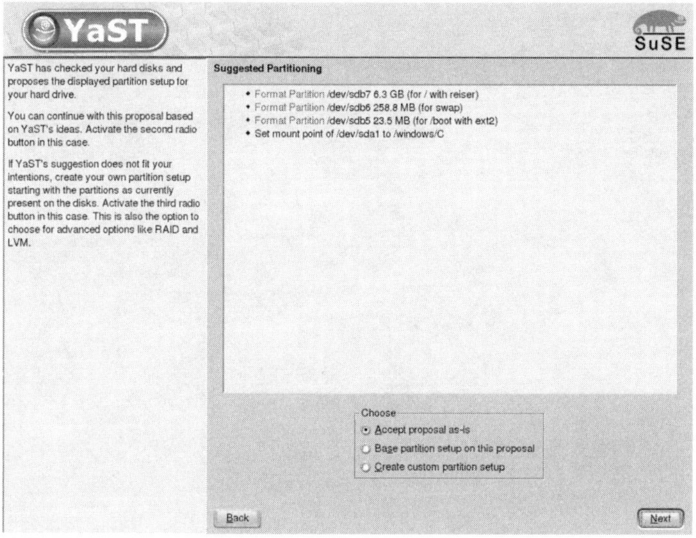

Figure 3.6: *Editing the Partitioning Setup*

installation. If a Windows operating system was found on the disk or if there is some other FAT file system, select whether to delete or resize the partition. Before doing so, read *Resizing a Windows Partition* on page 27. If desired, go to the 'Expert Partitioner' dialog to create a custom partition setup at this point (see *Expert Partitioning with YaST* on the current page).

Caution

If you choose 'Use entire hard disk', all data on that disk will be lost (as soon as the actual partitioning starts).

Caution

YaST checks during the installation whether the disk space is sufficient for the software selection made. If not, YaST automatically removes parts from the software selection as needed. The suggestion window then includes a notice to inform you about this. As long as there is suffient disk space available, YaST simply accepts your settings and partitions the hard disk accordingly.

Expert Partitioning with YaST

With the expert dialog, shown in Figure 3.8 on page 25, the partitioning of your hard disk can be modified manually. Partitions can be added, deleted, or edited.

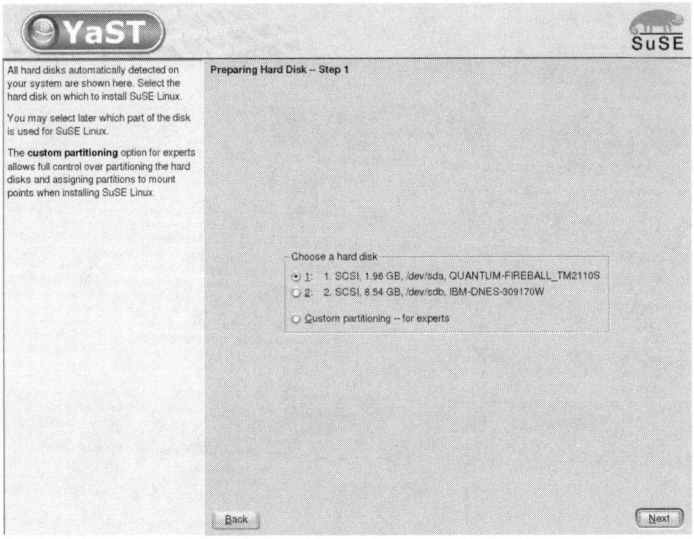

***Figure** 3.7: Selecting the Hard Disk*

All existing or suggested partitions on all connected hard disks are displayed in the list of the expert dialog. Entire hard disks are listed as devices without numbers, such as `/dev/hda` or `/dev/sda`. Partitions are listed as parts of these devices, such as `/dev/hda1` or `/dev/sda1`. The size, type, file system, and mount point of the hard disks and their partitions are also displayed. The mount point describes where the partition is mounted in the Linux file system tree.

Any free hard disk space is also listed and automatically selected. To allocate additional storage space to ☞*Linux*, free the needed space starting from the bottom toward the top of the list (starting from the last ☞*partition* of a hard disk toward the first). For example, if you have three partitions, you cannot use the second exclusively for Linux and retain the third and first for other operating systems.

Creating a Partition

1. Select 'New'. If several hard disks are connected, a selection dialog appears in which to select a hard disk for the new partition. Then, specify the partition type (primary or extended). Create up to four primary partitions or up to three primary partitions and one extended partition. Within the extended partition, you can create several logical partitions (see *Partition Types* on page 19).

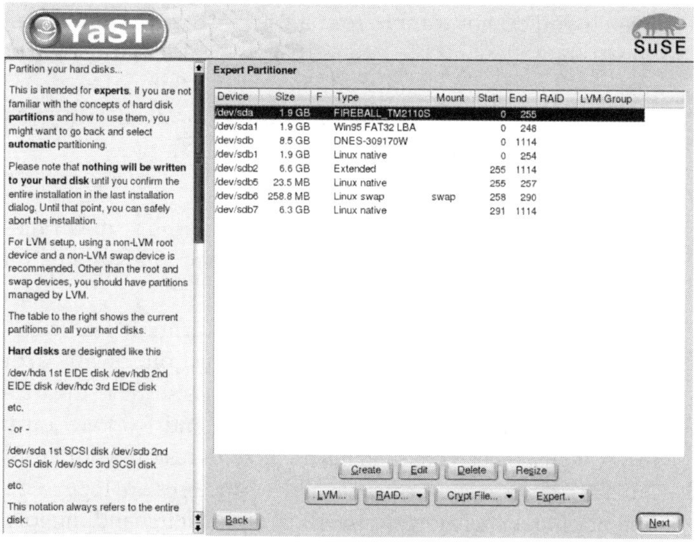

Figure 3.8: The YaST Partitioner in Expert Mode

2. Select the file system to use to format the partition and a mount point, if necessary. YaST suggests a mount point for each partition created. Details of the parameters are provided in the next section.
3. Select 'OK' to apply your changes.

The new partition is then listed in the partition table. If you click 'Next', the current values are adopted and you are returned to the suggestion screen.

Partitioning Parameters

If you create a new partition or modify an existing partition, various parameters can be set in the partitioning tool. For new partitions, suitable parameters are set by YaST and usually do not require any modification. To perform manual settings, proceed as follows:

1. Select the partition.
2. 'Edit' the partition and set the parameters:
   - File System ID

Even if you do not want to format the partition at this stage, specify one of the following file system IDs to ensure that the partition is registered correctly: 'Linux', 'Linux swap', 'Linux LVM', or 'Linux RAID'. Refer to the *Administration Guide* for details on LVM and RAID.

- File System

  To format the partition immediately within the scope of the installation, you can specify one of the following file systems for the partition: 'Swap', 'Ext2', 'Ext3', 'ReiserFS', or 'JFS'.

  Swap is a special format that makes the partition usable as virtual memory. Every system should have at least one swap partition of at least 128 MB (see on the facing page). ReiserFS is the default for Linux partitions. ReiserFS as well as JFS and Ext3 are journaling file systems. These file systems are able to restore your system very quickly after a system crash, as write processes are logged during the operation. Furthermore, ReiserFS is very fast in handling lots of small files. Ext2 is not a journaling file system. It is "rock solid" and good for smaller partitions, as it does not require too much disk space for management.

- File System Options

  Here, specify various parameters for the selected file system. Depending on the file system used, various options are offered. Only make changes if you are absolutely sure what you are doing.

- Encrypt File System

  If you activate the encryption, all data is written to the hard disk in encrypted form. This increases the security of sensitive data, but reduces the system speed, as the encryption takes some time.

- fstab Options

  Here, specify various parameters for the administration file of the file systems (`/etc/fstab`). These options should only be modified by experts.

- Mount Point

  This specifies the directory at which the partition should be mounted in the file system tree. Various YaST suggestions can be expanded at the respective entry field. If you accept these suggestions, the default file system structure is implemented. However, you can also specify any other names.

3. Select 'Next' to activate the partition.

Note

If you partition manually, you have to create a swap partition. The swap partition is used to free the main memory from data that is not used at the present moment. This keeps the main memory free for the most frequently-used important data.

Note

Resizing a Windows Partition

If your partition setup includes a hard disk that also has a Windows FAT partition, YaST offers either to delete or shrink it. Using this option allows you to install SuSE Linux on a disk where the current setup does not provide enough space for another operating system. This is commonly the case on computers with only one ☞*partition* that covers the entire hard disk. This setup is sometimes found on computers where Windows comes preinstalled.

The following discussion is based on the assumption that your Windows system is installed on a FAT partition (FAT or FAT 32). If YaST sees that there is not enough space on the selected hard disk, but that space could be made available by deleting or shrinking a Windows partion, it presents a dialog in which to choose one of these two options.

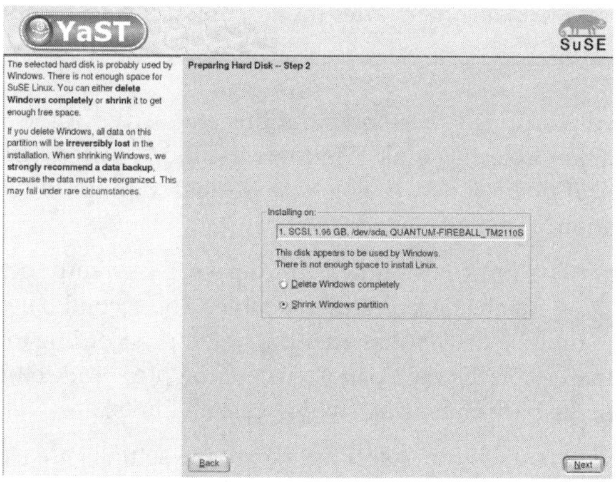

Figure 3.9: Possible Options for Windows Partitions

If you select 'Delete Windows completely', the Windows partition is marked for deletion to use the space for the installation of SuSE Linux.

Caution

If you delete Windows, all data will be lost beyond recovery as soon as the formatting starts.

Caution

To shrink the Windows partition, interrupt the installation for now and boot into Windows first to prepare the partition from there. Although this step is not strictly required, it speeds up the resizing process and also makes it safer.

In Windows, first run scandisk to make sure the FAT partition is free of lost file fragments and crosslinks, which are not that uncommon under Windows. After that, run defrag to move files to the beginning of the partition. This will make the resizing faster.

Note

If you have optimized virtual memory settings for Windows in such a way that a contiguous swap file is used with the same initial (minimum) and maximum size limit, consider another step. With these Windows settings, the resizing might have the effect that the swap file is split into many small parts scattered all over the FAT partition. Also, the entire swap file would need to be moved during the resizing, which makes the process rather slow. It is therefore useful to unset these Windows optimizations for the time being and reenable them after the resizing has been completed.

Note

When you have performed these preparations and arrive at the Linux partitioning setup again, select 'Shrink Windows Partition'. After a quick check of the partition, YaST opens a new dialog with a suggestion for the resizing of the Windows partition.

The first bar graph shows how much disk space is currently occupied by Windows and how much space is still available. The second bar graph shows how the space would be distributed after the resizing, according to YaST's current proposal (Figure 3.10 on the next page). Accept the proposed settings or use the slider to change the partition sizing (within certain limits).

When you leave this dialog by selecting 'Next', the settings are stored and you are returned to the previous dialog. The resizing takes place later — shortly before the disk formatting.

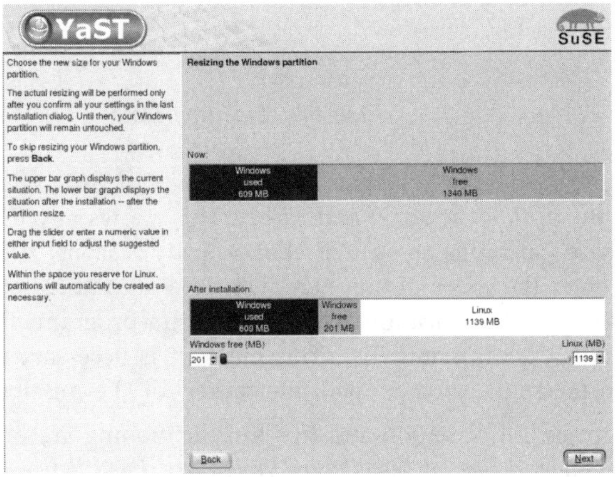

Figure 3.10: Resizing the Windows Partition

Note

The Windows versions NT, 2000, and XP are installed on an NTFS file system by default. If you have such a system installed, YaST may be unable to resize the file system, so there may not be enough space for the installation. To install SuSE Linux, either delete Windows from the hard disk or reinstall Windows on a smaller partition.

If Windows came preinstalled on your computer and uses the NTFS file system, the best option is probably to reinstall Windows on a smaller partition, but using the FAT 32 file system. Doing so makes it possible to resize the Windows partition later, if the need arises.

Note

More Partitioning Tips

If the partitioning is performed by YaST and other partitions are detected on the system, these partitions are also entered in the file `/etc/fstab` to enable easy access to this data. This file contains all partitions in the system with their properties (parameters), such as the file system, mount point, and user permissions.

```
/dev/sda1        /data1  auto    noauto,user 0 0
/dev/sda8        /data2  auto    noauto,user 0 0
```

File 1: /etc/fstab: Partition Data

The partitions, regardless of whether they are Linux or FAT partitions, are specified with the options `noauto` and `user`. This allows any user to mount or unmount these partitions as needed. For security reasons, YaST does not automatically enter the `exec` option here, which is needed for executing programs from the respective location. However, to run programs from there, you can enter this option manually. This measure is necessary if you encounter system messages such as "bad interpreter" or "Permission denied".

Detailed background information and tips for partitioning are provided in the *Administration Guide* in *Special Installation Procedures, Partitioning for Experts*.

Software

Here, select the software to install on your machine. The default selection includes KDE and OpenOffice. If you click 'Software', a dialog is displayed in which to choose one of three basic system setups:

- Minimum System (only recommended for experts)
- Minimum Graphical System (without KDE)
- Default System (with KDE and office package)

After selecting the desired setup, you can click 'Detailed selection' to start the software installation module. This module is shown in Figure 3.11 on the facing page).

Preselection

The module starts with the selection filter — 'Filter:' in the upper left is set to 'Selection' by default. Selections are entire groups of program packages that can be marked for installation or removal as a group by clicking the respective check box. Some of them are preselected because they belong to the default installation of SuSE Linux.

The right part of the window displays a table listing the individual packages included in the current selection. The leftmost table column shows the current status of each package. In the initial installation process, only two status

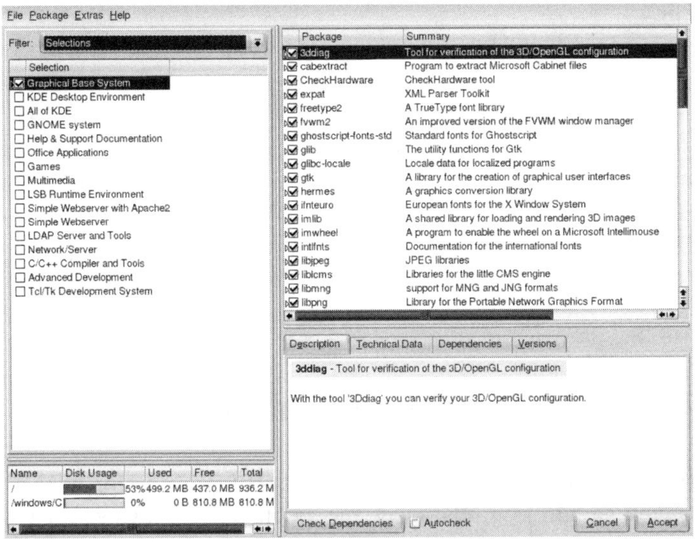

Figure 3.11: Installing and Removing Software

settings are normally used: "Selected for Installation" (the box in front of the package name is checked) and "Do Not Install" (the box is empty). To select or deselect individual software packages, simply go through the list and click in the boxes until they are checked or empty as desired.

The other status options are not really relevant for the initial installation. A description of the status flags and detailed instructions for this module are provided in *Install and Remove Software* on page 47.

Caution

The software preselected for installation has been chosen according to SuSE's experience and should meet the needs of most newcomers and advanced home users. In general, there is no immediate need to change anything here. However, if you decide to select additional packages and especially if you deselect any packages, you should be aware of the effects your decisions might have on the system. In particular, observe any warnings and avoid deselecting any parts of the base system (these are mostly found in the package group 'System').

Caution

Other Filters

Click the 'Filter' drop-down box to see a number of other filters that can be used to arrange the package list in different ways. When starting this YaST module from within the installed system, the list will be filtered according to 'Package Groups' by default. This view is also useful during the installation. It lists the software packages in the left part of the window in a tree structure, with the branches representing different categories or topics. The more you unfold the tree's branches, the more fine-grained the selection will become.

Booting (Boot Loader Installation)

During the installation, YaST proposes a boot configuration for your system. Normally, you should leave these settings unchanged. However, if you need a custom setup, modify the proposal for your system.

One possibility is to configure the boot mechanism to rely on a special boot floppy. Although this has the disadvantage of requiring the boot floppy in the drive for boot, it allows you to leave an existing boot mechanism untouched. This should not normally be necessary, however, because YaST can configure the SuSE Linux boot loader to boot coexisting operating systems as well. Another possibility with the configuration is to change the location of the boot mechanism on hard disk.

To change the boot configuration proposed by YaST, select 'Booting'. A dialog opens in which to change many details of the boot mechanism. Because the consequences of your changes could be severe, read *Boot Loader Configuration with YaST* on page 99 before modifying boot loader settings.

Note

The boot method should only be changed by experienced computer users.

Note

Time Zone

In this dialog, shown in Figure 3.12 on the next page, choose between `Local Time` and `UTC` under 'Hardware clock set to'. The selection depends on how the hardware (BIOS) clock is set on your machine. If it is set to `GMT`, which corresponds to UTC, your system can rely on SuSE Linux to switch from standard time to daylight savings time and vice versa.

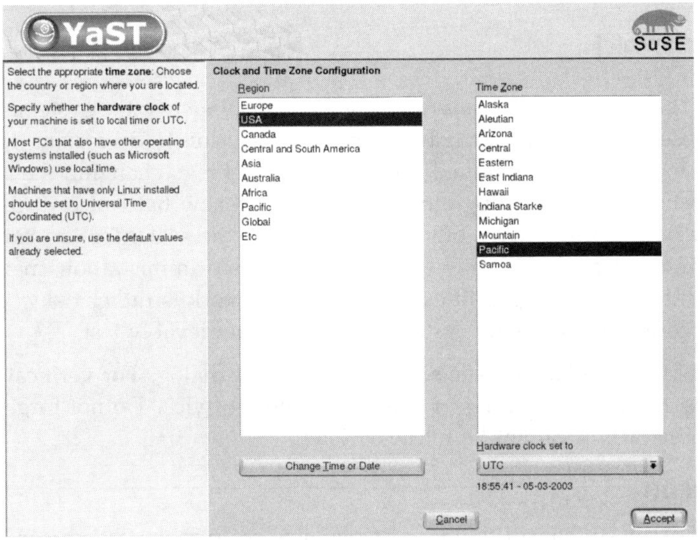

Figure 3.12: Selecting the Time Zone

Starting the Installation

When satisfied with the installation settings, click 'Next' to begin the installation. Confirm with 'Yes' in the green dialog that opens. Installation usually takes between fifteen and thirty minutes, depending on system performance and the software selected.

Finishing the Installation

After completing the basic system setup and the installation of all selected software packages, provide a password for the account of the system administrator (the "root" user). Then configure your Internet access and network connection, if available. With a working Internet connection, it is possible to update the system with security patches and software updates during installation. If desired, configure a name server settings for centralized user administration in a local network. Also configure any hardware devices, such as printers and scanners.

root Password

☞*root* is the name of the ☞*superuser*, the ☞*administrator* of the system. Unlike regular users, which may or may not have permission to do certain things on the system, `root` has unlimited power to do anything: changing the system configuration, installing programs, and setting up new hardware. If users forget their passwords or have other problems with the system, `root` can help. The `root` account should only be used for system administration, maintenance, and repair. Logging in as `root` for daily work is rather risky: a single mistake could lead to many system files being irretrievably lost.

Figure 3.13 on the facing page shows the relevant dialog. For verification purposes, the password for `root` must be entered twice. Do not forget the `root` password. It cannot be retrieved later.

Caution

The user `root` has all the permissions needed to make changes to the system. To carry out such tasks, the `root` password is required. You cannot carry out any administrative tasks without this password.

Caution

Network Configuration

In this step, configure network devices for a connection to the outside world. If you have these devices, such as network cards, modems, and ISDN or DSL hardware, it is a good idea to configure them now. An Internet connection allows YaST to retrieve any available SuSE Linux updates.

Directions for configuring network hardware is available in *Network Devices* on page 78, where the necessary steps are described. If preferred, configure your network devices later from the installed system. To do so, select 'Skip Network Configuration' then 'Accept'.

Testing the Internet Connection

If you configured an Internet connection, YaST can now test it for you by trying to establish a connection with SuSE's servers. It then checks whether any

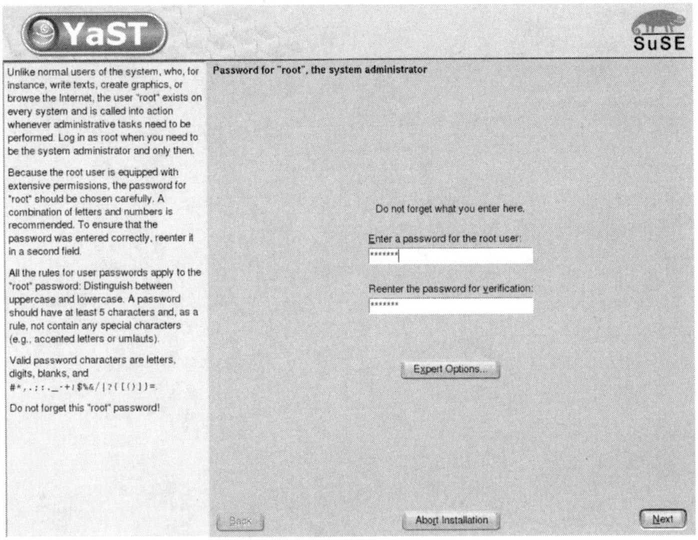

Figure 3.13: Setting the root Password

product updates are available for your version of SuSE Linux. If the connection works and updates are available, select whether to download and install the updates in the next step. The most recent release notes — information about the software — are also downloaded.

If you do not want to test the connection at this point, select 'Skip Test' then 'Next'. This also skips downloading product updates and release notes.

Loading Software Updates

If YaST was able to connect to the SuSE servers, select whether to perform a YaST online update. If there are any patched packages available on the servers, you can download and install them now to fix known bugs or security issues.

> **Note**
>
> The download of updates might take quite some time, depending on the bandwidth of the Internet connection and on the size of the update files.
>
> **Note**

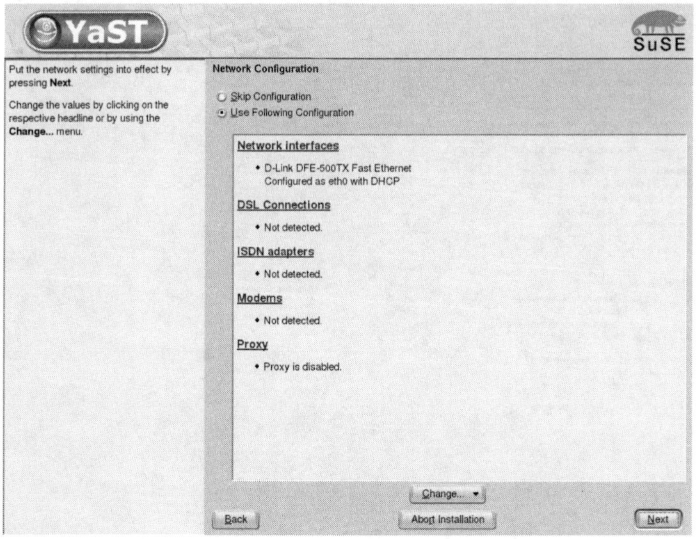

Figure 3.14: Configuring the Network Devices

To perform a software update immediately, select 'Perform Update Now' and click 'OK'. This opens YaST's online update dialog with a list of the available patches (if any), which can be selected and loaded. To learn about the details of the process, read *YaST Online Update* on page 45. This kind of update can be performed at any time after the installation. If you prefer not to update now, select 'Skip Update' then click 'OK'.

User Authentication

If the network access been configured successfully during the previous steps of the installation, you now have two different possibilities for managing user accounts on your system.

Local User Administration Using this method, users are managed locally — on the installed machine. This is the typical solution for stand alone workstations.

User Administration with NIS or LDAP This method is mostly used in organizations to manage workstations on a department-wide basis. The user administration for the entire department is carried out on a central

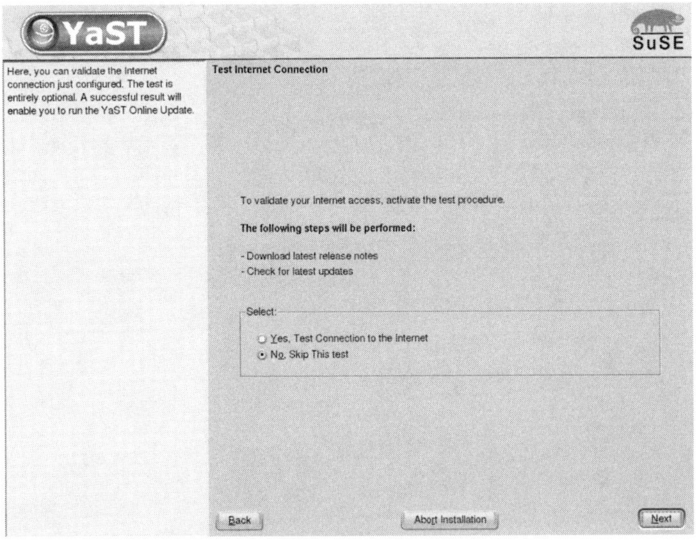

Figure 3.15: Testing the Internet Connection

host or name server, making the creation of local accounts unnecessary. In fact, the method could be chosen because local accounts are undesirable.

If all requirements are met, YaST opens a dialog in which to select the user administration method. It is shown in Figure 3.16 on the next page. If you do not have the necessary network connection in place, set up local user accounts.

Configuring the Host as a NIS Client

If you have decided to manage user accounts through NIS, configure the host as a NIS client. A NIS-enabled network requires some expert knowledge. The details of NIS are explained in the *Administration Guide*. The following only explains the basic setup of the client side.

In the following dialog, shown in Figure 3.17 on page 39, first select whether the host has a fixed IP address or gets one via DHCP. DHCP also provides the NIS domain and the NIS server. For further information about DHCP, see *DHCP* in the *Administration Guide*. If a static IP address is used, specify the NIS domain and the NIS server manually.

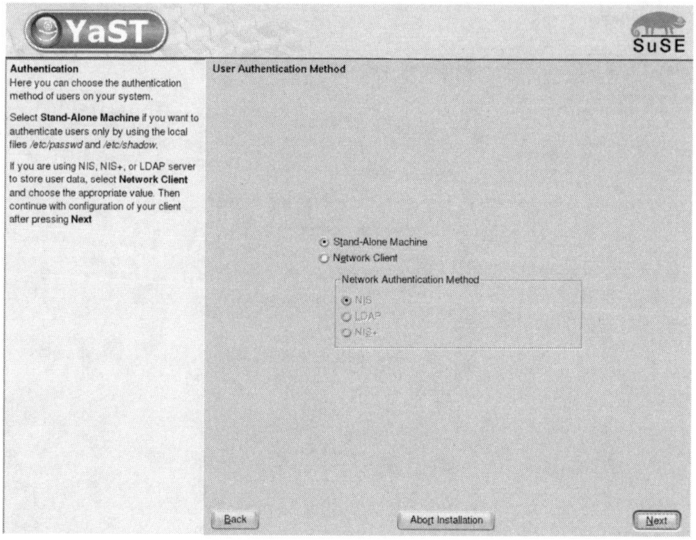

Figure 3.16: *User Authentication*

To search for any NIS servers broadcasting in the network, check the relevant check box. You can also specify several NIS domains and set a default domain. For each domain, you can select 'Edit' to specify several server addresses or enable the broadcast function on a per-domain basis.

In the expert settings, check 'Answer to the Local Host Only' ,if you do not want other hosts to be able to query which server your client is using. By checking 'Broken Server', no answers from servers on unprivileged ports are accepted. This is recommended for security reasons. For more information, see `man ypbind`.

Creating Local User Accounts

When user accounts are created locally, any data related to user accounts (name, login, password, and so on) are stored and managed locally on the host configured.

Linux is an operating system that allows several users to work on the same system at the same time. For each user, there needs to be a ☞*user account* to log in to the system. By having user accounts, the system gains a lot in terms of security. Regular users are not allowed to change or delete files needed for the system to work properly — regardless of whether they really intended to

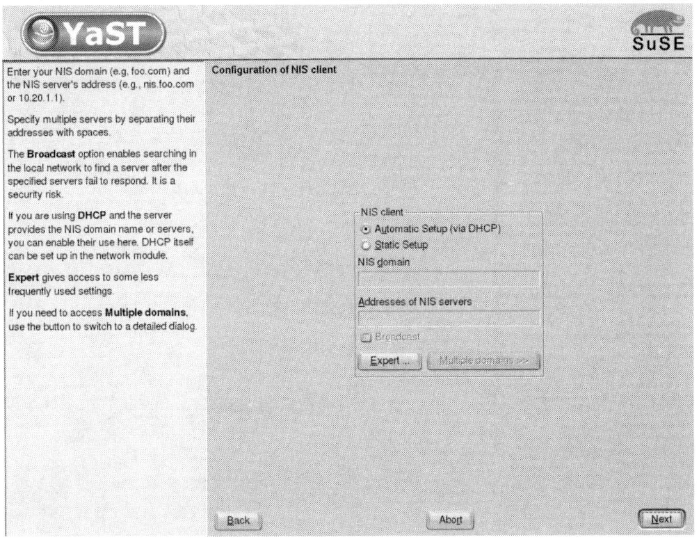

Figure 3.17: *NIS Client Configuration*

do so in the first place. Similarly, the personal data of a given user cannot be modified, viewed, or tampered with by other users. Each user can set up his own working environment and will always find it unchanged when logging back in.

A user account can be created using the dialog shown in Figure 3.18 on the next page. After entering the first name and last name, specify the user name (login). If you cannot think of a suitable user name, simply click 'Suggestion' for the system to generate one automatically.

Finally, enter a password for the user. Reenter it for confirmation (to ensure that you did not type something else by mistake). The user name tells the system who you are and the password is used to verify this identity.

To provide effective security, a password should be between five and eight characters long. The maximum length for a password is 128 characters, but if no special security modules are loaded, only the first eight characters are used to identify the password.

Linux distinguishes between lowercase and uppercase letters in the password. Accented characters and umlauts are not allowed. Special characters (such as: * . # ;) and the digits 0–9 may be used.

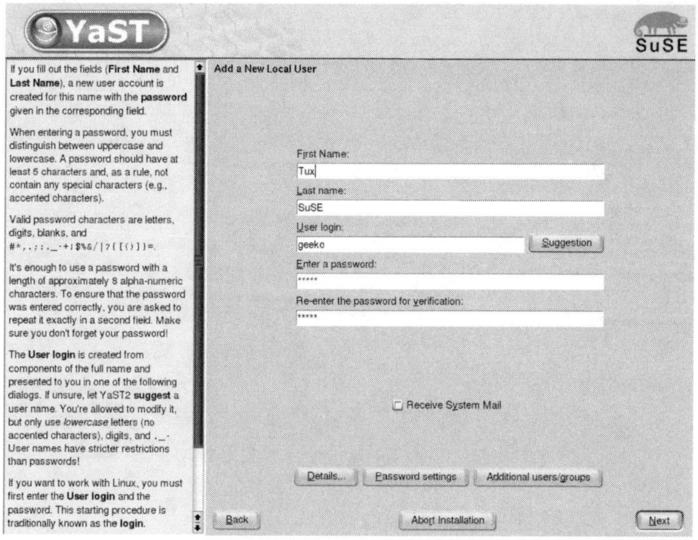

Figure 3.18: Entering the User Name and Password

Reading the Release Notes

After completing the user authentication setup, YaST displays the release notes. They contain important up-to-date information not available when the manuals were printed. If you have installed update packages, the most recent version of the release notes is available.

Hardware Configuration

Configure the graphics card and, if desired, other hardware devices, such as the printer and the sound card. Just click a component to start its configuration. For the most part, YaST then detects and configures the devices automatically.

You may skip any periphal hardware devices and configure them later. However, you should configure the graphics card right away. Although the display settings as autoconfigured by YaST should be generally acceptable, most users have very strong preferences as far as resolution, color depth, and other graphics features are concerned. To change these settings, select 'X Configu-

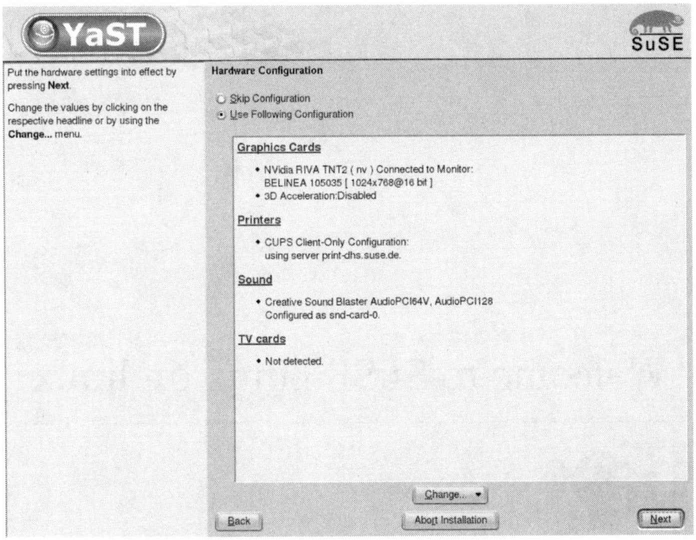

Figure 3.19: Configuring the System Components

ration'. The configuration is explained in *Display and Input Devices (SaX2)* on page 62. When finished, click 'Finish Installation'.

Graphical Login

SuSE Linux is now installed and ready for your first login. On your screen, you should see the graphical ☞*login* as shown in Figure 3.20 on the next page. Enter the user name created during installation then the respective password.

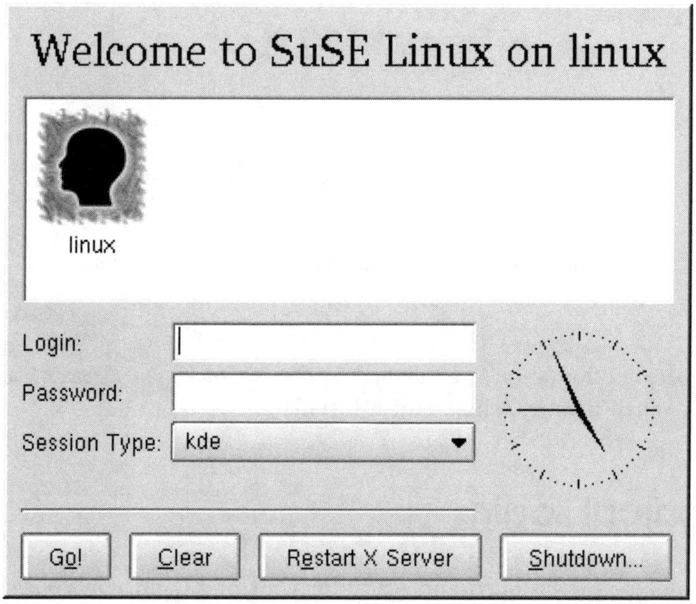

Figure 3.20: The Login Screen

YaST — Configuration

YaST, which you already used for the installation, is also the configuration tool for SuSE Linux. This chapter covers the configuration of your system with YaST2, which enables comfortable configuration of the main system components. This includes most of the hardware, the graphical user interface, Internet access, security settings, user administration, installation of software, and system updates and information. This chapter also provides instructions for using YaST in text mode.

Starting YaST

The 'K' menu and the 'SuSE' menu (the icons at the bottom left on the KDE panel) offer several ways to access YaST: via the 'Control Center', via 'SuSE' → 'Administration' →'Configuration', and via 'Preferences'.

In the K menu, you can directly select the needed configuration module. At start-up, YaST first opens a small dialog in which to enter the password for the user `root` (the system administrator). The configuration is performed as `root` because only `root` can modify Linux system files.

You can also start YaST from the command line, but this is a bit more complicated. In the shell, change to the user `root` with `sux` (enter the root password) and execute the `yast2`. After you terminate YaST, use the command `exit` to change from the user `root` to the normal user.

To change the language of YaST and your entire system, select 'System' → 'Select Language' in the YaST Control Center. Choose a language, exit the YaST2 Control Center, log out from your computer, then log in again and restart YaST.

The YaST Control Center

When you start YaST in the graphical mode, the YaST Control Center, as shown in Figure 4.1 on the facing page, opens first. In the left frame, see the categories 'Software', 'Hardware', 'Network Devices', 'Network Services', 'Security & Users', 'System', and 'Miscellaneous'. If you click one of icons, the respective contents are listed on the right-hand side. For example, if you select 'Hardware' then click 'Sound' to the right, a configuration dialog opens for the sound card. The configuration of the individual items usually comprises several steps. Press 'Next' to proceed to the following step.

The left frame displays a help text for the respective topic, explaining the entries required. After the necessary specifications have been made, complete the procedure by pressing 'Finish' in the last configuration dialog. The configuration is saved.

Software

Change Installation Source

The installation source is the medium containing the software to install. Install from CD or DVD (the usual approach), from a network server, or from

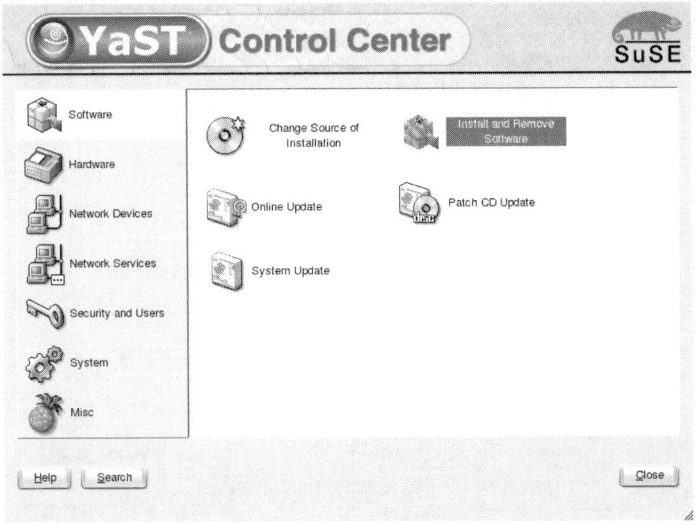

Figure 4.1: The YaST Control Center

the hard disk. Refer to the detailed YaST help text.

When you exit the module with 'Save and Exit', the settings are saved and applied to the configuration modules 'Install and Remove Software', 'System Update', and 'Boot and Kernel Configuration'. This module also offers the possibility to proceed with 'Install' to install or remove packages.

YaST Online Update

The YaST Online Update (YOU) enables the installation of important upgrades and improvements. The respective patches are made available for download on the SuSE FTP server. Under 'Installation Source', select the server. Activate 'Manual Update' to install only certain patches. Deactivate this option to install all available update packages.

If you activate 'Download All Patches Again', all patches, installable packages, and descriptions are downloaded from the server. If this box is not activated, you will merely receive the patches that are not yet installed on your system.

Use 'Configure Fully Automatic Update' to set up a cron job that checks for updates and patches on a regular basis.

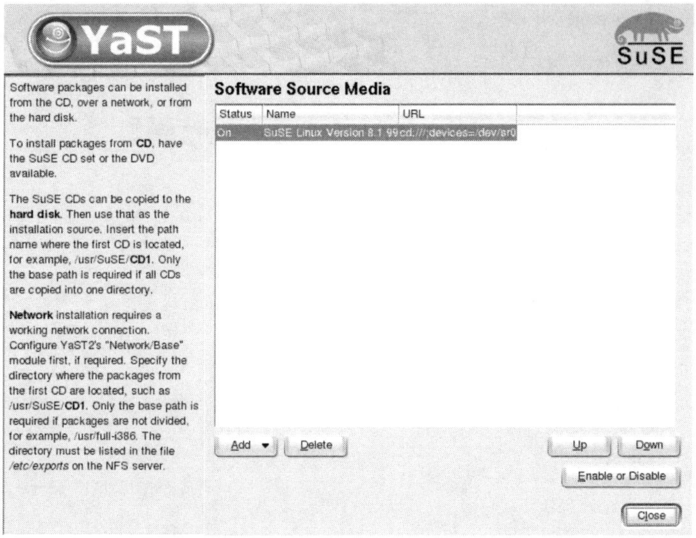

Figure 4.2: *Change Installation Source*

Press 'Next' to download a list of all available patches (if you selected 'Manual Update'). Subsequently, the software installation module (see Section *Install and Remove Software* on the next page) starts, listing all available patches. Select the packages for installation or simply accept the suggested patches already marked for installation.

First, all packages are downloaded from the server then installed on your machine. If errors occur, they are displayed in a window. In this case, you can skip the respective patches. Some patches open an information window before they are installed, allowing you to install or skip the package. Following the successful installation of all patches, a summary is displayed. Click 'Close' to exit the overview and 'Finish' to exit the YOU menu. Subsequently, SuSEconfig is executed.

Patch CD Update

The Patch CD Update is for "SuSE Linux Enterprise Server" customers. Patches are installed from CD instead of downloaded from a FTP server.

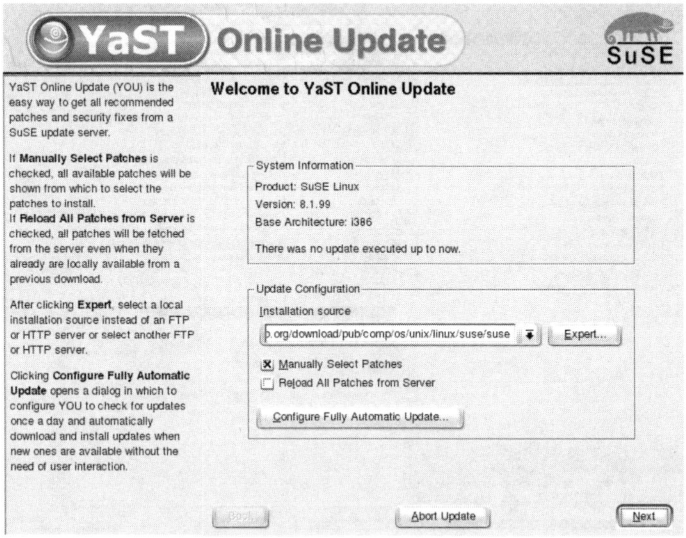

Figure 4.3: *YaST Online Update*

Install and Remove Software

This module enables you to install, update, or remove software. See Figure 3.11 on page 31. To install from CD or DVD, insert the first CD or the DVD in the drive.

The Menus

At the top left in the software module window (package manager), there are three menus: 'File', 'Packages', and 'Help'. Under 'File', you can use 'Export' to write a list of all installed packages to a text file. You will be prompted to specify a path and file name or confirm the default setting. Use 'Exit — Discard Changes' to exit the package manager. Select 'Quit — Save Changes' to save your settings.

Items under 'Packages' are only available if a package is currently selected. To apply the action to all packages of a package group, click the respective group and select 'All in This List'. The following actions are possible:

Install The status is changed to 'Install'. If you click 'Accept', the package or all packages of a group will be installed.

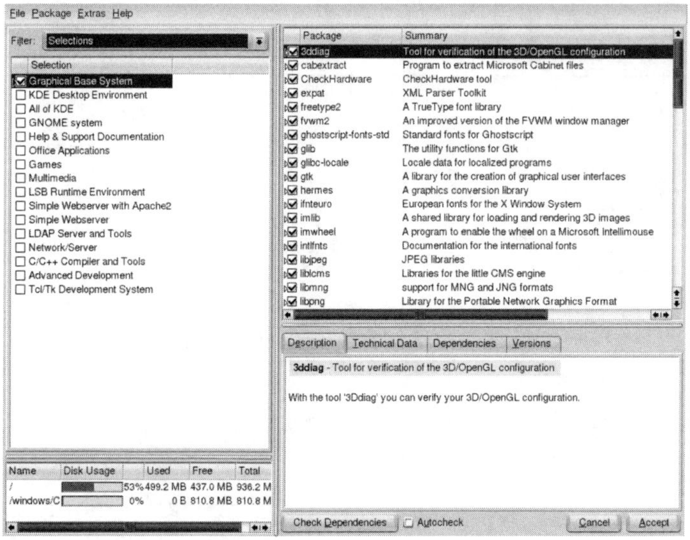

Figure 4.4: Installing and Removing Software

Do Not Install The status is set to 'Do Not Install', so the package will not be installed.

Keep The status is changed to 'Keep'. The package is already installed and is retained in this form.

Delete The status is changed to 'Delete'. The package is removed as soon as you click 'Accept'.

Update The status is changed to 'Update'. The package is replaced by a newer version.

Taboo — Never Install The status is changed to 'Taboo'. This means that the package is never installed, even if it is needed by another package that you install.

Install All Available Sources Source code will also be installed.

Do Not Install Any Sources The sources will not be installed.

These actions can also be executed by means of the keys indicated in the menu to the right of the menu items. Alternatively, change the package status by clicking the check boxes. An empty box precedes packages that are not installed. A box with a blue check mark precedes packages that are already installed and will be retained. Packages to install have a black check mark. If you click an installed package, the status first changes to 'Update', represented by a recycling symbol. If you click once more, the package status changes to 'Delete' and is marked with a wastebasket symbol. If you click the package again, it is marked with the blue check mark and will be retained. Packages that are not installed can also be set to 'Taboo'. In this case, the package will be marked with a do not enter sign. If you right-click a package, a context menu is displayed, enabling direct selection of the desired status for the package. If you are not sure about the meaning of a symbol, go to the help menu. Here, find a description of the YaST package manager, an explanation of the symbols, and the mapping of the various keys to the individual actions.

The Selection Filter

Using the filter drop-down box to the top left of the main dialog, determine how packages are displayed. The default setting is display according to 'Selections'.

1. With the selection filter, predefined selections of specific application areas can be installed or selected for installation by clicking the check boxes of the selections. For each selection, the packages of the selection and their current statuses are displayed to the right. You can also select or deselect individual packages. The range of selections includes 'Development', 'Games', 'KDE', 'GNOME', 'Multimedia', 'Web server', and 'Documentation'.

2. Another option is to list according to package groups. These package groups are displayed in a tree structure on the left-hand side. If you click one of the main groups (for example, 'Development' or 'Documentation'), all program packages belonging to this main group are listed at the top of the right frame. If you click one of the subgroups, the right frame only displays the packages of the subgroup.

Caution

You have the possibility to mark installed packages for deletion. Observe the alerts and do not delete any packages of the Linux base system (mostly located in the package group 'System').

Caution

3. The easiest way to find a specific package is to use the search function, which can also be accessed here. Enter a search string and use the check boxes to set the search method (only in the name, in the description, in the package dependencies). For example, use this feature to determine which packages use a specific "library".

4. After selecting the packages for installation, update, or deletion, view the installation summary available under Filter to see exactly what happens to which packages when you click 'Accept'. Using the check boxes to the left, list the packages according to the actions. To check only which packages are deleted manually or automatically, deactivate all other check boxes. The automatic installation, uninstallation, or update is performed whenever a package selected requires other packages.

The Information Window

The tabs in the bottom right frame provide various information about the selected package. The description of the selected package is automatically active. Click the other tabs to view technical data, the list of dependencies from other packages, or the version information.

Checking Dependencies

Under the information window, find 'Check dependencies' and, next to it, 'Autocheck'. If 'Autocheck' is activated and you select a package for installation, other required programs are displayed automatically. If preferred, simply disable the automatic check and use 'Check Dependencies' after selecting packages. If automatic checking is disabled and you do not check the dependencies manually, the package dependencies will be checked as soon as you click 'Accept'.

Apart from dependencies, there might also be conflicts. Some packages cannot be installed together with certain other packages. For example, this is the case with the packages package `sendmail` and package `postfix`. Figure 4.5 on the next page shows the conflict alert that prompts you to make a decision. The package `postfix` is already installed, so you can cancel the installation of package `sendmail`, remove package `postfix`, or take the risk and ignore the conflict. In most cases, ignoring the conflict is strongly discouraged, as the system stability and operability can no longer be guaranteed under these conditions.

Consumption of Hard Disk Space

Monitor the space consumed on the hard disk partitions in the overview at the bottom left. If you select too many packages, an alert is displayed.

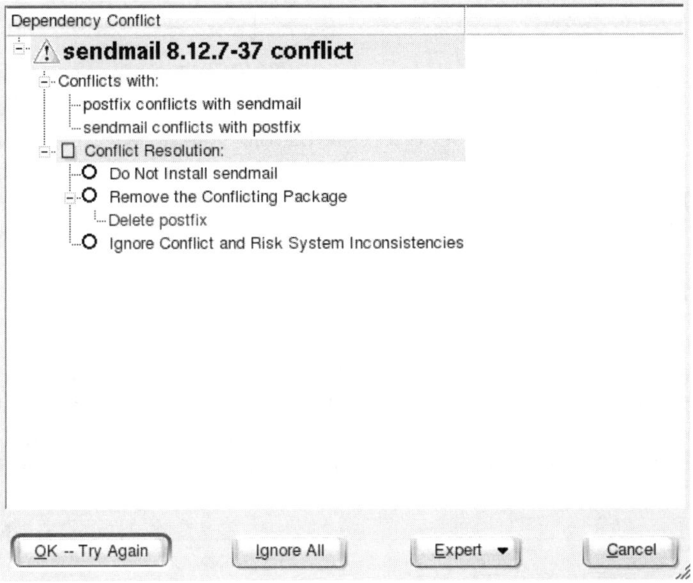

Figure 4.5: Conflict Management of the Software Module

System Update

This module enables you to update your system. The process consists of several steps. YaST checks which packages to update. If desired, decide individually for each package whether to perform an update. This approach cannot be used for the base system, which requires a boot from the installation medium, such as from CD.

Note

The system update is a very complex procedure. For each program package, YaST2 must check which version is installed on the computer and what needs to be done to replace the old version with the new version correctly. YaST2 also tries to adopt any personal settings of the installed packages. However, some configurations may cause problems after the update if the old configuration is unable to handle the new program version as expected or if unexpected inconsistencies arise between various configurations.

The older the existing version is and the more the configuration of the packages to update diverges from the standard, the more problematic the update will be. Sometimes, the old configuration cannot be adopted correctly. In this case, an entirely new configuration must be made. Before starting the update, the existing configuration should be saved.

Note

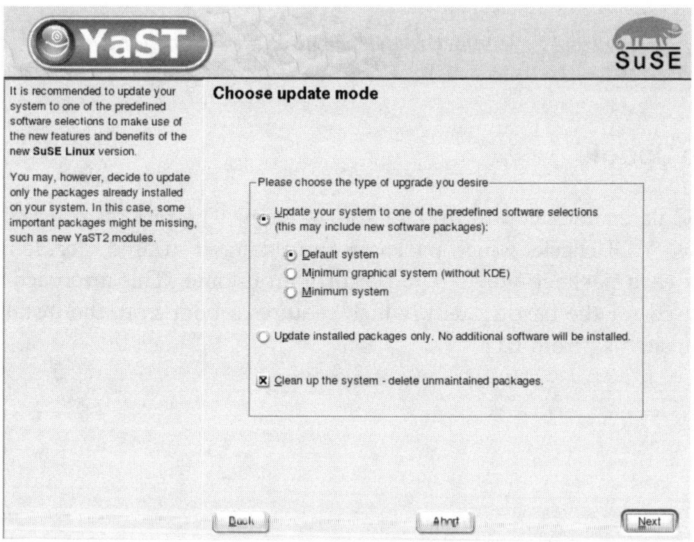

Figure 4.6: System Update

Hardware

New hardware must first be installed or connected as specified by the vendor. Switch on external devices, such as the printer or the modem, and start the respective YaST module. Most devices are automatically detected by YaST and the technical data is displayed. If the automatic detection fails, YaST offers a list of devices (model, vendor, etc.) from which to select the suitable device. Consult the documentation enclosed with your hardware for information.

Note

Use caution with model designations. If your model is not included in the device list, try a model with a similar designation. However, in some cases the model must match exactly, as similar designations do not always indicate compatibility.

Note

CD-ROM Drives

Within the scope of the installation, all detected CD-ROM drives are integrated in the installed system by means of entries in the file `/etc/fstab` and the respective subdirectories are created in `/media`. This YaST module can be used to integrate additional drives in the system.

When the module is started, a list of all detected drives is displayed. Mark your new drive using the check box at the beginning of the line and complete the integration with 'Finish'. The new drive is integrated in the system and can be used.

Printer

Linux Printing Basics

A Linux system manages printers through printer queues. Before any data is printed, it is sent to a printer queue for temporary storage. From there, it is retrieved by a print spooler, which sends it to the printer device in the required order.

However, for the most part this data is not available in a form that can be processed by the printer. A graphical image, for instance, first needs to be converted into a format the printer can understand. This conversion into a printer language is achieved with a printer filter, a program called by the print spooler to translate data as needed, so the printer can handle it.

Some Standard Printer Languages

- ASCII text

  Every normal printer should at least be able to print out ASCII text directly. However, there are devices that cannot print ASCII text directly, but are able to handle one of the other standard printer languages mentioned below.

- PostScript

  PostScript is the established printer language on Unix and Linux systems. Many programs produce PostScript output that can then be directly printed by a PostScript printer.

- PCL3, PCL4, PCL5e, PCL6, ESC/P, ESC/P2, and ESC/P raster

  If a PostScript printer is not available, the print filter can use the program Ghostscript to convert PostScript data into one of these other standard printer languages. Ghostscript uses different drivers for different printers to make use of specific features, such as color settings, offered by the various models as much as possible.

Processing a Print Job

1. The user or an application generates a new print job.
2. The print data is temporarily stored in the print queue. The print spooler sends it from there to the printer filter.
3. Now the printer filter performs the following steps:
   (a) It determines the type of print data.
   (b) The print data is converted into PostScript, if not in PostScript already. ASCII text, for example, is normally converted into PostScript by the filter program a2ps.
   (c) If necessary, the PostScript data is converted to another printer language.
      - If the printer is a PostScript model, the PostScript data is sent directly to the printer.
      - If the printer is not a PostScript model, Ghostscript uses a driver suitable for the respective printer to generate the printer-specific data that is subsequently sent to the printer.
4. After the entire print job has been sent to the printer, the print spooler removes the print job from the print queue.

Available Printing Systems

SuSE Linux supports two different printing systems:

LPRng and lpdfilter This is a traditional printing system that consists of the print spooler LPRng and the printer filter lpdfilter. The entire configuration of this printing system is left to the system administrator. Regular users can only choose between the different print queues that have already been set up. To allow users to choose between different options for a given printer, a number of print queues must be defined, each with a different printer configuration.

CUPS By contrast, the CUPS printing system allows users to set different options for each print job and the configuration of printer queues is not entirely predefined by the system administrator. Rather, printer options are stored in a PPD (PostScript printer description) file for each queue.

Because of conflicts between these two printing systems, you cannot have both of them installed at the same time.

For more information about CUPS, see `http://www.cups.org/` and the *Administration Guide*.

Print Queues

In most cases, more than one print queue is required for the following reasons:

- Different printer devices must be addressed through different print queues.
- The printer filter can be configured differently for each print queue. By having different queues for one printer, it can be operated with a different set of options. However, this is not required when using the CUPS printing system, because CUPS allows users to set options individually for each print job.

One standard queue is sufficient for plain black-and-white printers, such as most laser printers, but color ink jet printers usually require at least two queues (configurations):

- A standard "lp" configuration for quick and inexpensive black-and-white printouts. An `lp` queue should always be defined, because this is also the traditional name of the default queue.
- A `color` queue for color printing.

Supported Printers

Because most Linux printer drivers are not written by the maker of the hardware, it is crucial that the printer can be driven through one of the generally known languages. Normal printers understand at least one of these common languages. In the case of a GDI printer, however, the manufacturer has built a device that relies on its own special control sequences. Many inexpensive ink jet models belong to this group. Such a printer only runs "out of the box" under the versions of the operating systems for which the manufacturer has included a driver. As the device cannot be operated through one of the standard languages, it cannot be used with Linux or can only be used with difficulties.

Nevertheless, a number of these printers are supported by SuSE Linux. However, their use is often rather problematic and some features might not be available at all, for example, the printer could be limited to low resolution monochrome printing. The following list includes the GDI models that can be directly configured with YaST. Because SuSE does not test GDI printers, there is no guarantee that the list is correct.

- Brother HL 720/730/820/1020/1040, MFC 4650/6550MC/9050, and compatible models
- HP DeskJet 710/712/720/722/820/1000 and compatible models
- Lexmark 1000/1020/1100/2030/2050/2070/3200/5000/5700/7000/7200, Z11/42/43/51/52, and compatible models: Linux drivers from Lexmark are available at `http://www.lexmark.com/printers/linuxprinters.html`.
- Oki Okipage 4w/4w+/6w/8w/8wLite/8z/400w and compatible models
- Samsung ML-200/210/1000/1010/1020/1200/1210/1220/4500/5080/6040 and compatible models

To our knowledge, the following GDI printers are not supported by SuSE Linux. This list is by no means complete.

- Brother DCP-1000, MP-21C, WL-660
- Canon BJC 5000/5100/8000/8500, LBP 460/600/660/800, MultiPASS L6000
- Epson AcuLaser C1000, EPL 5500W/5700L/5800L

- HP LaserJet 1000/3100/3150
- Lexmark Z12/22/23/31/32/33/82, Winwriter 100/150c/200
- Minolta PagePro 6L/1100L/18L, Color PagePro L, Magicolor 6100DeskLaser/2DeskLaserPlus/2DeskLaserDuplex
- Nec SuperScript 610plus/660/660plus
- Oki Okijet 2010
- Samsung ML 85G/5050G, QL 85G
- Sharp AJ 2100, AL 1000/800/840/F880/121

Configuration with YaST2

To set up a printer, go to the 'Hardware' item in the YaST Control Center then select 'Printer'. This will open the main printer configuration window in which the detected devices are listed in the upper part. The lower part lists any queues that have been configured so far. If your printer was not detected, restart the autodetection. If it fails again, select 'Configure' to configure the printer manually. Not every printer can be configured for both printing systems. Certain configurations are only supported by either CUPS or LPRng and lpdfilter. YaST will inform you about this whenever necessary.

Note

In SuSE Linux, the default printing system is CUPS, but you can switch from CUPS to LPRng and back at any time. To do so, select 'Change' → 'Advanced' in the YaST printer configuration module. Then select either printing system and configure it.

Note

Automatic Configuration

YaST configures the printer automatically if these requirements are met:

1. The parallel or USB port can be set up automatically in the correct way and the connected printer can be autodetected.
2. The ID string of the printer, as supplied to YaST during hardware autodetection, is included in the printer database. As this ID may be different from the actual name of the model, you may need to select the model manually.

To make sure everything works properly, each configuration should be checked with the print test function of YaST. The YaST test page also provides important information about the configuration selected.

Manual Configuration

If one of the requirements for automatic configuration is not met or if you want a custom setup, configure the printer manually.

Depending on how successful the autodetection is and how much information about the printer model is found in the database, YaST may be able to determine the right settings automatically or at least make a reasonable preselection.

The following parameters must be configured:

Hardware Connection (Port) The configuration of the hardware connection depends on whether YaST has been able to find the printer during hardware autodetection.

- If YaST is able to detect the printer model automatically, it can be assumed that the printer connection works on the hardware level and no settings need to be changed in this respect.
- If YaST is unable to autodetect the printer model, there may be some problem on the hardware level and some manual intervention is required to configure the connection. To learn about the steps involved in this, refer to the Administration Guide.

Name of the Queue The queue name is used when issuing print commands. The name should be relatively short and consist of lowercase letters and possibly numbers only.

Ghostscript Driver or Printer Language (Printer Model) The Ghostscript driver and the printer language depend on your printer model. YaST lets you select a predefined configuration suitable for the model. Selecting a manufacturer and a model basically means selecting a printer language and a Ghostscript driver suitable for this language with some default settings for the driver. These settings may then be changed in an additional dialog as needed.

For non-PostScript models, all printer-specific data is produced by the Ghostscript driver. The driver configuration — both choosing the right driver and the correct options for it — is the single most important factor determining the output quality. The settings made at this point affect the printout on a queue-by-queue basis.

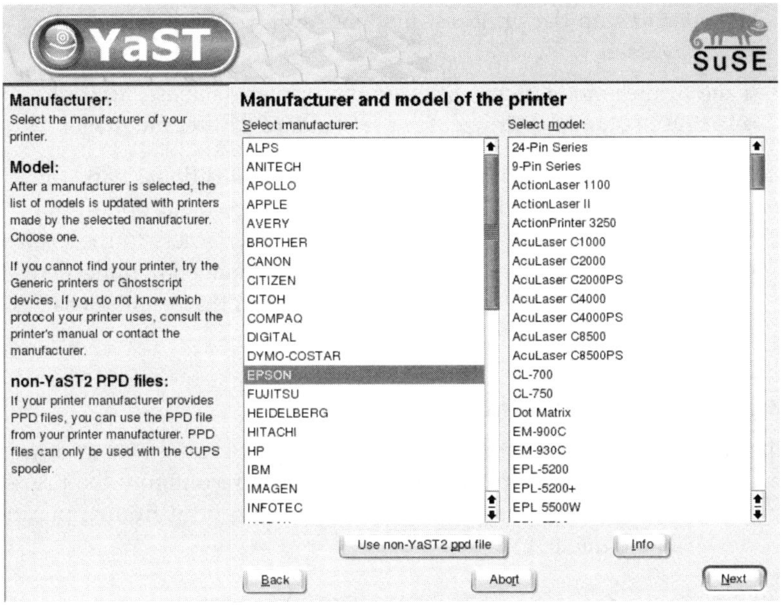

Figure 4.7: Selecting the Printer

If your printer was autodetected (using the printer database) or if the model has been selected manually, YaST presents a choice of suitable Ghostscript drivers, usually with a number of predefined configurations for each of them, for instance:

- monochrome
- color 300 dpi
- photo 600 dpi

A predefined configuration includes a suitable Ghostscript driver and, if available, a set of options for the driver related to output quality. Not all selectable combinations of driver settings work with every printer model. This is especially true for higher resolutions.

Always check whether your settings work as expected by printing the test page. If the output is garbled, for example, with several pages being almost empty, you should be able to stop the printer by first removing all paper then stopping the print test from YaST. However, in some cases the printer will refuse to resume work if you do so. It may then be better to stop the print test first and wait for the printer to eject all pages by itself.

If the printer model is not listed in the printer database, YaST offers a selection of standard drivers for the standard printer languages.

Advanced Settings Use this dialog to access some additional hardware-dependent (driver-specific) and hardware-independent options. If needed, change special queue settings or restrict access to the printer. However, normally there should be no need change anything here. Details about the possible settings are provided in the printing chapter of the *Administration Guide*.

Configuration for Applications

Applications rely on the existing printer queues in the same way as any command-line tools do. There is usually no need to reconfigure the printer for a particular application and you should be able to print from applications using the available queues.

Printing from the Command Line Print from the command line using the command `lpr -Plp filename`, where `filename` is the name of the file to send to the printer. In this example, the default printer queue `lp` is used, but the `-P` option allows you to specify another queue. For instance, the command `lpr -Pcolor filename` tells the printing system to use the `color` queue.

Using the LPRng Printing System With this printing system, applications can use the `lpr` command for printing. To make this work, tell the application to use one of the existing queues (such as `lp` or `color`) or use the application's print dialog to enter the corresponding command, for example, `lpr -Plp` or `lpr -Pcolor`.

Using the CUPS Printing System The CUPS printing system provides command-line tools, such as the `lpr` command, so the approach as described above works with CUPS, too.

To enable the above for KDE programs, it is necessary to use the 'Print through an external program' option in the print dialog. There are also several graphical tools, such as xpp and the KDE program krpinter, which provide a graphical interface to choose among queues and to change both CUPS standard options and printer-specific options as made available through the PPD file.

If desired, configure applications to use kprinter as the standard printing interface by specifying kprinter or kprinter --stdin as the printing command in the respective dialogs of these applications. Which of the two commands to use depends on the behavior of the application itself. If this is set up in the correct way, the application should call the kprinter dialog whenever a print job is issued from it, so you can use kprinter to select the queue and to set other options. This requires that the application's own print setup does not conflict with that of kprinter and that the setup is left unchanged after kprinter has been enabled.

Troubleshooting

If there is some kind of error in the communication between the computer and the printer, the printer may no longer be able to interpret data correctly. This can cause the output to be garbled and use up large amounts of paper.

1. To stop the printing, take out all paper or open the paper trays.
2. As the print job will be removed from the printer queue only after having been sent completely to the printer, it will usually still be there. Even a reboot will not remove it. To delete the print job, use a tool like kprinter. Instructions for managing print jobs from the command line are provided in the *Administration Guide*.
3. It is possible that some data is still transmitted to the printer even though the print job has been deleted from the queue. To stop all processes still using the printer device, use the `fuser` command. For a printer connected to the first parallel port, enter:

   ```
   earth:~ #  fuser -k /dev/lp0
   ```

   To achieve the same for a USB printer, enter:

   ```
   earth:~ #  fuser -k /dev/usb/lp0
   ```

4. Do a complete reset of the printer by switching it off. Wait a few seconds before putting the paper back into the trays and switching the device back on. The printer should now be ready to accept new jobs.

For More Information

Details about the Linux printing systems are provided in the Chapter *Printer Operation* in the *Administration Guide*, which should already be installed on your system. To read the manual, start SuSE Help then click *Administration Guide*. The PDF file is also available in `/usr/share/doc/packages/suselinux-adminguide_en` and can be opened with a viewer.

The above-mentioned chapter in the *Administration Guide* discusses printing issues and solutions in general terms. For more specific problems and troubleshooting hints, consult the Support Database.

If you have printer problems, check the Support Database articles *Installing a Printer* and *Printer Configuration with SuSE Linux 8.02 and Above*, which you can find by searching for the keyword "installation" or online at:
`http://sdb.suse.de/en/sdb/html/jsmeix_print-einrichten.html`
`http://sdb.suse.de/en/sdb/html/jsmeix_print-einrichten-82.html`
The Support Database can be accessed through the SuSE Help Center. The latest version is available online at `http://sdb.suse.de/en/`.

The most important issues of the current version are summarized in a central article, *Known Problems and Special Features in SuSE Linux 8.2* at `http://sdb.suse.de/en/sdb/html/bugs82.html`.

Hard Disk Controller

Normally YaST configures the hard disk controller of your system during the installation. If you add controllers, you can integrate these into the system with this YaST module. You can also modify the existing configuration, but this is generally not necessary.

The dialog presents a list of detected hard disk controllers and enables the assignment of the suitable kernel module with specific parameters. Use 'Test Loading of Module' to check if the current settings work before they are saved permanently in the system.

Caution

This is an expert tool. Do not modify the settings unless you know what you are doing. Your system may no longer boot if you specify incorrect settings. In any case, you should make use of the test option.

Caution

Display and Input Devices (SaX2)

The graphical user interface or X server handles the communication between hardware and software. Desktops, like KDE and GNOME, and the wide variety of window managers use the X server for interaction with the user.

The graphical user interface is initially configured during installation. To change the settings afterwards, run this YaST module. In the configuration dialog, choose between 'Text mode only' and the graphical user interface. The current settings are saved and you can reset to them anytime. The current values are displayed and offered for modification: the screen resolution, the color depth, the refresh rate, and the vendor and type of your monitor, if it was autodetected. If you have just installed a new graphics card that you want to initialize, a small dialog appears asking whether to activate 3D acceleration for your graphics card.

Click 'Edit'. SaX2, the configuration tool for the input and display devices, is started in a separate window. This window is shown in Figure 4.8.

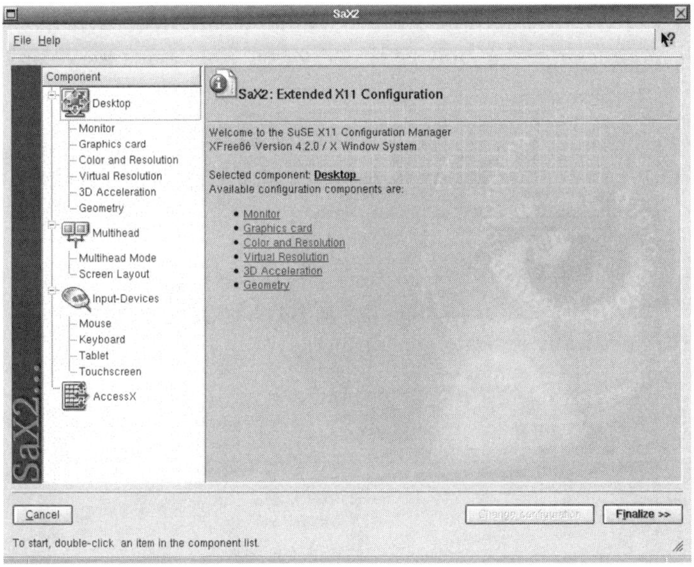

Figure 4.8: The Main Window of the New SaX2

SaX2 — Main Window

In the left navigation bar, there are four main items: 'Display', 'Input devices', 'Multihead', and 'AccessX'. Configure your monitor, graphics card, color depth, resolution, and the position and size of the screen under 'Display'. The keyboard, mouse, touchscreen monitor, and graphics tablet can be configured under 'Input devices'. Use 'Multihead' to configure multiple screen operation (see *Multihead* on page 68). Here, set the multihead display mode and the layout of the screens on your desk. 'AccessX' is a useful tool for controlling the mouse pointer with the number pad.

Select your monitor and your graphics card. Usually, these are automatically detected by the system. In this case, you do not need to modify anything. If your monitor is not autodetected, continue to the monitor selection dialog. Most likely, you can find your monitor in the comprehensive vendor and device list. Alternatively, manually enter the values specified in the monitor documentation or select one of the preconfigured VESA modes.

After you click 'Finish' in the main window following the completion of the settings for your monitor and your graphics card, test your settings. Thus, ensure that your configuration is suitable for your devices. If the image is not steady, terminate the test immediately by pressing (Esc) and reduce the refresh rate or the resolution and color depth. Regardless of whether you run a test, all modifications are only activated when you restart the X server.

Display

If you go to 'Edit configuration' → 'Properties', a window with the tabs 'Monitor', 'Frequencies', and 'Expert' appears.

- 'Monitor' — In the left part of the window, select the vendor. In the right part, select your model. If you have floppy disks with Linux drivers for your monitor, install these by clicking 'Driver disk'.

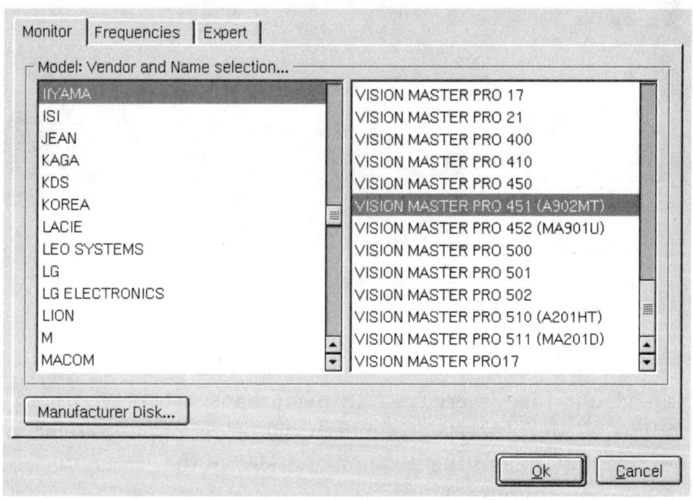

Figure 4.9: *SaX2: Monitor Selection*

- 'Frequencies' — Here, enter the horizontal and vertical frequencies for your screen. The vertical frequency is another designation for the image refresh rate. Normally, the acceptable value ranges are read from the model and entered here. Usually, they do not need to be changed.
- 'Expert' — Here, enter some options for your screen. In the upper selection field, define the method to use for the calculation of the screen resolution and screen geometry. Do not change anything unless the monitor is addressed incorrectly and the display is not stable. Furthermore, you can change the size of the displayed image and activate the power saving mode DPMS.

Graphics Card

The graphics card dialog has two tabs: 'General' and 'Expert':

- In 'General', select the vendor of your graphics card on the left side and the model on the right.

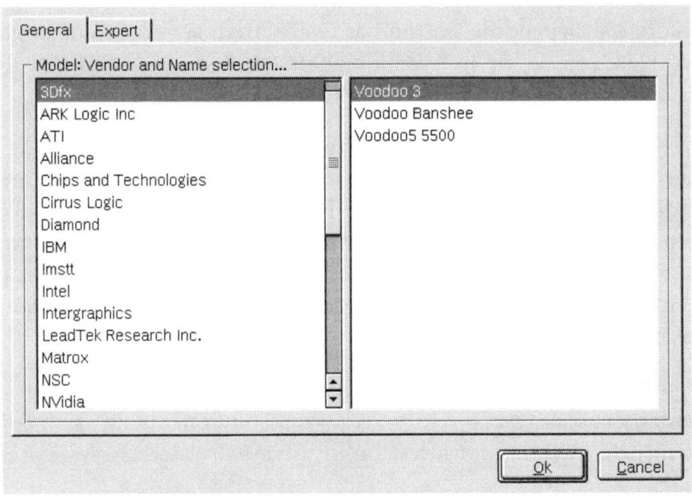

Figure 4.10: Selecting the Graphics Cards

- 'Expert' offers more advanced configuration possibilites. On the right side, turn your screen to the left or to a vertical position (useful for some turnable TFT screens). The entries for the BusID are only relevant if you operate several screens. Normally, nothing needs to be changed here. You should not modify the card options unless you have experience in this field and know what the options mean. If necessary, check the documentation of your graphics card.

Note

The configuration of graphics cards exclusively supported by XFree86 3.3.6 is no longer included in the installation. This affects cards like older S3 PCI cards. Instead, depending on the graphics card, YaST2 configures the framebuffer without acceleration or the generic 16-color VGA driver for these graphics cards. If your card is affected, repeat the configuration with XFree86 3.3.6 using SaX1. For this purpose, enter the command `sax` on the command line.

Note

Colors and Resolutions

Here, three tabs, 'Colors', 'Resolution', and 'Expert', are available.

- 'Colors' — Depending on the hardware used, select a color depth of 16, 256, 32768, 65536, or 16.7 million colors (4, 8, 15, 16, or 24 bit). For a reasonable display quality, set at least 256 colors.
- 'Resolution' — When the hardware is detected, the resolution is queried. Therefore, the module usually only offers resolution and color depth combinations that your hardware can display correctly. This keeps the danger of damaging your hardware with wrong settings very low in SuSE Linux. If you change the resolution manually, consult the documentation of your hardware to make sure the value set can be displayed.
- 'Expert' — In addition to the resolutions offered in the previous tab, this tab enables you to add your own resolutions, which will subsequently be included for selection in the tab.

Virtual Resolution

Every desktop has a certain resolution that is displayed over the full screen of the monitor. Additionally, it is possible to set the resolution larger than the visible area of the screen. If you move the mouse beyond the margins of the desktop, the virtual part of the desktop is displayed on screen. This increases the available work space.

The virtual resolution can be set in two different ways:

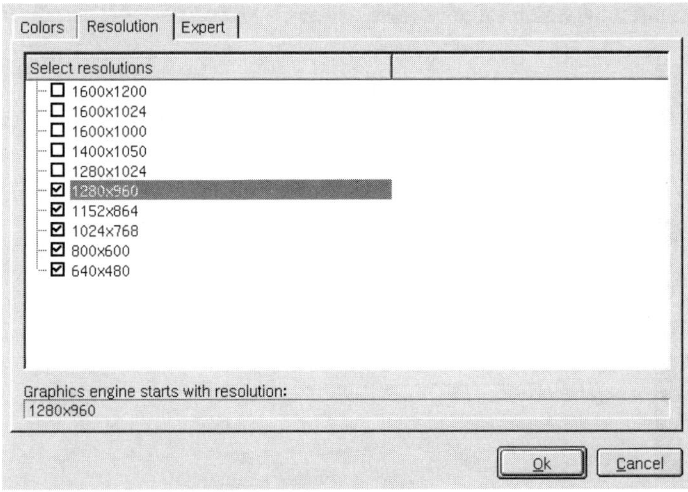

Figure 4.11: Configuring the Resolution

- 'By Drag&Drop' – Move the mouse pointer over the monitor image and the mouse will turn into crosshairs. Keep the left mouse button pressed and move the mouse to enlarge the raster image, which corresponds with the virtual resolution. This method is best if you are not quite sure how much virtual space you want on your desktop.
- 'By selection from the pop-up menu' — In the pop-up menu in the middle of the raster image, the currently used virtual resolution is displayed. To use one of the default virtual resolutions, select one from the menu.

3D Acceleration

Optionally, activate the 3D acceleration of your graphics card. A dialog is displayed in which to activate the 3D properties of your graphics card.

Image Position and Size

Under these two tabs, precisely adjust the size and the position of the image with the arrows. See Figure 4.13 on page 69. If you have a multihead environment (more than one screen), use 'Next screen' to switch to the other monitors to adjust their size and position. Press 'Save' to save your settings.

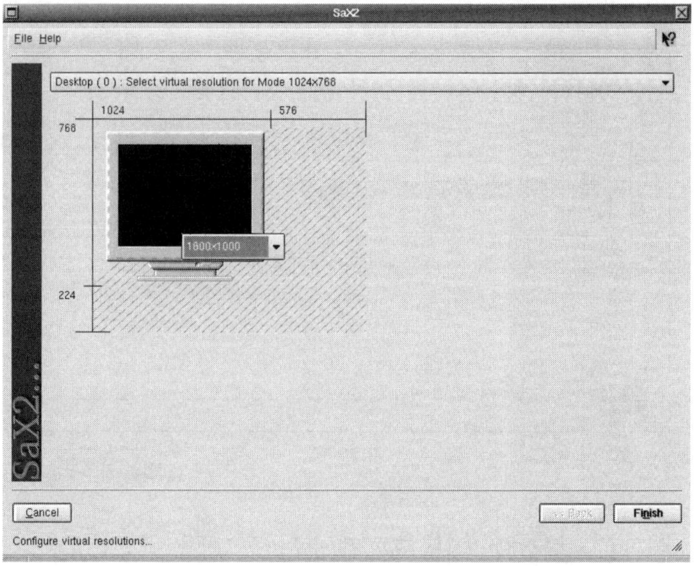

Figure 4.12: Configuring the Virtual Resolution

Caution

There are safety mechanisms, but you should still be very careful when manually changing the allowed frequencies. False values may destroy your monitor. If in doubt, refer to the manual of the monitor.

Caution

Multihead

If you have installed more than one graphics card in your computer or a graphics card with multiple outputs, you can connect more than one screen to your system. If you operate two screens, this is referred to as "dualhead". More than two is referred to as "multihead". SaX2 automatically detects multiple graphics cards in the system and prepares the configuration accordingly. Set the multihead mode and the arrangement of the screens in the multihead dialog. Three modes are offered: 'Traditional' (default), 'One screen (Xinerama)', and 'Clone mode'.

- 'Traditional multihead' — Each monitor represents an individual unit. The mouse pointer can switch between the screens.

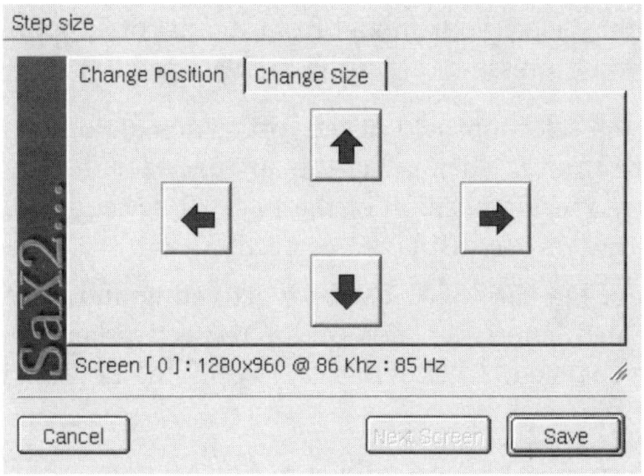

Figure 4.13: Adjusting the Image Geometry

- 'Cloned multihead' — In this mode, all monitors display the same contents. The mouse is only visible on the main screen.
- 'Xinerama multihead' — All screens combine to form a single large screen. Program windows can be positioned freely on all screens or scaled to a size that fills more than one monitor.

The layout of a multihead environment describes the arrangement of and the relationship between the individual screens. By default, SaX2 configures a standard layout that follows the sequence of the detected graphics cards, arranging all screens in a row from left to right. In the 'Layout' dialog of the multihead tool, determine the way the monitors are arranged by using the mouse to move the screen symbols in the grid.

After you have completed the layout dialog, verify the new configuration by clicking 'Test'.

Linux currently does not offer 3D support for Xinerama multihead environments. In this case, SaX2 deactivates the 3D support.

Input Devices

Mouse If the mouse already works, you do not need to do anything. However, if the mouse does not work, control it with the number pad of the keyboard as described in *AccessX* on page 71.

If the automatic detection fails, use this dialog to configure your mouse manually. Refer to the documentation of your mouse for a description of the model. Select your model from the list of supported mouse types and confirm by pressing ⑤ on the number pad.

Keyboard Use the selection field at the top of this dialog to specify the kind of keyboard to use. Then select the language for the keyboard layout (the country-specific position of the keys). Use the test field to check if special characters are displayed correctly.

The status of the check box used for activating and deactivating the entry of accented letters depends on the respective language and does not need to be changed. Click 'Finish' to apply the new settings to your system.

Touchscreen Currently, XFree86 only supports Microtouch and Elo TouchSystems touchscreens. SaX2 can only autodetect the monitor, not the toucher. The toucher is treated as an input device. Configure the toucher as follows:

1. Start SaX2 and select 'Input devices' → 'Touchscreens'.
2. Click 'Add' and add a touchscreen.
3. Save the configuration by clicking 'Finish'. You do not need to test the configuration.

Touchscreens feature a variety of options and usually must be calibrated first. Unfortunately, there is no general tool for this purpose in Linux. The standard configuration contains suitable default values for the dimensions of the touchscreen. Normally, no additional configuration is required.

Graphics Tablet Currently, XFree86 only supports a limited number of graphics tablets. SaX2 enables the configuration of graphics tablets connected to the USB port or the serial port. From the configuration perspective, a graphics tablet is just an input device like a mouse. The following procedure is recommended:

1. Start SaX2 and select 'Input devices' → 'Graphics tablet'.
2. Click 'Add', select the vendor from the following dialog, and add a graphics tablet from the selection list.
3. Mark the check boxes to the right if you have connected a pen or eraser.
4. If your tablet is connected to the serial port, verify the port. `/dev/ttyS0` refers to the first serial port. `/dev/ttyS1` refers to the second. Additional ports use similar notation.
5. Save the configuration by clicking 'Finish'.

AccessX

If you do not use a mouse on your computer, start SaX2 and activate AccessX. The mouse pointer can now be controlled with the keys on the number pad as follows:

- *Button 1* correponds to the key %
  This key activates the left mouse button.
- *Button 2* corresponds to the key X
  This key activates the middle mouse button.
- *Button 3* corresponds to the key -
  This key activates the right mouse button.
- A *Click* is emulated with the key 5
  This key equals a click of the previously activated mouse button. If no mouse button was activated, the left mouse button is used.
- *Double Click* equals the key +
  This key works like the key5, except that it invokes a double click.
- *Button Lock* equals the key 0
  This works like the key5, except that it keeps the button pressed.
- *Button Release* equals the key Del
  This key works like a mouse click invoked by the key 0.
- *Arrow up and left* works like the key 7
  The mouse pointer moves up and left.
- *Arrow up* acts like 8
  The mouse pointer moves up in a straight line.
- *Arrow up and right* acts like the key 9
  The mouse pointer moves up and right.
- *Left arrow* works as the key 4
  The mouse pointer moves to the left.
- *Right arrow* acts like the key 6
  The mouse pointer moves to the right.
- *Down arrow* corresponds to the key 1
  The mouse pointer moves down.
- *Down arrow* corresponds to the key 2
  The mouse pointer moves down in a straight line.

- *Arrow down and right* corresponds to the key ③
  This key moves the mouse pointer down and right.

With the slider, set the speed of the mouse pointer movement when a key is pressed.

For More Information

For more information about the X Window System, its history, and its properties, refer to *Configuration of the X Window System with SaX2* in the *Administration Guide.*

Hardware Information

YaST performs a hardware detection for the configuration of hardware components. The detected technical data is displayed in this screen. This is especially useful, for example, if you want to submit a support request for which you need information about your hardware.

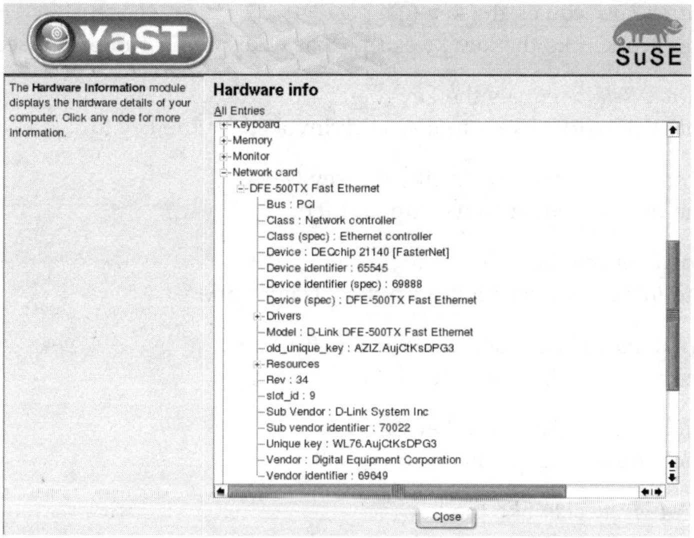

Figure 4.14: Displaying Hardware Information

IDE DMA Mode

This module enables you to activate and deactivate the DMA mode for your IDE hard disks and your IDE CD/DVD drives in the installed system. This module does not have any function for SCSI devices. DMA modes can substantially increase the performance and data transfer speed in your system.

During the installation, the current SuSE Linux kernel automatically activates DMA for hard disks but not for CD drives, because default DMA activation for all drives often caused problems with CD drives. Use the DMA module to decide whether to activate DMA for your drives. If the drive supports the DMA mode smoothly, the data transfer rate of your CD drive can be increased by activating DMA.

Note

"DMA" (*D*irect *M*emory *A*ccess) means that your data can be transferred directly to the RAM, bypassing the processor control.

Note

Joystick

Use this module to configure your joystick by selecting the manufacturer and the model from the displayed list. With 'Test', check if your joystick responds correctly. The test dialog shows three charts for the analog axes of the joystick and marks for the four standard buttons. When you move the joystick or press the buttons, you should be able to see a reaction in the test dialog. As joysticks are usually connected to the sound card, you can also access this module from the sound card configuration.

Select Mouse Model

Configure your mouse with this YaST module. As the procedure for the selection of the mouse was already explained within the scope of the user-defined installation, refer to *Mouse* on page 19.

Scanner

If your scanner is connected and switched on, it should be detected automatically when this YaST module is started. In this case, the dialog for the installation of the scanner appears. If no scanner is detected, the manual configuration dialog appears. If you have already installed one or several scanners, a table listing existing scanners that can be modified or deleted appears. Press 'Add' to configure a new device.

Next, an installation is performed with default settings. If the installation is successful, a corresponding message appears. Now, test your scanner by inserting a document and clicking 'Test'.

Scanner Was Not Detected

Only supported scanners can be autodetected. Scanners connected to another network host will not be detected. The manual configuration distinguishes three types of scanners: USB scanners, SCSI scanners, and network scanners.

- USB scanner: Specify the vendor and model. YaST attempts to load USB modules. If your scanner is very new, the modules may not be loaded automatically. In this case, you will be taken to a dialog that enables you to load the USB module manually. Refer to the YaST help text for more information.
- SCSI scanner: Specify the device (such as `/dev/sg0`). SCSI scanners should not be connected or disconnected when the the system is running. Shut the system down first.
- Network scanner: Enter the IP address or the host name.

You can use a scanner that is connected to a host in your network and configured as a network scanner. To configure a network scanner, refer to the Support Database article "Scanning in Linux" (`http://sdb.suse.de/en/`, keyword "scanner"). When selecting a network scanner, enter the host name or the IP address of the host to which the scanner is connected in the dialog.

If your scanner was not detected, probably the device is not supported. However, sometimes even supported scanners are not detected. If that is the case, proceed with the manual scanner selection. If you can identify your scanner in the list of vendors and models, select it. If not, select 'Cancel'. Information about scanners that work with Linux is provided at `http://cdb.suse.de/index.php?LANG=en`, `http://sdb.suse.de/en/`, and `http://www.mostang.com/sane`.

Caution

Only assign the scanner manually if you are absolutely sure. A wrong selection could damage your hardware.

Caution

Troubleshooting

Your scanner may not have been detected for one of the following reasons:

- The scanner is not supported. Check `http://sdb.suse.de/en/` for a list of devices compatible with Linux.
- Your SCSI controller was not installed correctly.
- There are termination problems with your SCSI port.
- Your SCSI cable is too long.
- Your scanner has a SCSI Light Controller that is not supported by Linux.
- Your scanner is defective.

Caution

SCSI scanners should not be connected or disconnected when the the system is running. Shut the system down first.

Caution

For more information about scanning, refer to *Kooka — The Scanning Application* on page 271.

Sound

When the sound configuration tool is started, YaST tries to autodetect your sound card. Configure one or multiple sound cards. To use multiple sound cards, start by selecting one of the cards to configure. Press 'Configure' to enter the 'Setup' dialog. 'Edit' opens a dialog in which to edit sound cards already configured. 'Finish' saves the current settings and completes the sound configuration. If YaST is unable to autodetect your sound card, press 'Add Sound Card' in 'Sound Configuration' to open a dialog in which to select a sound card and module.

Setup

With 'Quick Automatic Setup', you will not be required to go through any of the further configuration steps and no sound test is performed. The sound card is configured automatically.

With 'Normal Setup', you have the possibility to adjust the output volume and play a test sound.

With 'Options', you can manually customize the sound card options.

Set up your joystick by clicking the respective check box. Select the joystick type in the following dialog and click 'Next'. The same dialog appears when you click 'Joystick' in the YaST2 Control Center.

Sound Card Volume

Test your sound configuration in this test screen. Use the '+' and '-' buttons to adjust the volume. Start at about ten percent to avoid damage to your speakers or hearing. A test sound should be audible when you press 'Test'. If you cannot hear anything, increase the volume. Press 'Continue' to complete the sound configuration. The volume setting will be saved.

Sound Configuration

Use 'Delete' to remove a sound card. Existing entries of configured sound cards are deactivated in the file `/etc/modules.conf`. Click 'Options' to open a dialog in which to customize the sound module options manually. In 'Volume', configure the individual settings for the input and output of each sound card. 'Next' saves the new values and 'Back' resets to the default configuration. Under 'Add Sound Card...', configure additional sound cards. If YaST autodetects another sound card, continue to 'Configure a Sound Card'. If YaST does not detect a sound card, you are directed to 'Manual Sound Card Selection' automatically.

If you use a Creative Soundblaster Live or AWE sound card, automatically copy SF2 sound fonts to your hard disk from the original Soundblaster driver CD-ROM with 'Install Sound Fonts'. The sound fonts will be saved in the directory `/usr/share/sfbank/creative/`.

The start-up of ALSA when booting the machine can be enabled or disabled with 'Start ALSA'. For playback of MIDI files, activate 'Start Sequencer'. This way, the sound modules required for sequencer support will be loaded along with the ALSA modules.

The volume and configuration of all sound cards installed will be saved when you click 'Finish'. The mixer settings are saved to the file `/etc/asound.conf` and the ALSA configuration data appended at the end of the file `/etc/modules.conf`.

Configuring a Sound Card

If multiple sound cards were detected, select your preferred card under 'List of Automatically Recognized...'. Continue to 'Setup' with 'Next'. If the sound card was not autodetected, click 'Select from List' and, with 'Next', proceed to 'Manual Sound Card Selection'.

Manual Sound Card Selection

If your sound card was not autodetected, a list of sound card drivers and models are shown from which to choose. With 'All', see the entire list of supported cards.

Refer to your sound card documentation for the information required. A reference list of sound cards supported by ALSA with their corresponding sound modules is available in `/usr/share/doc/packages/alsa/cards.txt` and at `http://www.alsa-project.org/\char126{}goemon/`. After making your selection, click 'Next' to return to 'Setup'.

TV and Radio Cards

After starting and initializing this YaST module, the 'TV and Radio Cards' dialog appears. If your card was autodetected, it is shown in the list at the top. In this case, highlight the line with the mouse then select 'Configure'.

If your card was not detected, select "Other (not recognized)". If you press 'Configure', continue to the manual selection in which to select your card from the manufacturer and model lists.

If you have already configured TV or radio cards, modify existing configurations with 'Change'. In this case, a dialog presents a list of all configured cards. Select a card and start the manual configuration with 'Edit'.

During the automatic hardware detection, YaST attempts to assign the correct tuner to your card. If you are not sure, simply keep the setting 'Default (recognized)' and check whether it works. If you are not able to set all channels, this might be due to a failure of the automatic detection of the tuner type. In this case, click 'Select Tuner' and highlight the correct tuner type in the list.

If you are familiar with the technical details, you can use the expert dialog to specify settings for a TV or radio card. A kernel module and its parameters can be selected in this dialog. Also check all parameters of your TV card driver. To do this, select the respective parameters and enter the new value in the parameter line. Confirm the new values with 'Apply' or restore the default values with 'Reset'.

The dialog 'TV and Radio Cards, Audio' enables you to connect your TV or radio card with the installed sound card. You must use a cable to connect the output of the TV or radio card with the external audio input of the sound card. This only works if the sound card is already configured and the external input is active. If you have not yet configured your sound card, select 'Configure Sound Card' to go to the respective dialog (see *Sound* on page 75.

If your TV or radio card has loudspeaker jacks, you can also connect the loudspeakers directly without configuring the sound card. There are also TV cards without any sound function, which do not require an audio configuration (e.g., for CCD cameras).

Network Devices

Basic Information about Internet Access

This section explains a number of important terms in connection with Internet access, briefly introducing their aim and function.

All the machines connected to the Internet form a large network in which various operating systems run with different hardware. The Internet uses a standard communication protocol that can be understood regardless of the hardware or software used. This is made possible by means of the Internet Protocol (IP) together with the Transmission Control Protocol (TCP), the User Datagram Protocol (UDP), and the Internet Control Message Protocol (ICMP). These protocols comprise the common "language" used by all machines on the Internet. The abbreviation for this is TCP/IP.

Every machine on the Internet has an ID number — the IP address. It can only be addressed by TCP/IP with this number. Normally, a machine also has a text name. The Domain Name System (DNS) is responsible for converting the IP address to a text name. This particular service is offered by name servers. A machine or an application offering a service is called a server (for example, DNS server) and a machine or application making use of a service is called a client.

Under TCP/IP, there are various standardized protocols for forwarding the appropriate TCP/IP data transfers to the given transmission method. For network connections via a network card, the ethernet protocol is used. For modem and ISDN telephone connections, it is the Point-to-Point Protocol (PPP). For ADSL and T-DSL connections, the Point-to-Point over Ethernet Protocol (PPPoE) is used.

To establish an Internet connection, the ethernet, PPP, or PPPoE connection between your host and a host of the Internet provider must be established first, followed by the TCP/IP connection.

On top of TCP/IP, there are various standardized protocols for proper data transfer to the application.

- The HyperText Transfer Protocol (HTTP) serves for the transfer of web sites in HyperText Markup Language (HTML) format.
- The Simple Mail Transfer Protocol (SMTP) is responsible for sending e-mails to another machine and the Post Office Protocol (POP3) for downloading e-mails from a mail server.
- The File Transfer Protocol (FTP) is used to transfer files.

For several application programs, such as a web browser and an e-mail program, to use the same Internet connection at the same time, separate TCP/IP connections are used for each application. Large amounts of TCP/IP data are also divided into small packets, so HTTP packets from the web browser can be sent over its TCP/IP connection while alternating with SMTP or POP3 packet transfers from the e-mail program via other TCP/IP connections.

Because several applications are using the same Internet connection, the IP address, which only identifies the machine, is not sufficient. A port number is needed to sort out which TCP/IP data belong to which application. These standard services are usually provided on servers at the following port numbers:

- DNS on port 53
- HTTP on port 80
- SMTP on port 25 and POP3 on port 110
- FTP on port 20 and 21

The client can only use services if it addresses the correct port number on the server.

Information about the Internet Dial-Up

If you activate 'Dial on demand' or 'Automatic dial-up' in the YaST modules, the Internet connection is established automatically whenever necessary, for example, when an external URL is entered in the browser or when e-mail is sent and retrieved. 'Dial on demand' or 'automatic' is only advisable if you have a flat rate for Internet access. With 'manual', the computer only establishes a connection to the Internet when you want it to do so. Background processes, such as retrieval of e-mail in regular intervals, frequently establish connections to the Internet, which can be expensive.

Network Card

When the YaST module is started, see an overview of the network configuration. The top part of the dialog lists all network cards that were autodetected or manually configured. If your card was detected correctly when the system was booted, the name of the card appears here. Devices that were not recognized are listed as 'Other (not detected)'. The lower part of the screen lists configured devices including the network type and the address. You can configure new network cards or modify the configuration of a configured device.

Manual Configuration of the Network Card

Make the following basic settings to configure a network card that was not recognized:

Network interface Specify the network type and the device number.

Support for Wireless Connections If you are located in a wireless LAN and your network card supports this connection type, activate 'Wireless Device'. Press 'Wireless settings' to enter the dialog in which to configure the operating mode, network name (ESSID), network ID (NWID), encryption key, and nickname. Press 'OK' to finish the configuration of your card.

Kernel Module and Selection of the Network Card If your network card is a PCMCIA or USB device, activate the respective check boxes and exit the dialog with 'Next'. If not, select the network card model 'Select from list'. YaST automatically selects a suitable kernel module. Exit this dialog with 'Next'.

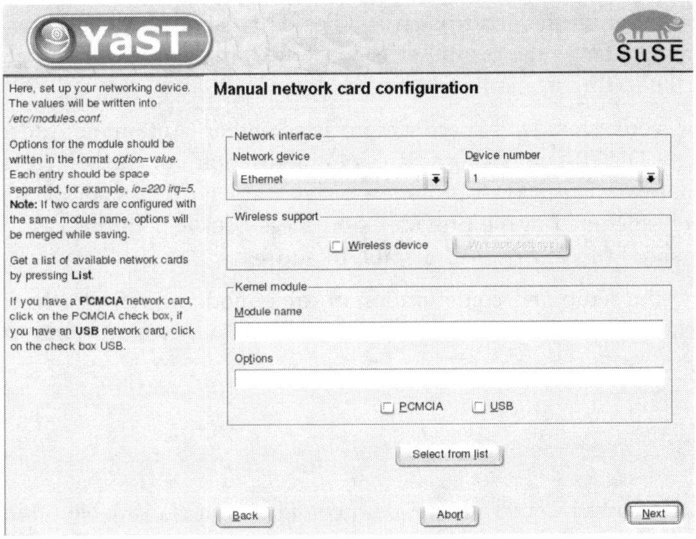

Figure 4.15: Configuration of the Network Card

Configuration of the Network Address

Specify the address allocation method for your network card:

'Automatic Address Setup (with DHCP)' If there is a DHCP server within your network, automatically retrieve the configuration data for your network card from there. You should also activate the address setup with DHCP if your DSL provider has not given you a static IP address for your system.

'Static Address Configuration' Enter the IP address and the correct subnet mask for your network. The preset value for the subnet mask should meet the requirements of a typical home network.

Exit this dialog with 'Next' or configure the host name, name server, and routing (see *Host Name and DNS* on page 88 and *Routing* on page 89).

Cable Modem

In some countries (US, Austria), Internet access via cable modems has become relatively widespread. The cable subscriber gets a modem-like device from the ISP, which is connected to the TV cable network on one side and to the computer on the other using a 10BaseT (twisted pair) cable and a network card. As far as the computer is concerned, this is basically a permanent network link with a static IP address.

Following your provider's specification, select either 'Automatic Address Setup (with DHCP)' or 'Static Address Configuration' for the configuration of your network card. Most providers today use DHCP. A static IP address is generally included in the provider's business package. In this case, the provider should have assigned a static IP address.

Regarding the setup and configuration of cable modems, refer to the Support Database article available online at `http://sdb.suse.de/en/sdb/html/cmodem8.html`.

Modem

In the YaST Control Center, the modem configuration is available under 'Network Devices'. If the autodetection fails, select the manual configuration. In the screen that opens, enter the port under 'Device'.

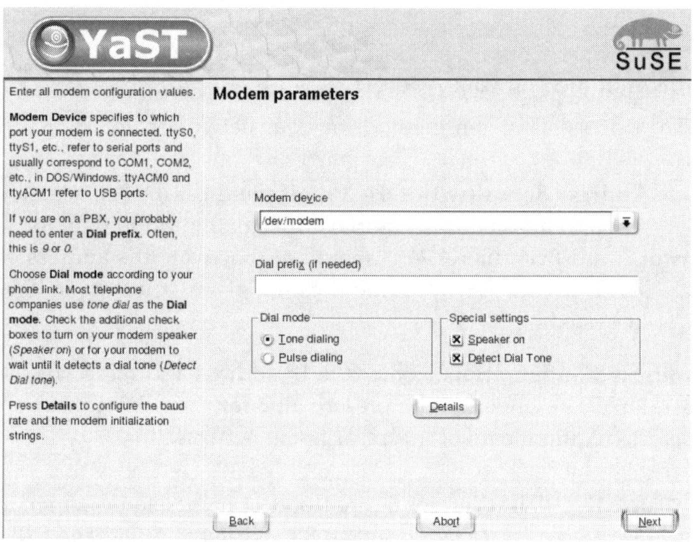

Figure 4.16: Modem Configuration

If a PBX is interposed, you may need to enter an extra number to dial external numbers (usually a zero, but you can find this out in the operation instructions for your telephone system). Also decide between tone and pulse dialing, whether the speaker should be switched on, and whether it should wait for the dial tone. The last option should not be used if your modem is connected to a PBX.

The baud rate and the initialization string settings for the modem can be specified under 'Details'. Only make changes if your modem has not automatically been recognized and special settings must be made for data transfer. This is primarily the case for ISDN terminal adapters. Exit this dialog with 'OK'.

Select the ISP (Internet Service Provider) in the following dialog. If you want to select your provider from a list of preconfigured providers in your country, activate 'Countries'. You can also configure the ISP parameters manually by pressing 'New'. In the dialog that opens, enter the name of the dial-up connection, the provider, and the provider's phone number. Furthermore, enter the user name and the password assigned to you by the provider. Activate 'Always ask for password' if you want to be prompted for the password every time a connection is established.

Enter the connection parameters in the final dialog:

'Dial-on-demand' Refer to *Information about the Internet Dial-Up* on page 80. Enter at least one name server to use dial-on-demand.

'Modify DNS when connected' This check box is activated by default. Accordingly, the name server is adjusted each time a dial-up connection is established. Deactivate this setting and specify static name servers for 'Automatic dial-up'.

'Stupid mode' This option is activated by default. Input prompts by the dial-up server are ignored to facilitate the establishment of the connection.

'Activate firewall' Here, activate the SuSE Firewall to implement protection against intruders when connected to the Internet.

'Idle time (seconds)' Here, specify the period after which the connection should be terminated if there is no data transfer.

IP details With this button, enter the address configuration dialog. If your provider has not assigned a dynamic IP address, deactivate 'Dynamic IP Address' and enter the local IP address of your host and the remote IP address. Contact your provider for information about these settings. Leave the 'Default route' setting active and exit the dialog with 'OK'.

Press 'Next' to return to the overview and see what you configured. Finish the configuration with 'Finish'.

DSL

Your network card must be properly configured to configure ADSL access. With YaST, you can only set up connections based on the Point-to-Point-over-Ethernet protocol (PPPoE). The DHCP protocol is not used for the automatic assignment of IP addresses. Therefore, you should not use 'Automatic address setup (with DHCP)'. Instead, use a static "dummy IP address" like `192.168.22.1`. In 'Subnet mask', enter `255.255.255.0`. For a stand-alone system, be certain that you do not make any entries in the 'Default gateway' field. The values for the 'IP address' of your machine and 'Subnet mask' are only placeholders. They do not have anything to do with setting up a connection with ADSL. They are only required for activating the network card.

In this screen, enter the user ID, the personal password, and the ethernet card to which your modem is connected (usually `eth0`). The recommended 'Idle time' is 60 seconds to terminate the connection automatically if no data transfer has occurred. Click 'Finish' to finish the procedure. To use 'Dial-on-demand' (see page 80) if you have a stand-alone system, you must enter a name server. Most providers today support dynamic DNS assignment, so a current IP address is forwarded to the name server each time the connection is set up. However, a suitable dummy name server IP must be entered in this dialog, for example, `192.168.22.99`. If you do not receive a dynamic name server assignment, enter the IP addresses of the name servers of your provider here.

Proceed for T-DSL (German Telecom) as you would for ADSL. To configure your T-DSL, you will need the following data: attachment identification, T-Online number, shared user ID, and your personal password. This information can be obtained from your T-DSL login sheet.

ISDN

If your ISDN card is successfully autodetected, a dialog appears in which to make your 'Selection of ISDN protocol'. 'Euro-ISDN (EDSS1)' is the standard for this (refer to scenarios 1 and 2a below) in Europe. '1TR6' is a protocol used by older and larger phone systems (refer to scenario 2b below). 'NI1' is the standard in the USA. If this automatic detection fails, choose the correct ISDN card and specify the ISDN protocol. Furthermore, enter area code and country code of your location for the ISDN connection, e.g., `+44 208`. Enter the prefix for external calls if necessary. Then confirm your settings with 'OK'.

The interface is configured in the following dialog. Theoretically, you can configure several interfaces. However, this is usually not necessary for home

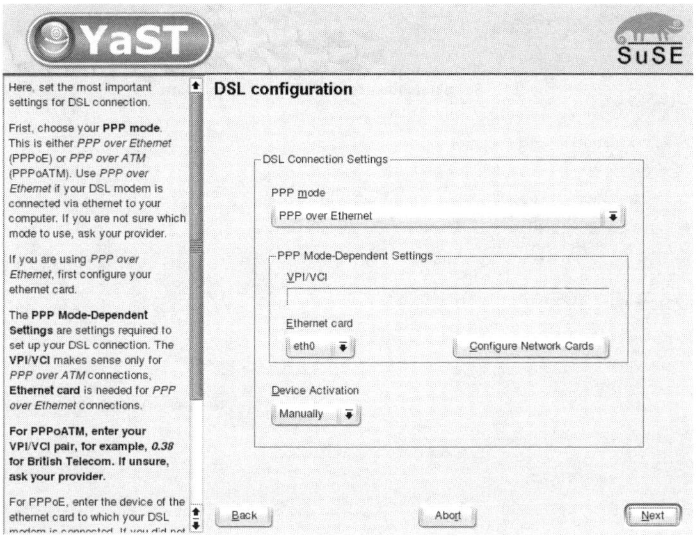

Figure 4.17: ADSL Configuration

users, as several providers can be set up for one interface. The first configured interface is `ippp0`. The specification of the 'Phone Number' depends on which of the following connection scenarios is used:

The ISDN card is connected directly to the socket (NTBA) By default, ISDN offers three numbers (MSN — Multiple Subscriber Number). On request, up to ten numbers can be made available for your line. Here, assign one of the MSN numbers to your ISDN card. The number is specified without the prefix. If you enter the wrong number, your telecom provider will automatically use the first MSN assigned to your ISDN line.

The ISDN card is connected to a PBX Various specifications are required depending on the constellation.

- For private use: Usually the Euro-ISDN/EDSS1 protocol is used for the internal ports of small phone systems. These phone systems use an internal S0 bus and use internal numbers for the connected devices.

  Use one of the internal numbers to specify the MSN. One of the MSNs of your phone system should work, provided external access is possible with this MSN. As a final resort, a single zero

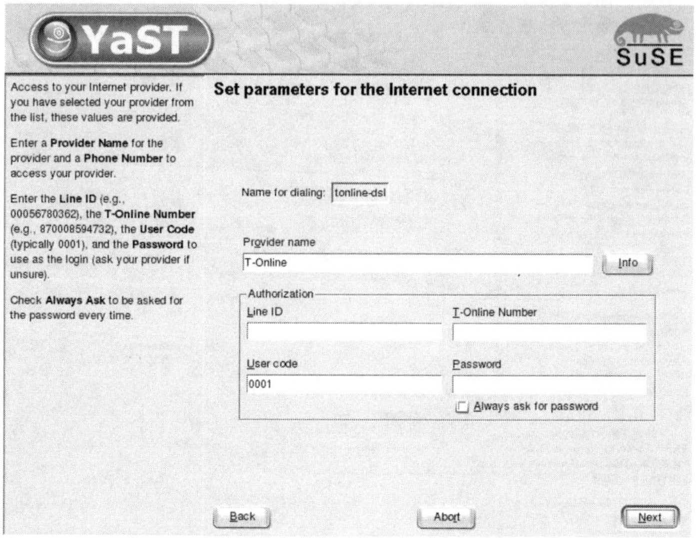

Figure 4.18: T-DSL Configuration in Germany

might work. For more information, refer to the documentation of your phone system.

- For commercial use: Normally the 1TR6 protocol is used for the internal ports of large phone systems. Here, the MSN is called EAZ and is usually the extension. For the Linux configuration, the last digit of the EAZ is normally sufficient. If this does not work, try the digits 1 to 9.

Select the desired start mode. 'OnBoot' causes the ISDN driver to be initialized when the system is booted. If you decide for 'Manual', the ISDN driver must be initialized manually by the user with `rcisdn start`. The option 'Hotplug' loads the driver when the PCMCIA card or the USB device is connected.

By means of a check box, determine whether you want existing connections to be terminated prior to the next charge increment ('ChargeHUP'). However, this does not yet work with all providers. For 'Channel bundling' (multilink PPP), activate the respective check box. For SuSEfirewall2 to be started, mark the check box 'Activate firewall'.

'Details' opens a dialog that enables the implementation of more complex connection scenarios. Normal home users do not need this dialog. Exit the dialog with 'Next'.

In the following dialog, specify the settings for the assignment of the IP address. If your provider has not assigned a static IP address, select 'Dynamic IP address'. If you have a static IP address, enter the local IP address of your host and the remote IP address as specified by the provider in the respective fields. If the interface is to be used as standard route to the Internet, activate 'Default Route'. Only one interface per system can be used as the default route. Exit the dialog with 'Next'.

Specify your country and your provider in the following dialog. The listed providers are call-by-call providers. To use a provider that is not listed here, click 'New'. The dialog 'ISP parameters' is then displayed, enabling you to enter all settings for the desired provider. The default setting for 'ISDN type' is 'ISDN SyncPPP'. Under 'Provider name ', enter the name of the provider and, in the next field, the phone number of the provider.

If a PBX is interposed, you may need to enter an extra number to dial external numbers (usually zero). The entire phone number should not be separated by commas or spaces. Furthermore, enter the user name and the password you received from your provider.

Subsequently, select a dial mode. Read page 80 for the dial mode 'Automatic dial-up'. If you do not mark 'Automatic dial-up', you can easily connect to the Internet using an application, such as kinternet. This program allows you to switch between the configured providers. From the console, dial with `/usr/sbin/isdnctrl dial ippp0` and hang up with `/usr/sbin/isdnctrl hangup ippp0`.

To use 'Dial on demand' (see page 80) if you have a stand-alone system, you must enter a name server. Most providers today support dynamic DNS assignment, so a current IP address is forwarded to the name server each time the connection is set up. However, a suitable dummy name server IP must be entered in this dialog, for example, `192.168.22.99`. If you do not receive a dynamic name server assignment, enter the IP addresses of the name servers of your provider here. Also set the time after which the connection should be terminated automatically if no data exchange has occurred. Finally, confirm your settings with 'Next'. You will be taken to an overview of the configured interfaces. Activate your settings with 'Finish'.

Network Services

This group mostly contains tools for professionals and for the system administrator. If you have SuSE Linux Personal Edition, some of the tools covered

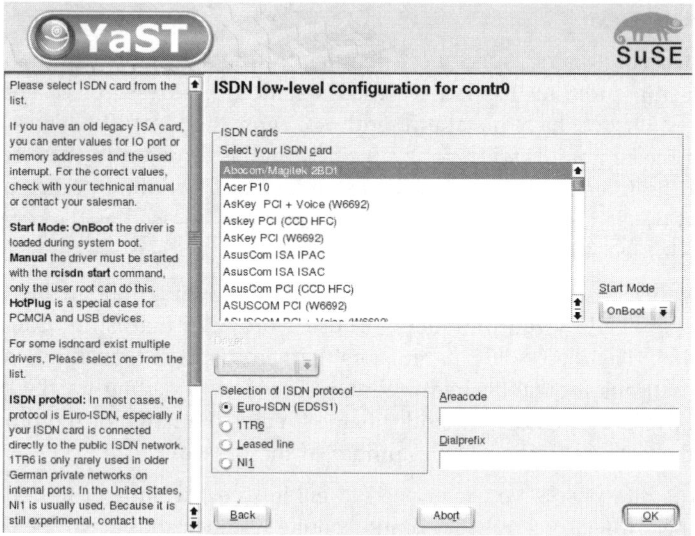

Figure 4.19: ISDN Configuration

in this section will not exist in this group, as they are only installed in the Professional Edition.

Note

The tools 'LDAP Client', 'NIS Server', 'NIS Client', 'NIS+ Client', and 'Proxy' will not be addressed here, as these are genuine expert tools that are usually only used in company networks. More information about these modules is provided in the *Administration Guide*.

Note

Host Name and DNS

The host name and the domain name can be changed here. If the provider has been configured correctly for DSL, modem, or ISDN access, the list of name servers contain entries made automatically as they were retrieved from the provider data. If you are located in a local network, most likely you will receive your host name via DHCP, in which case you should not modify the name.

NFS Client and NFS Server

You need these two tools only if you are located in a network. In this case, you have the possibility to operate a file server that can be accessed by members of your network. On this file server, make programs, files, or storage space available for users. Use the 'NFS Server' module to set up your computer as an NFS server and to determine which directories to export for use by the network users. The NFS server should be set up by an expert. To configure an NFS server, refer to the brief instructions in the *Administration Guide* under *Linux in the Network: NFS*.

Subsequently, any user (with the needed permissions) can mount these directories in his own file tree. The easiest way to do this is by means of the 'NFS Client' module, in which the user merely needs to enter the host name of the computer acting as NFS server and the mount point on his computer. To do this, select 'Add' in the first dialog and enter the said data (see Figure 4.20).

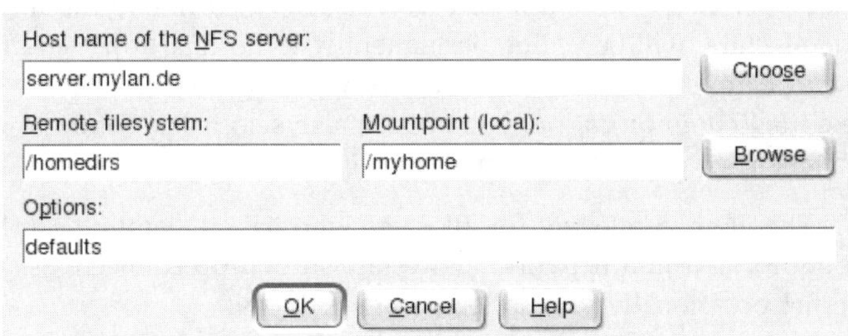

Figure 4.20: Configuration of NFS Clients

Routing

This tool is only needed if you are located in a local network or are connected to the Internet by way of a network card, as is the case with DSL. As indicated in *DSL* on page 84, for DSL the gateway data is only needed to configure the network card correctly. However, the entries are dummies that do not have any function. The value is important only if you are located in a local network and use your own computer as gateway (the gateway to the Internet).

E-Mail Communication

The configuration module allows you to adapt your mail settings if you send your mail with sendmail, postfix, or the SMTP server of your provider. Retrieve mail via SMTP or the fetchmail program, for which you can also enter the details of the POP3 server or IMAP server of your provider.

You can also use a mail program of your choice, such as KMail or Evolution, to set your POP and SMTP access data as usual (to receive mail with POP3 and send mail with SMTP). In this case, you do not need this module.

Connection Type

If you want to specify your mail settings with YaST, the desired type of connection to the Internet must be specified in the first dialog of the e-mail configuration module. Choose one of the following options:

'Permanent' Select this option if you have a dedicated line to the Internet. Your machine will be online permanently, so no dial-up is required. If your system is part of a local network with a central e-mail server for the e-mail communication, you should also select this option to ensure permanent access to your e-mail messages.

'Dial-up' This item is relevant for all users who have a computer at home, are not located in a network, and establish dial-up connections with the Internet occasionally via modem, DSL, or ISDN.

No connection If you do not have access to the Internet and are not located in a network, you cannot send or receive e-mail.

Furthermore, you can activate virus scanning for your incoming e-mail with AMaViS by activating the respective check box. The package is installed automatically as soon as you activate the mail filtering feature. In the following dialogs, specify the outgoing mail server (usually the SMTP server of your provider) and the parameters for incoming mail. If you use a dial-up connection, you can specify diverse POP or IMAP servers for mail reception by various users. By means of this dialog, you can also assign aliases, implement masquerading, or set up virtual domains. Click 'Finish' to exit the mail configuration.

Starting or Stopping System Services

This tool allows you to determine which network services (such as telnet, finger, talk, and ftp) should start when SuSE Linux boots. These services enable external hosts to connect to your computer. Also configure various parameters for each service. By default, the master service that manages the individual services (inetd or xinetd) is not started.

When this module starts, choose which of the two services to configure. The selected daemon can be started with a standard selection of network services or you can 'Add', 'Delete', or 'Edit' services to compose your own selection of services.

Caution

This is an expert tool. Only make modifications if you are familiar with network services.

Caution

Security and Users

A basic aspect of Linux is its multiuser capability. Consequently, several users can work independently on the same Linux system. Each user has a user account identified by a login name and a personal password for logging in to the system. All users have their own home directories where personal files and configurations are stored.

User Administration

Use the check boxes to decide whether to edit users or groups.

YaST offers an overview of all local users in the system. If you are part of an extensive network, use the 'Filter' to list all system users (e.g., `root`) or NIS users. To add new users, fill in the required blanks in the following screen. Subsequently, the new user can log in to the host with the login name and password. Under 'Edit', the user profile can be fine-tuned with 'Details'. The validity of the password is configured in 'Password settings'. To delete a user, select the user from the list and click 'Delete'.

For advanced network administration, define the default settings for the creation of new users by means of 'Set defaults'. Use 'Expert ...' to select the authentication and user administration method (NIS, LDAP, or Kerberos) as well as the algorithm for the password encryption. However, these settings are not intended for private networks, but for large (corporate) networks.

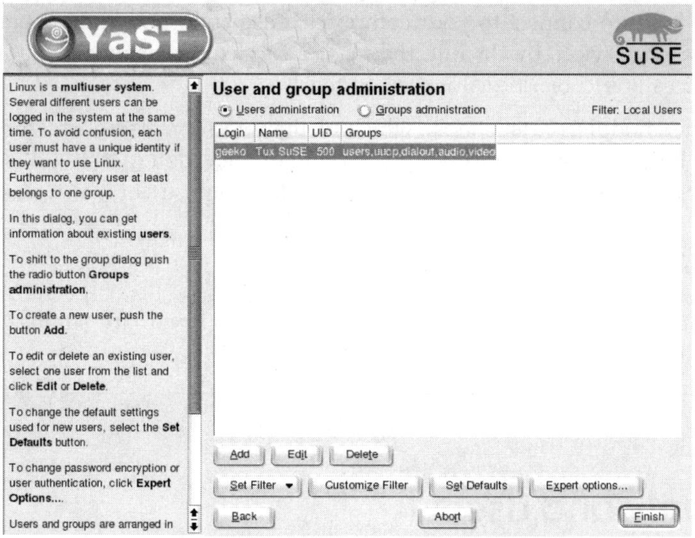

Figure 4.21: User Administration

Group Administration

When this module is started, you will see the screen 'User and group administration'. Decide whether to edit users or groups. The user administration is performed by means of the 'User administration' module and is described there.

YaST provides a list of all groups, which greatly facilitates the group administration. To delete a group, select it from the list (the line will be highlighted dark blue) and click 'Delete'. To 'Add' and 'Edit' users, enter the name, group ID (gid), and members of the group in the respective YaST screen. You can set a password for the change to this group.

Security Settings

In the start screen 'Local security configuration', which can be accessed under 'Security&Users', you can select one of the following four options:

Level 1 is for stand-alone computers (preconfigured). Level 2 is for workstations with a network (preconfigured). Level 3 is for a server with a network (preconfigured). Use 'Custom Settings' for your own configuration.

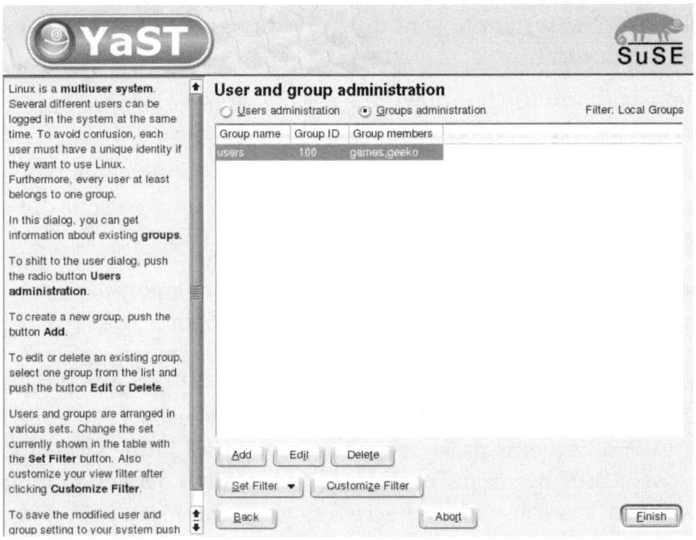

Figure 4.22: Group Administration

If you click one of the three items, have the option of incorporating one of the levels of preconfigured system security options. To do this, simply click 'Finish'. Under 'Details', access the individual settings that can be modified. If you choose 'Custom settings', proceed to the different dialogs with 'Next'. Here, find the default installation values.

'Password settings' If you want new passwords to be checked by the system before they are accepted, mark the two check boxes'Checking new passwords' and 'Plausibiliy test for password'. Set the minimum and maximum length of passwords for newly created users. Moreover, define the period for which the password will be valid and how many days in advance an expiry alert is to be issued when the user logs in to the text console.

'Boot settings' How do you want the key combination (Ctrl) (Alt) (Del) to be interpreted?

Usually, this combination, entered in the text console, causes the system to reboot. Do not modify this setting unless your machine or server is publicly accessible and you are afraid someone could carry out this action without authorization. If you select 'Stop', this key combination will cause the system to shut down. With 'Ignore', this key combination is ignored.

Who is allowed to shut down the system from KDM (KDE Display Manager — the graphical login)?

'Only root' (the system administrator), 'All users', 'Nobody', or 'Local users'. If 'Nobody' is selected, the system can only be shut down via the text console.

'Login settings' Typically, following a failed login attempt, there is a waiting period lasting a few seconds before another login is possible. The purpose of this is to make it more difficult for "password sniffers". In addition, you have the option of activating 'Record failed login attempts' and 'Record successful login attempts'. If you suspect someone is trying to find out your password, check the entries in the system log files in `/var/log`. By means of the check box 'Allow remote graphical login', other users are granted access to your graphical login screen via the network. However, as this access possibility represents a potential security risk, it is inactive by default.

'Add user settings' Every user has a numerical and an alphabetical user ID. The correlation between these is established via the file `/etc/passwd` and should be as unique as possible.

Using the data in this screen, define the range of numbers assigned to the numerical part of the user ID when a new user is added. A minimum of 500 is suitable for users. Proceed in the same way with the group ID settings.

'Miscellaneous settings' For 'Setting of file permissions', there are three selection options: 'Easy', 'Secure', and 'Paranoid'. The first one should be sufficient for most users. The YaST help text provides information about the three security levels.

The setting 'Paranoid' is extremely restrictive and should serve as the basic level of operation for system administrator settings. If you select 'Paranoid', remember that some programs might not work or not work correctly, because you no longer have the permissions to access certain files. In this dialog, also define which user should start the `updatedb` program. This program, which automatically runs either on a daily basis or after booting, generates a database (locatedb) where the location of each file on your computer is stored (locatedb can be searched by running the `locate` command). If you select 'Nobody', any user can find only the paths in the database that can be seen by any other (unprivileged) user. If `root` is selected, all local files are indexed, because the user `root`, as superuser, may access all directories.

Finally, make sure the option 'Current directory in root's path' is deactivated (default).

Press 'Finish' to complete your security configuration.

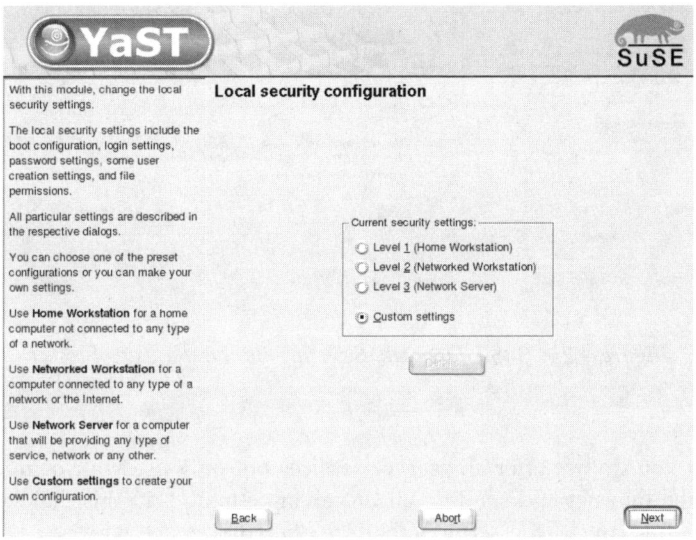

Figure 4.23: Security Settings

Firewall

Use this module to configure SuSEfirewall2 to protect your machine against attacks from the Internet. When the module is started, four dialogs appear consecutively. In the first dialog, select the interface to protect (see Figure 4.24 on the following page). 'External interface' is the interface for the Internet. 'Internal interface' is only required if you are located in an internal network and intend to use the firewall to protect your computer against internal attacks. In this case, your computer would be in a "demilitarized zone" (DMZ). Normally, a configuration with DMZ is only used for company networks.

After selecting your interface, selectively activate the services of your computer for which to allow access from the Internet (see Figure 4.25 on the next

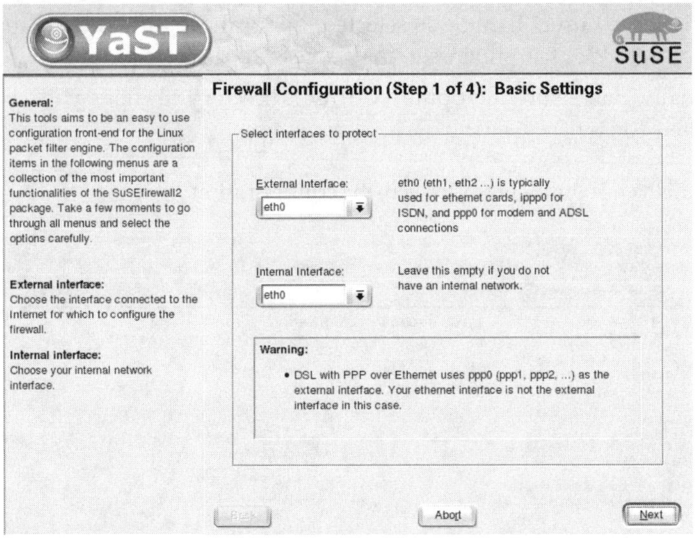

Figure 4.24: *SuSE Firewall: Selecting the Interfaces to Protect*

page). If you do not offer any server services but only use your computer for surfing the Internet and sending and receiving e-mail, skip this dialog without activating any of the services that are offered.

If you are not familiar with the terms masquerading and traceroute, simply accept the third dialog without any modifications. You can also accept the final dialog, as the default log options are usually sufficient.

When you click 'Next', a small window asks for confirmation. Then the new configuration is saved to your hard disk. The next time your Internet connection is started, your computer is protected effectively against attacks.

For more information about the SuSE Firewall, refer to the *Administration Guide* under *Network Security → Firewall*.

System

Creating a System Backup

The YaST backup module enables you to create a backup of your system. The backup created by the module does not comprise the entire system, but only

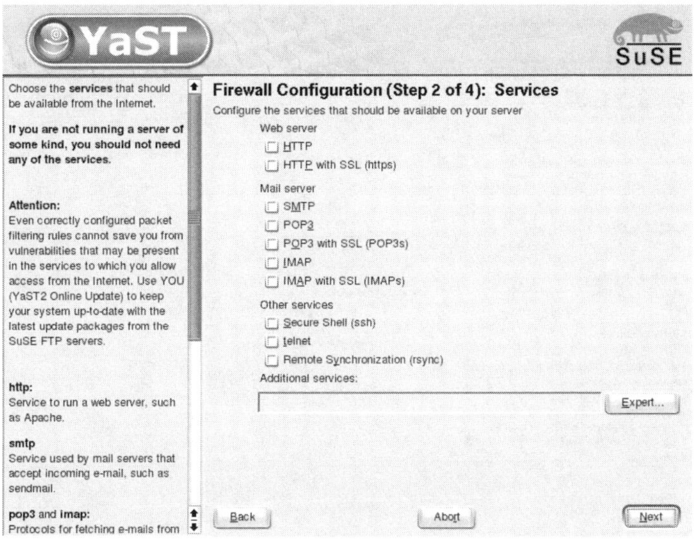

Figure 4.25: SuSE Firewall: Externally Accessible Services

saves information about changed packages and copies of critical storage areas and configuration files.

Define the kind of data to save in the backup. By default, the backup includes information about any packages changed since the last installation run. In addition, it may include data that does not belong to packages themselves, such as many of the configuration files in `/etc` or in the directories under `/home`. Apart from that, the backup can include important storage areas on your hard disk that may be crucial when trying to restore a system, such as the partition table or the master boot record (MBR).

Creating a Boot, Rescue, or Module Disk

With this YaST module, easily create boot disks, rescue disks, and module disks. These floppy disks are helpful if the boot configuration of your system is damaged. The rescue disk is especially necessary if the file system of the root partition is damaged. In this case, you might also need the module disk with various drivers to be able to access the system (e.g., to access a RAID system).

'Standard boot disk' Use this option to create a standard boot disk with

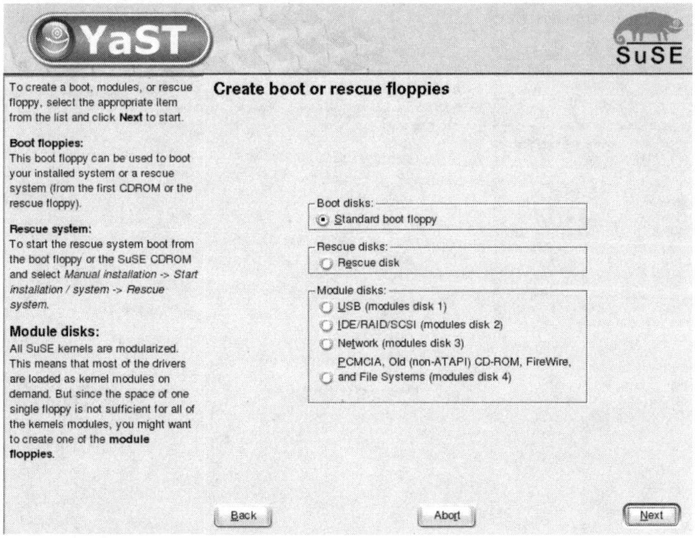

Figure 4.26: Creating a Boot, Rescue, or Module Disk

which you can boot an installed system. This disk is also needed for starting the rescue system.

'Rescue disk' This disk contains a special environment that allows you to perform maintenance tasks in your installed system, such as checking and repairing file system and updating the boot loader.

To start the rescue system, boot with the standard boot disk and select 'Manual Installation', 'Start Installation/System', and 'Rescue System'. You will then be prompted to insert the rescue disk. If your system was configured to use special drivers (such as RAID or USB), you might need to load the respective modules from a module disk.

'Module disks' Module disks contain additional system drivers. The standard kernel only supports IDE drives. If the drives in your system are connected to special controllers (such as SCSI), load the needed drivers from a module disk.

- USB modules

  This floppy disk contains the USB modules you might need if USB drives are connected.

- IDE, RAID, and SCSI modules

As the standard kernel only supports normal IDE drives, you will need this module disk if you use special IDE controllers. Furthermore, all RAID and SCSI modules are provided on this disk.

- Network modules

  If you need access to a network, load the suitable driver module for your network card from this floppy disk.

- PCMCIA, CDROM (non-ATAPI), FireWire, and file systems

  This floppy disk contains all PCMCIA modules used especially for laptop computers. Furthermore, the modules for FireWire and some less common file systems are available here. Older CDROM drives that do not comply with the ATAPI standard can also be operated with drivers from this floppy disk.

To load drivers from a module disk to the rescue system, select 'Kernel modules (hardware drivers)' and the desired module category (SCSI, ethernet, etc.). You will be prompted to insert the respective module disk and the contained modules will be listed. Select the desired module. Watch the system messages carefully: 'Loading module <modulename> failed!' indicates that the hardware could not be recognized by the module. Some older drivers require specific parameters to be able to address the hardware correctly. In this case, refer to the documentation of your hardware.

To create one of the above-mentioned floppy disks, select the respective option and click 'Next'. You will be asked to insert a floppy disk. If you click 'Next' again, the content will be written to the floppy disk.

Boot Loader Configuration with YaST

This YaST module greatly simplifies the configuration of the boot loader. However, you should not experiment with this module unless you understand the concepts behind it. Read the corresponding parts of the *Administration Guide* before changing the boot loader configuration. The following discussion is focused on GRUB, the default boot loader of SuSE Linux.

Note

Do not change the boot method from a running system unless you really know what is going on behind the scenes.

Note

In the YaST Control Center, go to 'System' and start the 'Boot Loader Configuration' module. This opens a window in which the current boot loader configuration is displayed and can be changed. The table listing the configuration data (white background) has three columns, Under 'Ch.' (to the left), there are flags to mark whenever an option has been changed. These options are listed in the center column. The current values or settings are listed in the column to the right. To add an option, click 'Add'. To change the value of an existing option, click 'Edit'. If you do not want to use an existing option at all, select it then click 'Delete'.

Selecting an option and clicking 'Edit' opens a dialog in which to change the settings according to your needs. Leave the dialog and confirm any changes made by clicking 'OK'. Back in the main window, select other options and repeat these steps to change them. However, the available options themselves differ according to the type of boot loader used. The following list explains some options of the GRUB boot loader:

Boot Loader Type: Use this option to switch between GRUB and LILO. The dialog opened lets you specify the way in which this change should be performed. For instance, specify that a current GRUB configuration should be converted into a similar LILO configuration. However, some settings may be lost, because LILO has no equivalent for them. You can also create a new configuration from scratch or generate a suggested configuration that may then be changed as needed.

The following two options are not available when SuSE Linux is being installed, but only after the installation, at which point you may also tell the module to read in the existing configuration as stored on the hard disk. This reloads the configuration of the previous boot loader and is useful if you want to switch back to the original setup for some reason. This possibility only exists as long as you do not close the boot loader module.

Location of the Boot Loader: Use this dialog to define where the boot loader should be installed: in the master boot record (MBR), in the boot sector of the boot partition, in the the boot sector of the root partition, or on a floppy. Use 'Others' to specify a custom boot sector as the location of the boot loader.

Hard Disk Sequence: If your computer has more than one hard disk, specify the boot sequence of the disks as defined in the BIOS setup of the machine.

Default Entry: This option lets you specify which kernel or operating system to boot by default, if no active selection is made in the boot menu before the time-out has elapsed. Click this option then 'Edit' to see a list of all the entries in the boot menu. Then select one entry from the list and click 'Set as Default'. Also use this dialog to change any entry by clicking 'Edit'. In fact, this dialog is identical to the one opened after selecting 'Current Entries'. It allows you to perform all the actions provided by the latter — changing the order of entries in the boot menu, adding, changing, and deleting entries, and setting a default entry.

Current Entries The existing entries of the boot menu are listed under this option in the main window. If you select this option then click 'Edit', a dialog opens that is identical to the 'Default Entry' dialog.

Make Boot Loader Partition Active Use this option to activate the partition whose boot sector holds the boot loader, independently from the partition on which the directory with the helper files of the boot loader are stored (`/boot` or the root directory `/`).

Write to MBR Specify whether to overwrite the MBR, which may be necessary if you have changed the location of the boot loader.

To learn more about the options and configuration of boot loaders, refer to *Administration Guide*.

LVM

The "Logical Volume Manager" (LVM) is a tool for individually partitioning hard disks by means of logical drives. As this is a genuine expert tool, no additional information is provided within the scope of this user guide. For information, refer to the *Administration Guide*.

Partitioning

Although it is possible to modify the partitions in the installed system, this should be handled by experts who know exactly what they are doing, as otherwise the risk of losing data is very high. If you decide to use this tool, refer to the description in the installation part of this book in *Partitioning* on page 19 (the partitioning tool during the installation is the same as in the installed system).

Profile Manager (SCPM)

The SCPM (System Configuration Profile Management) module offers the possibility to create, manage, and switch between entire individual system configurations. This is especially useful for mobile computers that are used in different locations (in different networks) and by different users. Nevertheless, this feature is useful even for stationary machines, as it enables the use of various hardware components or test configurations. Although the module with the accompanying help is easy to use, the configuration of profiles is a task that should be performed by experts or system administrators. For more information about SCPM basics and handling, refer to the respective sections in the *Administration Guide*.

Restore

The restore module (Figure 4.27 on the next page) enables you to restore your system from a backup archive. Follow the instructions in YaST. Press 'Next' to proceed to the individual dialogs. First, specify where the archives are located (removable media, local hard disks, or network file systems). As you continue, a description and the contents of the individual archives is displayed, so you can decide what to restore from the archives.

Additionally, there are two dialogs for uninstalling packages that were added since the last backup and for the renewed installation of packages that were deleted since the last backup. These two steps enable you to restore the exact system state at the time of the last backup.

Caution

As this module normally installs, replaces, or uninstalls many packages and files, you should use it only if you have experience with backups, as otherwise you may lose data.

Caution

Runlevel Editor

The Runlevels in SuSE Linux

SuSE Linux can be operated in several runlevels. By default, the system boots to runlevel 5, which offers multiuser mode, network access, and the graphical user interface (X Window System). The other runlevels offer multiuser mode with network but without X (runlevel 3), multiuser mode without network (runlevel 2), single-user mode (runlevel 1 and S), system halt (runlevel 0), and system reboot (runlevel 6).

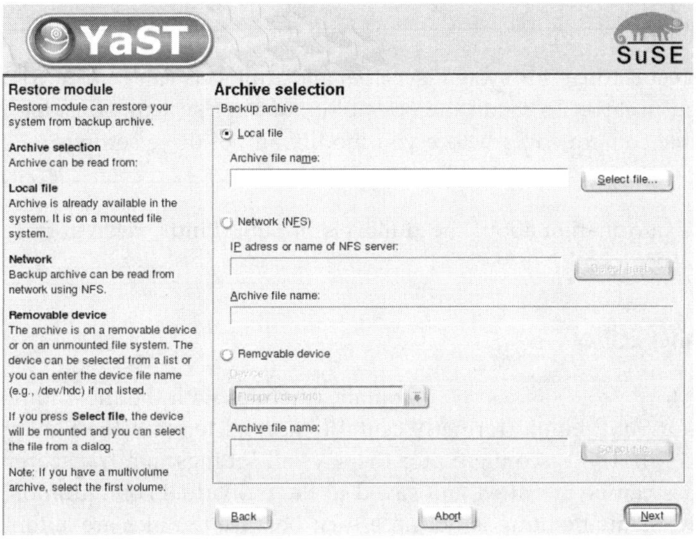

Figure 4.27: YaST: Start Window of the Restore Module

The various runlevels are useful if problems are encountered in connection with a particular service (X or network) in a higher runlevel. In this case, the system can be booted to a lower runlevel to repair the service. Moreover, many servers operate without a graphical user interface and must be booted in a runlevel without X, such as runlevel 3.

Usually home users only need the standard runlevel (5). However, if the graphical user interface freezes at any time, you can restart the X Window system by switching to a text console with Ctrl + Alt + F1, logging in as root, and switching to runlevel 3 with the command `init 3`. This shuts down your X Window system, leaving you with a text console. To restart the graphical system, enter `init 5`.

Setting the Runlevel in YaST2

In a default installation, runlevel 5 is selected. To start a different runlevel when the system is booted, change the default runlevel here. 'Runlevel properties' allows you to determine which services are started in which runlevel.

Caution

Incorrect settings for system services and runlevels can render your system useless. To retain the operability of your system, consider the possible consequences before you modify any of these settings.

Caution

For more information about the runlevels in SuSE Linux, refer to the *Administration Guide.*

Sysconfig Editor

The directory `/etc/sysconfig` contains the files with the most important settings for SuSE Linux (formerly centrally administered in the file `/etc/rc.config`). The sysconfig editor displays all settings in a transparent form. The values can be modified and saved to the individual configuration files. Generally, manual editing is not necessary, because the files are automatically adapted when a package is installed or a service is configured.

Caution

Do not edit the files in `/etc/sysconfig` if you do not know exactly what you are doing, as this could be very detrimental to the operability of your system.

Caution

More information is provided in the *Administration Guide* under *The Boot Concept*.

Time Zone Selection

The time zone was already set during the installation, but you can make changes here. Click your country or region in the list and select 'Local time' or 'GMT' (Greenwich Mean Time). 'GMT' is often used in Linux systems. Machines with additional operating systems, such as Microsoft Windows, mostly use the local time.

Language Selection

Here, select the language for your Linux system.

The language can be changed at any time. The language selected in YaST applies to the entire system, including YaST and the desktop environment KDE 3.

Keyboard Layout Selection

Note

Only use this module if you work on a system without the X Window System and a graphical user interface. If you use a graphical system (such as KDE), set up the keyboard with the module 'Display and Input Devices'. See *Display and Input Devices (SaX2)* on page 62.

Note

The desired keyboard layout usually matches the selected language. Use the test field to see if special characters, such as the pipe symbol `|`, are displayed correctly.

Miscellaneous

Submitting a Support Request

By purchasing SuSE Linux, you are entitled to free installation support. Information such as the scope, address, and phone number is listed in the support flyer.

YaST offers the possibility to directly send a support request by e-mail to the SuSE team. Registration is required first. Start by entering the respective data — your registration code is located at the back of the CD cover. Regarding your query, select the problem category in the following window and provide a description of the problem (Figure 4.28 on the next page). Also read the YaST help text, which explains how to best describe the problem so the support team can help you.

Tip

If you need advanced support (such as for special problems), consider using the SuSE Professional Services. Refer to `http://www.suse.de/en/support/` for details.

Tip

View Start-up Log

The start-up log contains the screen messages displayed when the computer is started. It is logged to `/var/log/boot.msg`. Use this YaST module to view the log, for example, to check if all services and functions were started as expected.

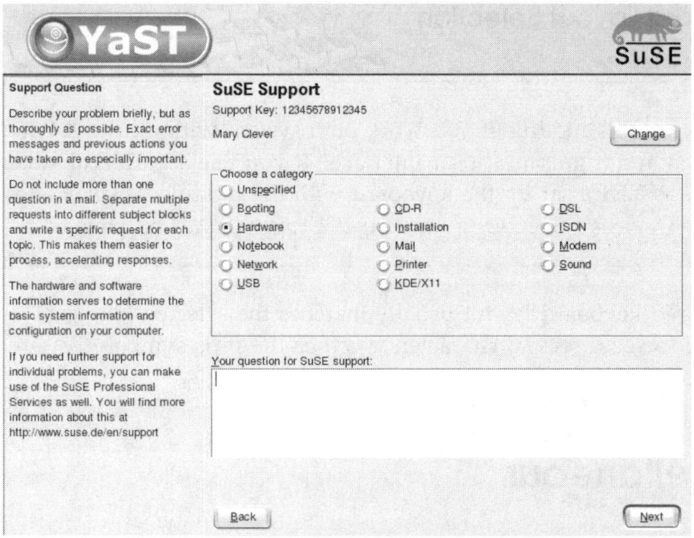

Figure 4.28: Submitting a Support Request

View System Log

The system log logs the operations of your computer to `/var/log/messsages`. Kernel messages are recorded here, sorted according to date and time.

Loading a Vendor's Driver CD

With this module, automatically install device drivers from a Linux driver CD that contains drivers for SuSE Linux.

When installing SuSE Linux from scratch, use this YaST module to load the required drivers from the vendor CD after the installation.

YaST2 in Text Mode (ncurses)

YaST can also be controlled by means of a text-based terminal. This is especially useful if the administrator does not have access to the graphical user interface.

Controls

The usage may be unfamiliar, but is very simple. Basically, the entire program can be controlled with Tab, Alt + Tab, Space, the arrow keys (↑ and ↓), ↵, and shortcuts. The YaST Control Center appears first, as shown in Figure 4.29.

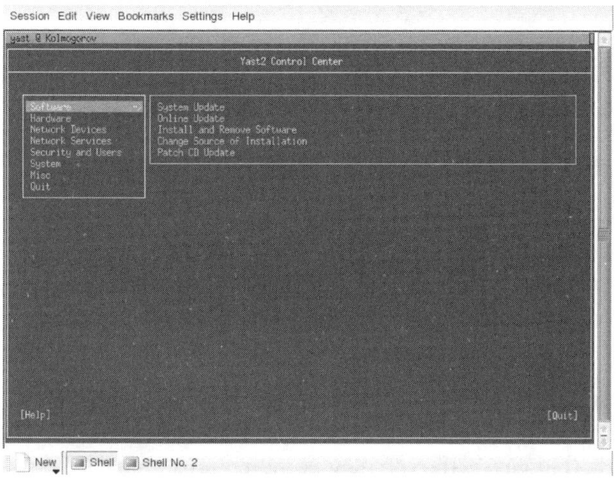

Figure 4.29: The Main Window of YaST2 ncurses

There are three areas here. The left frame, which is surrounded by a thick white border, features the categories to which the various modules belong. The active category is indicated by a colored background. The right frame, which is surrounded by a thin white border, provides an overview of the modules contained in the active category. The bottom frame contains the buttons for 'Help' and 'Exit'.

When the YaST Control Center is started, the category 'Software' is selected automatically. Use ↓ and ↑ to change the category. To start a module from the selected category, press →. The module selection then appears with a thick border. Use ↓ and ↑ to select the desired module. Keep the arrow keys pressed to scroll through the list of available modules. When a module is selected, the module title appears with a colored background and a brief description is displayed in the bottom frame.

Press Enter to start the desired module. Various buttons or selection fields in the module contain a letter with a different color (yellow by default). Use

Alt + yellow letter to select the respective button directly without navigating there with Tab.

Exit the YaST Control Center by pressing 'Exit' or by selecting 'Exit' in the category overview and pressing Enter.

Restriction of Key Combinations

If you have system-wide Alt key combinations when the X server is running, the Alt combinations in YaST might not work. Furthermore, keys like Alt or ⇑ Shift might be occupied by the settings of the terminal.

Replacing Alt with Esc: Alt shortcuts can be executed with Esc instead of Alt. For example, Esc + H replaces Alt + H.

Replacement of backward and forward navigation by Ctrl + F and Ctrl + B: If the Alt and ⇑ Shift combinations are occupied by the window manager or the terminal, the combinations Ctrl + F (forward) and Ctrl + B (backward) can be used instead.

Restriction of function keys: The F keys are also used for functions. Certain F keys might be occupied by the terminal so might not be available for YaST. However, the Alt key combinations and the F keys should always be fully available on a pure text console.

The following paragraphs assume that the Alt key combinations are functional.

Module Operation

Navigating Buttons and Selection Lists Tab and Alt + Tab navigate back and forth among buttons and frames.

Navigating in Selection Lists ↑ and ↓ always navigate among the single items within an activated frame containing a selection list. These can, for instance, be the single modules of a module group in the control center.

Checking Radio Buttons and Check Boxes Buttons with empty square brackets (check box) or empty parentheses (radio buttons) can be selected with Space or Enter. The buttons at the bottom of the individual modules are selected with Enter when they are selected (green background) or with the combination Alt + yellowkey (see Figure 4.30 on the next page).

The Function Keys Various functions are mapped to the F keys (F1 to F12). Which F keys are actually mapped to functions depends on which YaST module is active as the different modules offer different buttons (such as details, info, add, and delete). The buttons 'OK', 'Next', and 'Finish' are mapped to F10. The YaST help, which can be accessed with F1, provides information about the functions of the individual F keys.

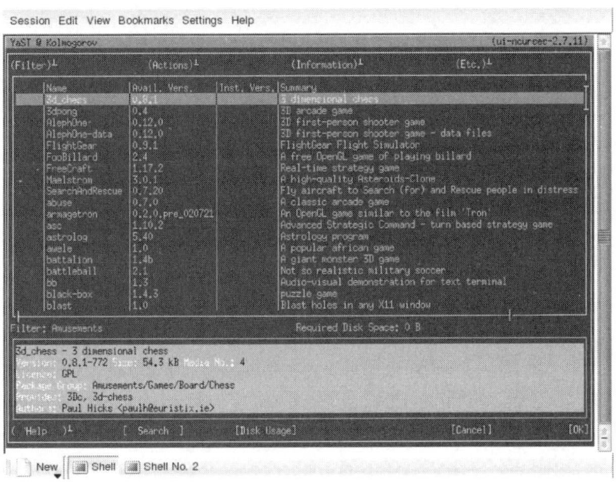

Figure 4.30: The Software Installation Module

Starting Individual Modules

To save time, the individual YaST modules can also be started directly. To start the modules, enter `yast` followed by the name of the module. The network module, for example, is started with the command `yast lan`. A list of the names of all modules available on your system can be viewed with `yast -l` or `yast --list`.

KDE — The Desktop

The K Desktop Environment (KDE for short) is the standard desktop for SuSE Linux. All information for optimizing your work with your desktop system can be found here. This chapter shows the graphical elements, summarizes some of the applications, and introduces KDE Internet connections.

The History of KDE

The story of KDE sounds like a modern fairy tale. A frustrated computer science student from Tübingen, Germany, was tired of the lack of uniformity of previous Unix and Linux desktops. For this reason, he developed the popular graphical user interface for the X Window System: KDE. In those days, Matthias Ettrich would have never guessed what his appeal in a newsgroup would start. He looked for some volunteers for his project "*K*Desktop *E*nvironment" (KDE) and met a lively reaction. Soon, the first executable version was compiled and KDE became more popular. Improvements followed, bringing the KDE project to a critical mass and allowing it to take off on its own. Hundreds of programmers all over world are involved in further improving KDE.

The First Start-Up

When you start KDE for the first time, the welcome dialog appears on the screen. In the first step, this dialog presents some information about SuSE. In the next step, arrange the global look and feel of KDE by activating or deactivating a number of features (preview function, magnification of icons, etc.). Save your settings with 'Finish'. Start the program manually by pressing Alt + F2 and entering `SuSEgreeter`.

Help

>When the mouse pointer is held over a button, text field, or other control element, a "tooltip", if available for the item, appears. The tooltip is a brief help text describing the item. >If you need more information about a graphical element, press ⇑ Shift + F1 and click it. If a help text exists, a frame displaying a more extensive help text is displayed. Additional information in HTML format can be accessed with 'Help' → 'Help on …'. The text is displayed in Konqueror.

Advanced users who need information for a Linux command can use the man and info pages. These can also be viewed in KDE. Simply press Alt + F2 and enter `info:` to get an overview of all info pages. To view a specific command, directly enter `info:cvs`. This also applies to man pages, with the only difference that you have to replace `info` with `man`.

Operating KDE

In KDE, there are various ways to change the configuration and open files and applications. The KDE desktop, the menu bar, title, window, and control panels are available for this purpose. These various options are introduced in the following subsections.

The KDE Desktop

The desktop is the central hub in KDE. On start-up, see various icons on the desktop, enabling you to access CD-ROM, floppy, or hard disk drives, save files, and insert links to directories and files. Actually, the desktop is merely a folder on your hard disk. It is located in your home directory under `Desktop`. KDE displays all files placed here on the desktop. *System Administration* on page 137 shows how to change the path.

The Menu Bar

If desired, place a menu bar at the top of the screen. To do this, start the KDE Control Center (press Alt + F2 and enter `kcontrol`) and select 'Look & Feel' → 'Style'. On the 'Miscellaneous' tab, activate 'Menubar at the top of the screen in the style of MacOS' and click 'Apply'. Following the activation, a menu appears at the top of the screen. Depending on which program is active, the menu bar changes.

Enter the KDE desktop menu by clicking a free space on the desktop. The desktop menu allows you to log out, create new directories and files, manage your bookmarks and desktops, arrange the windows, and get help.

The Title Bar

The title bar is the area at the top of a window containing its name and various icons, depending on the window decoration. The "KDE2 default" decoration, for example, has the following title bar layout: the window panel menu, the "pushpin" symbol, the respective window name, and the minimizing, enlarging, and closing symbols. Sometimes, a question mark may appear before the minimizing symbol, the "What's This?" symbol. Figure 5.1 on the next page shows the structure of the title bar.

Obtain more functions by right-clicking the title bar. A pop-up menu opens in which to configure the current window or create settings for the layout of all the windows. The pop-up menu contains the following items:

Figure 5.1: KDE Title Bar

'Move' The window follows the movement of the mouse until dropped by left-clicking.

'Size' Change the horizontal and vertical dimensions of the window by moving them with the mouse. Confirm with a left click.

'Minimize' Minimize the current window. The application remains open, but its window disappears from the desktop and only appears as an icon in the task bar. To reopen the window, click the icon in the taskbar.

'Maximize' Maximize the current window. The application now occupies the entire screen. By clicking it again, restore the window to its original size.

'Shade' The current window is reduced to just a title bar.

'Always on Top' The current window remains visible on your desktop until you deactivate this function or close the window.

'Store Settings' Saves your specifications.

'To desktop' By selecting from the submenu, move the window to another desktop.

'Settings...' Specify the properties and decoration in the window that opens.

'Close' Close the current window.

The Panel

After starting KDE, the panel appears on the lower margin (default setting). It contains the SuSE menu and various quick-start icons for frequently-used applications, such as a terminal, the file and web browser Konqueror, and others. Several "applets", introduced in *The Applets: Miniprograms* on the facing page, are also available.

The KDE and SuSE Menu Structure

The SuSE KDE packages include two menus: the normal K menu and the extended SuSE menu. The K menu is the "traditional" menu, which only contains KDE applications. The arrangement of the SuSE menu is a little different. This menu is set by default at the first start-up. The SuSE menu contains all KDE programs and more. For example, you can start all installed GNOME and X applications from here. The menu is sorted into the categories: development, games, graphics, Internet, multimedia, office programs, settings, system, and tools. Also find entries for the SuSE help system, the Control Center, and so on.

Switch from one menu to another in the Control Center under 'Look&Feel' → 'Menu settings'. Here, also integrate additional menus for the start panel, such as the task menu or the administrator menu. These offer a presorted listing of frequently used applications. Basically, all KDE applications are accessible from the K menu as well as from the SuSE menu. Decide for yourself which menu structure you prefer.

The Applets: Miniprograms

The panel also provides space for applets, which can be embedded there. For instance, display the time of day. Figure 5.2 shows, from left to right, switchboard, quickstarter, system monitor, eyes, newsticker, the system section of the panel, and clock.

Figure 5.2: A Selection of Applets

Next to every applet is a small arrow that opens a menu. The applet can be moved or deleted there. The menu can be also used to open a settings dialog if one exists for that program. To add similar useful applications, right-click an open space and select 'Add' → 'Applet'.

The Taskbar The taskbar helps to quickly and easily jump between open applications. Sort the applications according to desktops or group respective windows together. Select 'Look&Feel' → 'Taskbar' in the Control Center and explore the different setting options.

The Switchboard KDE provides multiple desktops. Configure up to sixteen "virtual desktops" to which you can even assign specific names.

Figure 5.3: The Taskbar Displaying All Active Desktop Windows

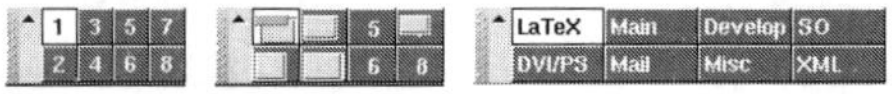

Figure 5.4: Three Different Switchboard Display Types

Figure 5.4 actually shows the same switchboard (from left to right), displayed with a numerical view, preview, and name view, respectively.

Right-clicking in the switchboard opens a pop-up menu. Here, select'Preview', 'Number', or 'Name'. By clicking 'Enable Desktop Preview', all windows appear as thumbnails.

Newsticker If you have an Internet connection, you can get the latest news. The news reports appear as a marquee text in an applet.

Selected KDE Applications

KDE offers many applications. Because of limited space, only a few applications are described here in detail. The selection in the list that follows by no means indicates a comparison of quality.

Hard Disk Management

Both kdf and kwikdisk help mount or unmount data media available on your system quickly and easily.

kwikdisk is an applet, so it can be integrated into the panel. When you right-click the icon, a menu opens with which to mount or unmount the respective data medium. For a graphical overview, select 'Start KDiskFree'.

kdf and KDiskFree show an overview of your data media obtained from the `/etc/fstab` file, similar to the `df` command. The window includes the data medium icon, the type, the size, the mount point, the available disk space, percentage of occupied disk space, and a graphical representation.

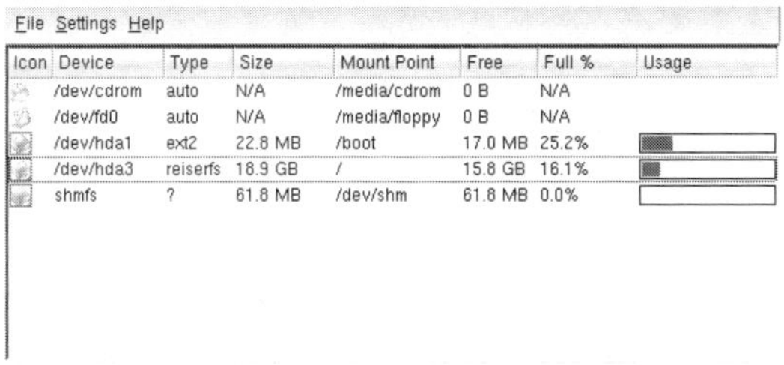

Figure 5.5: Overview of Data Media with kdf

If you right-click an entry, a pop-up menu opens. Integrate the data medium into your system with 'Mount device' or remove it with 'Unmount device'. 'Open data medium' starts a new Konqueror window listing the contents.

DVI, PostScript, and PDF Viewers

DVI and PostScript are two of the most important formats in Linux. They can be viewed comfortably with the DVI viewer kdvi or with the PostScript and PDF viewer kghostview. Both applications have a a clear structure that is easy to learn. Figure 5.6 shows the KDvi window.

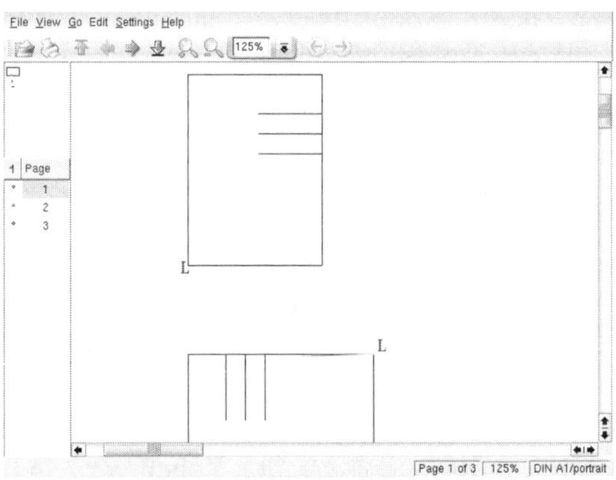

Figure 5.6: KDvi Document Viewer

One of the characteristics of these viewers is that they can be integrated in a Konqueror window. This makes it very easy to display files without needing to start the respective application manually. In kghostview, shown in Figure 5.7, load and view any PostScript or PDF document. To do this, select 'File' → 'Open' and select the document.

Figure 5.7: KGhostview Document Viewer

In the 'View' menu, choose various displays that automatically show the contents to size. To rotate the image by ninety degrees, use 'View' → 'Orientation'.

Viewing, Decompressing, and Creating Archives with Ark

To save space on the hard disk, use a "packer" that shrinks files and directories to a fraction of their original size. ark is a convenient program for managing these archives. It supports a number of common formats, such as zip, tar.gz, tar.bz2, lha, rar, and zoo.

To start the program, press Alt + F2 and enter `ark`. If you already have compressed files, you can move these from a Konqueror window to the ark window. ark will display the contents of the archive. You can achieve the same by selecting 'File' → 'Open'.

Once the archive has been opened, you can perform various actions. 'Action' offers a number of options, such as adding files or directories, deleting, extracting, viewing, editing, or opening with another program.

To create a new archive, use 'File' → 'New'. Enter the name of the new archive in the pop-up window. If you specify a file extension, the archive is created in that format. If you omit the extension, zip is used.

When the entry is completed, a blank window is displayed, allowing you to insert files or directories from Konqueror. ark compresses the files and lists them. For more information about ark, select 'Help' → 'Ark Handbook'.

Setting Appointments with KOrganizer

With korganizer, manage appointments and get easy reminders of birthdays and important events. Define tasks and record your progress. The application can be found in the `kdepim3` package. It can be installed using YaST2. Start the program by pressing (Alt) + (F2) and entering `korganizer`.

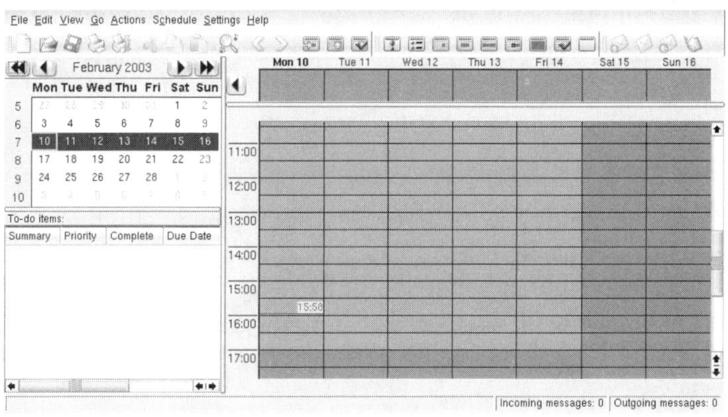

Figure 5.8: KOrganizer — the KDE Scheduler

To set a new appointment, click 'Actions' → 'New Appointment'. A window appears in which to enter general information about the appointment, who will attend, and frequency of recurrence. If an entry recurs weekly, for example, set this under the 'Recurrence' tab. For this, 'Recurring Event' must be checked under the 'General' tab.

Under the 'General' tab, enter a 'Summary' and set the beginning and ending date along with the start time. To be reminded of this appointment, activate 'Reminder' and set the time korganizer should remind you of your appointment. In the text field underneath, enter more detailed text. To organize your appointments, define categories. Click 'Categories' to open a window in which to select the corresponding event. If the type of event to schedule is not listed, add the new name in 'New Categories' and press (↵). Close the window by clicking 'OK'.

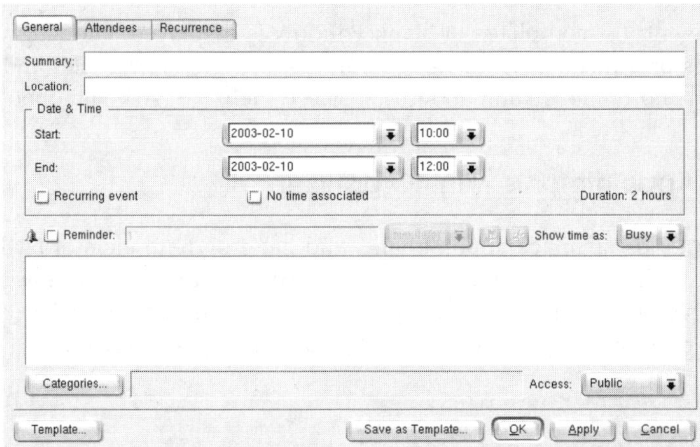

Figure 5.9: *Setting a New Appointment*

The following illustrates how to add a new appointment effectively. To do this, use 'Actions' → 'New Event'. First, schedule a simple appointment. To do this, enter the type of appointment in the 'Summary' field. Define the date with 'Start Date' and 'End Date'. Set a time that makes sense in 'Start Time' and 'End Time'. If you do not want to set a time, simply activate 'No time associated'.

To be reminded of this appointment, activate 'Reminder'. Now, the entry field next to it is available for setting the reminder in minutes, hours, or days. In the text field underneath, enter the details of the appointment. With 'Categories', calender entries can be sorted.

To specify other participants, click 'Attendees'. Enter their names and e-mail addresses. Define which role the participant has (such as participant only or organizer) and the participant's status (such as needs preparation, accepted, or confirmed). Select the participant with 'Address Book…' and the name and e-mail address are automatically added. When you click 'Apply', your appointment is added to the calendar. This button leaves the window open, so you can still make small changes. To close the window, click 'OK'.

With KOrganizer, not only manage appointments, but also organize tasks. In 'Actions', find 'New To-Do'.

KInternet — Connecting to the Internet

For surfing the Internet or sending and receiving e-mail, either a modem, ethernet, or ISDN card needs to be connected to a computer and be properly configured with SuSE Linux. This is done with the help of the installation and configuration tool YaST2. When the device has been properly configured, the application KInternet is used to control the dial-up Internet connection.

KDE loads KInternet at start-up. The application independently evaluates whether an Internet connection can be established. If so, the application icon automatically appears in the lower right corner of the KDE panel in the form of a connector plug. The following is a list of the symbols and their meaning:

 Currently not connected to the Internet.

 Making a connection.

 The connection has been established.

 Not currently connected to the Internet. A connection will be attempted when requests are made that require one.

 Data is being transferred either to or from the Internet.

Right-clicking the KInternet icon opens a menu with which to configure the application. To set up the access details for an Internet service provider, go to 'Settings...' → 'Configure with YaST'. Enter the root password when requested. Choose the corresponding configuration entry within YaST (modem, ISDN, network or DSL) and a list of the most common providers appears for selection.

Frequently Asked Questions and Answers

- *How can I access a CD or DVD?*

  An icon is located on your KDE desktop with an image of a CD. Insert your CD or DVD in your drive and left-click the icon. The CD will be mounted and its contents displayed in your Konqueror window.

- *There isn't a CD icon on my desktop. How do I create one?*

  Right-click the desktop. Select 'Create new...' → 'CD-ROM Device'. A window opens. Under 'General', rename the icon on the desktop. Enter the device name of your CD or DVD drive under 'Device'.

- *Can I put the panel somewhere else?*

  Yes, of course. Left-click a free space in the panel and drag it to any other edge. After you have released the mouse button, the panel will be placed there.

- *I want another panel. Is that possible?*

  Yes, right-click an open space in the already existing panel. Select 'Add' → 'Extension' → 'External Taskbar'. A taskbar opens. Now add files and directories there with the help of Konqueror. Alternatively, right-click the panel and select the corresponding items under 'Add'.

- *How can I add programs and other items to the panel?*

  For this, there are two options:

  1. Right-click a free space in the panel. A pop-up menu opens. Select 'Add' → 'Button' and you see the entries as they appear in the K menu. Add your preferred item to the control panel by clicking 'Add this menu'. Also select the desired program directly by clicking it. In both cases, the corresponding icon then appears in the control panel.
  2. Programs and folders can be added by selecting them straight from Konqueror with the left mouse button and, keeping the mouse button pressed, dropping the object into the panel and releasing the mouse again.

- *I want to find out more about my system. Where can I find this information?*

  There are two options. Press the key combination Alt + F2 and enter the command `ksysguard`. A window opens. Use the "sensor browser" on the left-hand side to click individual monitoring modules and drag them to the main window. The other possibility is to use the Control Center. All the resources and devices associated with your computer are located under 'Information'.

- *How can I display PostScript or PDF files?*

  In KDE, the program KGhostview serves this purpose. *DVI, PostScript, and PDF Viewers* on page 117 provides more details about this program.

- *How can I view graphics files?*

  Use kuickshow. Start it by pressing Alt + F2 and entering `kuickshow`. The application supports numerous graphics formats.

- *Can I play back my WAV, MP3, and other sound files in KDE?*

  Yes, press Alt + F2 and enter `xmms`. In the window that opens, press L and select the files to play.

- *How can I play back an audio CD?*

  Insert the audio CD into the drive and start the application xmms (press Alt + F2, then enter `xmms`). You may have to adjust the volume. This can be done with the volume slider of xmms or with kmix.

- *How can I play movies?*

  Movies in various file formats, such as mpeg1, avi, or DVDs (unencoded, mpeg2), can be played with gmplayer. The program can be started by pressing Alt + F2 and entering `gmplayer`.

  Note

  Images, sound, and videos can also be started automatically with the three programs by simply clicking the respective files in Konqueror.

  Note

- *How can I dial into the Internet?*

  Use the KInternet application. A detailed description is provided in *KInternet — Connecting to the Internet* on page 121.

- *How can I read my e-mail?* Use the program KMail, which is described in detail in *KMail — The KDE Mail Application* on page 207.

For More Information

Check out the KDE web site at `http://www.kde.org` for more information. `kde.themes.org` is good source for finding icons, themes, designs, and related eye candy.

Configuring KDE

This chapter is intended to illustrate how to change the look and feel of KDE using the Control Center. It also shows how to configure the file manager, web browser, and other tools to meet your individual demands.

KDE Control Center

Use the KDE Control Center to configure KDE according to your needs. Because an explanation of all individual options would exceed the scope of this chapter, the following sections only focus on the general framework and a brief overview.

The KDE Control Center can be accessed directly via the panel icon or in the K Menu or SuSE menu under 'Control Center'. The window shown in figure 6.1 opens.

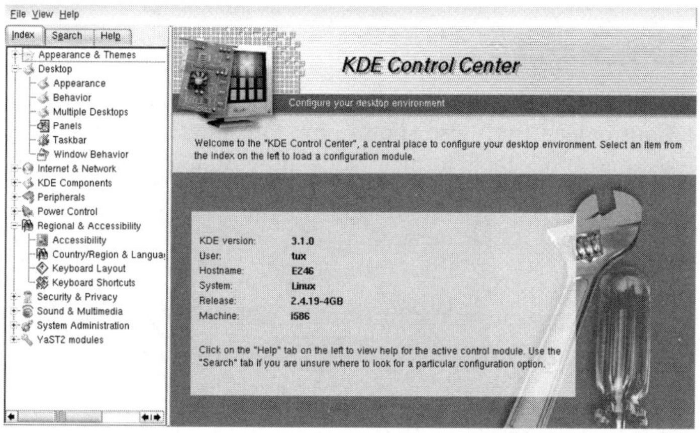

Figure 6.1: *The KDE Control Center*

The Control Center is divided into a menu bar and left and right panels. The left panel shows a list of configuration modules. After clicking a menu, the related modules in the right panel display some information. Clicking the module again starts the settings dialog in the panel to the right. Below it, there are usually up to four buttons:

'Help' View a short help text

'Use default settings' Restores the default settings

'Apply' Confirm changes

'Reset' Revert changes

The menu bar of the control center is structured as follows:

'File' Close the Control Center with 'Quit'

'View' Select the appearance of the Control Center. In 'Mode', decide whether to work with a structured 'Tree View' or with a simple 'Icon View'. The 'Icon Size' of the latter can then be specified.

'Help' In this menu entry, view the help pages of the Control Center via 'Contents' or use 'What is this?' to obtain information about a symbol or input field selected with the mouse. Additionally, you can write a 'Bug Report Regarding …' to the program author. Additional information about KDE and the Control Center is available under the respective entries.

If you are unsure what a particular setting does, consult the tool tips by pressing ⇑ Shift + F1 then clicking the element in question. This opens a corresponding help text.

Peripheral Devices

Digital Cameras This module allows configuration of the support for digital cameras. Already recognized cameras are featured in the list. Select 'Add' (the first icon to the left) if there is no entry. A dialog box appears with a list of supported camera models. Select the camera that best matches your model and connection (USB, serial, etc.).

The pictures stored in the camera can be accessed by entering camera: in Konqueror (and related KDE applications) if the camera was configured correctly.

Printer The 'Printer' module allows the comfortable configuration of all printing functions of the operating system through KDEPrint, the configuration interface to the `kprinter` application. The configuration should only be undertaken by experts. Configure your printers with YaST2.

Mouse The module offers the following configuration options:

The 'General' tab has settings for left-handed or right-handed mouse or trackball usage, whether files or folders are opened with a single-click or a double-click, and whether the mouse pointer should be larger and white.

The settings for the acceleration of the mouse pointer, the threshold time for recognizing a double-click, and others are located in

'Advanced'. Users with a wheel mouse can set how many lines are scrolled.

'Mouse Navigation' controls mouse navigation with the keyboard.

Keyboard This item holds the configuration options for keyboard repeat, audible keypress feedback, locking of the numeric keypad, and related items.

Desktop

Look and Feel 'Appearance' offers the customization of the font size, the default font type, the color display of plain text, and the corresponding background color as well as the underscoring of file names.

Window Behavior Customize how windows should behave when activated, moved, or resized. The settings are only valid for KWin, the default window manager for KDE.

Taskbar Select whether all windows should be displayed or just those of the current virtual desktop.

Control Panels The 'Position' tab offers the adjustment of the position, length, and size of the control panel.

'Hiding' offer options for the hiding behavior of the panel: the mode of hiding (only hide when the hide panel icon is clicked or hide automatically), the hide icons themselves, and animation options.

Settings in the 'Menus' tab determine the format of the menu entries (the order sequence of the names and descriptions).

Behavior This module determines for which special file types preview thumbnails should be displayed, how clicking events to the desktop are handled, and whether devices should be displayed on the desktop.

Virtual Desktops Set the number and names of the virtual desktops here.

Power Control

The modules in this menu item allow the activation of the energy-saving features of the computer. The execution of a certain command or a sound event on low power can be configured here. Modern computers can be switched to standby mode after a certain period of inactivity. This functionality requires APM support, which is standard issue in most contemporary PCs.

Look and Feel

This module offers a variety of configuration options for the KDE system.

Note

Keep the resources of your computer in mind when changing the look and feel of KDE. Styles with a lot of color variations and background images require more memory and processing power. This can slow down the system.

Note

Most dialogs are self-explanatory. However, the following discusses a few important modules.

Screensaver This module contains a list of common screensavers. Users whose computer is openly accessible should consider locking it with a timed screen saver. Activate the 'require password' option for this.

Theme Manager This module offers the possibility of creating, saving, or deleting themes (desktop designs). Select a theme from the list in 'Installation'. Fine adjustments can be made in the 'Contents' tab. This controls which elements, like colors, sound, and icons, should be ivolved.

Colors The color scheme of your KDE desktop can be changed here. Individual color adjustments can also be made, as shown in Figure 6.2), all of which will be adopted by most KDE applications. Some preset color schemes are already provided in the list. Clicking one of them opens a preview of the change in the upper display frame.

Window Decoration Decorate your window margins and title bars using this module. The following tabs ('Buttons', 'Configure [Quartz]', etc.) are activated, depending on the features of the decoration module selected. Then make your fine adjustments.

Background In this module, assign desktops a common background, different backgrounds, or color gradients.

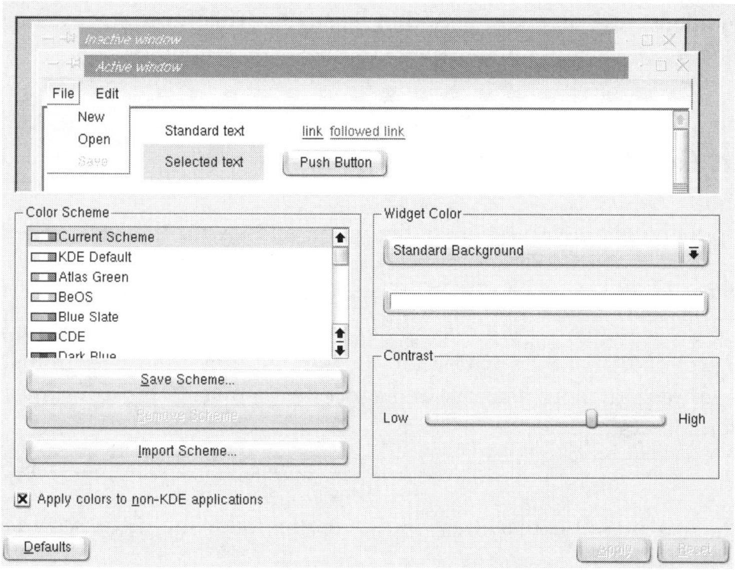

Figure 6.2: Color Adjustments to Your Desktop

To assign backgrounds or color gradients, select a desktop from the list. To the right of it is a preview window. At the bottom of the window, find the tabs 'Background', 'Wallpaper', 'Advanced', and 'Optimization'.

Under 'Background', configure a mode, such as a pattern or a horizontal or vertical color gradient. The colors for this are located just below the mode drop-down box.

'Wallpaper' specifies one or more wallpaper images for your desktop. Also define a mode here (centered, tiled, etc.). If you do not want to use these options, select 'No Wallpaper'.

'Advanced' provides options for blending your wallpaper background. Several options are available, including horizontal, vertical, and pyramidal.

'Optimization' provides options for memory optimization (for experts).

Control Panels The position, size, and appearance of your panel (or "kicker") are set in this module. This module has several tabs:

The position of the panel on your screen (left, right, above, below), its style (tiny, small, medium, large), and its size can be set in the 'Position' tab. The panel can also be set to hide automatically in the 'Hiding' tab.

'Look & Feel' defines various backgrounds for particular menus. First, make sure the box next to 'Enable background tiles' is checked (if it is not, click it) before the menus below are activated.

The 'Menus' tab defines how the K menu should be laid out and which additional items should appear there. Additional options include the integration of a quick browser menu, the configuration of a menu cache, and various other options.

The security level for the panel applets can be specified in the 'Applets' tab. They can be started in two ways: internally or externally. The internal method is preferable to the external one, but can lead to instability and security lapses if the applets are poorly programmed. Select the appropriate security level here.

The last tab is labeled 'Extensions' and is used for configuring additional external taskbars, such as their position, automatic hiding, or the presence of hiding buttons.

Preferences This module can be used to switch between the standard KDE menu and the SuSE menu. The KDE menu normally displays only KDE applications, while the SuSE menu includes others, such as GNOME applications.

Launch Feedback Various options can be activated in this module to provide visual feedback that an application is being launched. Set 'Enable Busy Cursor' to receive a feedback to your mouse cursor. It is possible to opt for a flashing feedback effect or for how long the feedback should be provided.

Optionally, have feedback that a program is starting. This is also displayed in the panel if 'Enable taskbar notification' is checked. Make settings here as to how long the launch feedback should be active.

Fonts The default fonts can be changed here. Click 'Select' next to the font to change. Set the font type, style, and size in the dialog and confirm the changes with 'OK'.

Style A style is the way that buttons, lists, menus, and other related desktop elements are presented. Some preset styles are provided and already listed. Additional settings can be made in 'Effects', for instance, whether the menus should appear to be transparent.

'Miscellaneous' determines even more style settings.

Icons Use this module to change all icons of the KDE environment. Some predefined icon designs can be chosen from the list.

The effects for the icons and their size settings for the various panels and desktops can be set in the 'Advanced' tab.

Internet and Networking

This menu contains modules for configuring e-mail, networking, and the web browser.

Releasing the Desktop This module assists in making your desktop available to other computers. "Desktop Sharing" uses the RFB protocol, which is better known as VNC.

To allow a trusted third party access to your desktop, select 'Make & manage invitations...'. A new personal invitation can be drafted with the 'New personal invitation...' option in the dialog box that opens. The relevant data (system, password, and end of lease) is displayed. A user must be told the password to enable access to the desktop. KDE informs you when a connection is requested and prompts for acceptance or refusal of the request. More information can be found at `http://www.tjansen.de/krfb/`.

File Sharing The settings in this module can only be changed by the user `root`. It allows the sharing of files in a network. The NFS (Network File System) and SMB (Server Message Block) protocols are used for this.

Email Enter user information in this module, such as name, organization, e-mail address, and reply address. Specify your preferred e-mail application.

Preferences The behavior of KDE applications in networks can be adjusted by setting time-out limits. The time until a time-out error is returned can be extended when working on slow connections.

LAN Browsing The LISa daemon for setting up LANs can be configured with this module.

Proxies & Cache The module 'Proxy' allows the configuration of interaction with any proxies your ISP supports.

The 'SOCKS' item provides options for data transfer through firewalls. The module should be activated only by skilled expert users.

Web Browser These options are described in *Konqueror — The KDE File Manager and Web Browser* on page 191.

KDE Components

File Manager The look and feel of Konqueror as a file manager is determined with this module.

File Associations The 'File associations' menu allows the association of data types (also called MIME types) to certain applications. A file association generally consists of a rule or a file pattern (for example, `*.sxd`), a brief description, an icon, and a list of applications that can process this data type.

Session Manager Lists some KDE services.

Selection of Components Regularly-used applications, like editors, mail clients, and terminal emulators, are stored in *components*. Other applications can also use this service.

Spell Checking Dictionaries, encoding, and applications necessary for spell checking can be configured with this module.

Session Manager This module determines the behavior of your system on login and logout. This includes whether logout needs to be confirmed and whether the computer is supposed to shut down immediately.

Regional Settings and Accessibility

Country & Language The language, number, and date format settings for your region can be set here. Selecting the respective 'Country' is usually sufficient. Any additionally desired modification to these settings can be made under 'Numbers', 'Money', and 'Time & Date'.

The absence of a desired language in the list is probably due to a missing KDE language package. The name of the package starts with `kde3-i18n-` and ends with an short code for the language, such as `de` for German or `es` for Spanish.

Tip

See how your settings will be applied in the module preview at the bottom of the window.

Tip

Keyboard Layout To use multiple keyboard layouts, check 'activate keyboard layouts'. The keyboard model can be set with 'Keyboard Model'. The default language is set with 'Primary Layout'. Additional languages are selected with 'Additional Layouts'.

Shortcuts If the previous keyboard shortcuts do not suit you, redefine the various key shortcuts for actions and applications in this module.

The 'Global Shortcuts' tab contains application-independent keyboard shortcuts. A key shortcut can be associated to an action in the list. For example, (Alt) + (F2) opens the 'Run command' dialog.

'Shortcut Sequences' defines the shortcuts to use for switching between desktops or moving a window to a certain desktop.

The 'Application Shortcuts' tab defines certain key combinations to use for various actions frequently occurring in many applications, such as deleting, cutting, copying, and pasting.

Accessibility For error messages to be issued by acoustic or visual signals other than the standard system bell, make these settings in the 'Bell' window of this module.

Set the key delays in the 'Keyboard' window. This sets the minimum time a key must be pressed before considered input.

Crypto

Passwords Decide whether blank spaces or asterisks should appear when entering your password. Restricting the storage time for any password is recommended.

Crypto This module provides SSL (Secure Socket Library) setup options, certificates, certificate authorities, authentication, and the configuration of other security-related aspects.

Sound and Multimedia

Use this module to configure use of your sound card.

Audio CD This item allows the configuration of the I/O module for your audio CDs. It is called by entering `audiocd:/` in the URL bar of Konqueror. Settings can be made for the automatic detection of audio CDs, error correction, the "Ogg-Vorbis" and "MP3" file formats, and for connecting to a music database on the Internet.

System Bell A system bell event with adjustable volume, pitch and duration can be generated instead of system notifications. The system bell is activated with 'Use System Bell instead of System Notification'.

Audio System This module sets up the KDE aRts sound server.

System Notifications This module offers settings for reporting or documenting occurring events. Figure 6.3 shows the details.

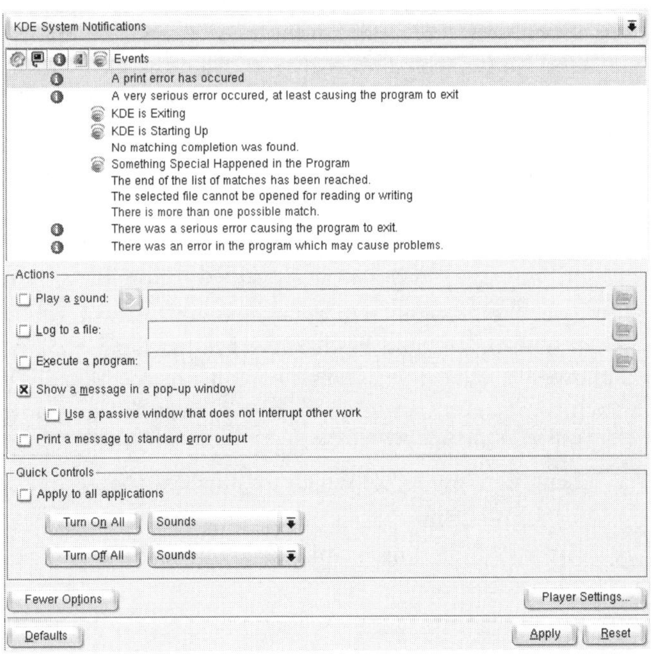

Figure 6.3: KDE System Notifications

Selecting 'More Options' displays additional options for creating a log file, playing a sound, or executing a command.

System Administration

The menu contains modules for settings regarding your system behavior.

Caution

Because the settings for the modules 'Login Manager' and 'Date & Time' affect the whole system, only `root` can make changes.

Caution

Login Manager The KDE graphical login procedure can be configured with this module. For example, control the appearance of the welcome screen and the list of users who are granted access to the login manager or have permission to shut down the system.

The 'Appearance' tab offers options for configuring the appearance of the login screen with a greeting and a logo. The visual display style and the language (which can be different from the individual user preferences) can also be set. A global or a customized setting for the position of the login manager can also be defined.

Use 'Font' to choose the fonts the login manager should use for the greeting text and user name.

The preferences for a special wallpaper image or a simple custom color gradient for the login screen can be specified in the 'Background' tab.

The settings in the 'Sessions' tab determine which session types, such as 'KDE' or 'failsafe', should be displayed in the login manager and who is allowed to shut down the system. It can additionally be specified which commands should be executed when shutting down or restarting the system.

Use the 'Users' window to set which existing users on the network appear in the login manager.

Automatic user login and other miscellaneous features can be defined under 'Convenience'.

Caution

Saving passwords presents a security risk. Therefore, avoid this type of "convenience".

Caution

Date & Time Define the system date, time, and time zone.

Paths This module determines the location of the desktop folder, the trash folder, and the autostart folder as well as the document path.

Font Installer At the first initialization of this module, an assistant program offers help with the installation of fonts. Nothing much needs to be changed here normally, as default settings are already provided for this feature.

Session Manager This module defines whether a confirmation dialog should precede a logout and whether the settings of the previous session should be restored on login.

7

GNOME — The Desktop

With the recent release of GNOME2, GNOME provides an amazingly fast option for the Linux desktop. This speed is offered without sacrificing features or convenience. GNOME (GNU Network Object Model Environment) is an effective desktop as well as a flexible and sophisticated developer's environment. It was developed to make the user interface more uniform, streamlining the various aspects of the look and feel. As well as components for managing the windows, additional components ensure that applications can share data with each other, featuring a uniform operating concept and help system. Modularization allows reusable program elements to be integrated into other applications so the wheel does not have to be reinvented for each individual scenario.

This chapter focuses on how to work with GNOME and how to customize the environment and applications. It also provides an overview of some of the core applications.

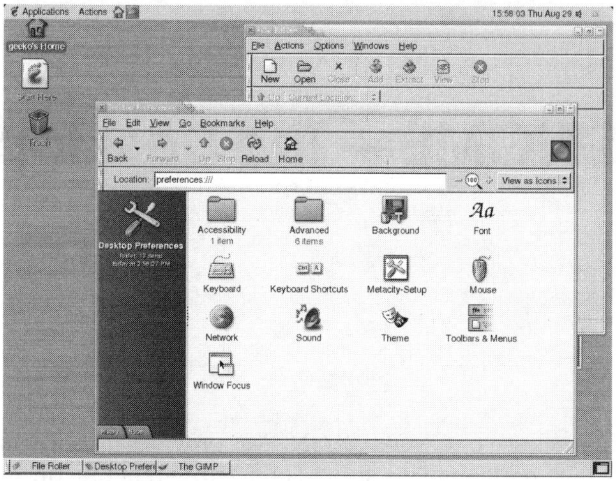

Figure 7.1: *GNOME2 Desktop with Open Applications*

Changing to GNOME2

Although the core GNOME2 desktop has been released, the changeover for applications is somewhat more time consuming. SuSE Linux 8.1 includes GNOME2 applications as much as possible. When the application has not yet been updated to the newer environment, the most recent GNOME 1.4 version is included.

These applications can be easily used in GNOME2, but do not offer the configuration integration provided by GNOME2 applications. Unfortunately, applets created for GNOME 1.4 are not compatible with the GNOME2 panels. As many applications and applets as possible are included in the distribution. To find additional GNOME2 packages, refer frequently to `http://www.suse.com` for updates.

For more information about changes between GNOME and GNOME2, refer to the release notes at http://www.gnome.org/start/2.0/releasenotes.html. These notes provide specific information about changes in the GNOME desktop from the developers themselves.

Starting GNOME2

A GNOME2 session is available from the graphical display managers included in SuSE Linux. It can also be started with `startx gnome2`. A reasonable default configuration is included for both regular users and the root user. It is also possible for the system administrator to modify this configuration or provide additional options.

GNOME2 and Window Managers

As well as GNOME2, a window manager must be used. The window manager controls how windows are drawn on the desktop. GNOME2 offers two window managers: Metacity and Sawfish2. Sawfish2 is a port of the Sawfish window manager commonly used with earlier GNOME versions. Metacity is a new window manager designed with GNOME2 in mind. It is lighter and faster than Sawfish and offers simplified configuration. Metacity is now the default GNOME2 window manager in SuSE Linux.

Help

GNOME2 includes extensive help and documentation. Yelp, the GNOME2 help browser, also provides easy access to other documentation on your system, like man pages. Access the help by selecting 'Help' from the menu. Many configuration dialogs and applications also offer help from menus or buttons.

Configuring GNOME

If the default configuration does not suit your needs, it can be modified extensively.

GConf

GNOME2 offers a new configuration method. The intention is to simplify and unify configuration in programs. For example, instead of changing the font in each application, you can change the font once and it will be applied to all applications compatible with GConf. GConf can also be used by system administrators to make configuration layouts. The GConf Editor can be useful for administrators and experienced users. The basic functionality of GConf is offered by the 'Desktop Preferences' and the individual application's configuration dialogs.

Desktop Preferences

If this is your first start, try the 'Start Here' icon on the desktop then select 'Desktop Preferences'. If this icon is not available, open Nautilus, the default GNOME file manager and viewer, by right-clicking the desktop and selecting 'New Window'. Under 'Location:', enter `preferences://`. Double-click the icon to access the dialog. The configuration options available here can also be opened from the menu.

Accessibility

GNOME2 is intended to be highly accessible for people with disabilities. Special accessibility options, such as keyboard controls, are in this folder.

Advanced

The 'Advanced' folder contains more complication configuration dialogs. Use them for selecting what applications are used for different file types, controlling access to a CD database, and other things. The subfolder 'Sawfish' contains the configuration for the Sawfish2 window manager. Unless you have specifically selected to use Sawfish, ignore this configuration and use the 'Metacity Setup' dialog described below.

The 'Preferred Applications' dialog is very useful. Use it to select your default web browser and text editor.

Background

Your GNOME background can be a picture or just a gradient. To select a picture, drag and drop one from an open Nautilus window or click the 'Picture' image to open a file browser. Select how the options are displayed under 'Picture Options'. Use 'No Picture' if you do not want a picture. Under 'Background Style' and 'Color', set the color background used with 'No Picture' or behind the picture.

Font

Select your 'Standard Application Font' and 'Desktop Font'. Click the listed font to open a selection dialog. The 'Standard Application Font' applies to all applications compatible with GNOME2 configuration.

Keyboard

In this dialog, make special settings for your keyboard. You can also configure the blinking of the cursor here.

Keyboard Shortcuts

It is possible to control a wide range of window manager functions with the keyboard. The default setup includes many reasonable keyboard shortcuts. To check the shortcuts or modify them to your own preferences, use this dialog. Two schemes are available: 'Default' and 'Emacs'. The Emacs scheme can be very convenient for emacs users. Either scheme can be modified to your needs. To enter a new shortcut, select the one to change. Press the keys to use for this function in the future.

Metacity Setup

This configuration tool only applies if you are using the Metacity window manager. This window manager is the default in SuSE Linux. Select a theme from the list. It will be used immediately, so you can see how it will look if used. To use a font other than that set in the 'Font Preferences' dialog, uncheck the 'Use Default Font' check box and select the desired font. With 'Focus Selector', set how windows are given focus. 'Click' gives focus only when a window is clicked. Both 'Mouse' and 'Sloppy' give focus when the mouse cursor is moved onto a window. When 'Mouse' is used, a window loses focus when the cursor leaves that window. Select how many workspaces to use with the 'Workspace Selector'.

Mouse

Use the 'Buttons' tab to configure your mouse for left-handed or right-handed use. Also set the 'Double-click Delay'. Under 'Cursor', configure the display of the mouse cursor and optionally set for an animated highlight around the cursor when Ctrl is pressed. 'Motion' contains settings for mouse acceleration and sensitivity and a threshold distance for dragging an item.

Network

If you use a proxy for accessing the web, configure its setup here. This will then be applied to all GConf-compliant applications.

Sound

Under 'General', select to enable or disable the sound server on start-up. If the sound server is enabled, optionally enable 'Sounds for events'. Use the list under 'Sound events' to configure individual sounds for events in compatible applications.

Theme

This selection controls the Gtk+ theme used in compatible applications. The Gtk+ theme selects the controls used in applications, including buttons, check boxes, and radio buttons. The titlebar and window borders are controlled by the window manager theme, set with the appropriate window manager configuration tool.

Toolbars & Menus

Use this to control the appearance and functioning of toolbars and menus. Select how text and icons are used in the toolbars, whether or not toolbars can be moved, and if menu items can have icons.

Panels

GNOME panels are easy to configure, add, and remove. A panel can be used to provide menus, applets, drawers, and launchers. Applets are small applications providing useful functionalities. Launchers are icons used to start a program. Drawers are like a subpanel that can contain other panel objects. To access panel controls, right-click an existing panel in an empty space to open the panel menu. If you right-click an existing launcher or applet, only the menu for that item is opened.

Configuring Panels

If available, use 'Properties' from the panel menu to make panel-specific settings. The settings available vary based on the panel type. The 'Hiding' settings are available with most panel types. 'Auto-hide' removes the panel from view when it is not being used. The panel is retrieved when the mouse moves to the panel location. Hide buttons enable the user to collapse and expand the panel as desired. The 'Background' tab has settings for the background color or image of the panel

Creating a Panel

GNOME offers five types of panels menu, edge, corner, sliding, and floating. The menu panel is the panel at the top of the screen with the menu and clock in it. Edge panels are full-length panels placed along one of the four edges of the screen. Corner panels are short panels that can be positioned in the ends or middle of an edge. Sliding panels are short panels that can be middle-clicked and dragged into the desired position along an edge. Floating panels can be middle-clicked and dragged anywhere on the screen.

To create a new panel, right-click an existing panel and select 'Create Panel'. Select the desired panel type. Right-click the new panel to configure it or add items. Middle-click and drag to move it.

Adding Items

To add something to a panel, right-click an empty space and select 'Add to Panel'. Available applets are listed by category in the submenus. Launchers can be added manually or from the menu. Select the item to add. If you select 'Launcher', a dialog opens. Enter a specific and generic name for the item. Also enter a comment if desired. For 'Command', enter the command used to start the program, such as `xchat` to start xchat. If the application should be run in a terminal, select the 'Run in Terminal' check box. Click 'No Icon' to select an icon for the application. Things under 'Advanced' are not required.

Rearranging Panel Items

Things like applets, launchers, and drawers can be rearranged. Just drag items into place or right-click the item and select 'Move'. Items can be dragged from one panel to another. Remove items by right-clicking and selecting 'Remove from Panel'.

Removing Panels

To remove a panel, right-click and select 'Delete this panel...'. When a panel is deleted, all items in the panel and all configuration settings are lost. If you want items in the panel to be available in a different panel, move them to another panel before deleting the panel.

Nautilus

Nautilus is the GNOME2 file manager and viewer. It also supplies the icons on the desktop. For GNOME2, Nautilus has undergone extensive changes that have drastically improved its speed. If you have tried Nautilus before and disliked it, you may want to give it another chance. The information provided here is just a brief overview of the basic functionality of Nautilus. Refer to the internal help for more information.

Controlling Your Desktop

The default configuration provides several useful icons on the desktop. Double-click the desktop icon to start the application or open the folder in Nautilus. To make changes to the icon, such as rename it, right-click the icon and select the appropriate option from the menu. Use 'Properties' to select a different icon or make other changes. 'Rename' can be used to simply rename an icon. To delete the icon that launches a program, just throw it into the trash. Use caution doing the same with icons representing folders or data. If the icon is a folder or file, the actual data is deleted. If the icon is a link to a directory or file, only the link will be deleted.

If you right-click an empty space on the desktop, a menu of options opens. To create a new folder on the desktop for storing items, select 'New Folder'. To create a launcher for an application, select 'New Launcher'. Enter the name and command for the application and select an icon. Check 'Run in Terminal' if the application needs to be run in a terminal window.

To create a link on the desktop to an existing folder or file, open to it in Nautilus (double-click your home icon then navigate to the correct location). Right-click the item to which to link and select 'Make Link'. Drag the link from the Nautilus window and drop it onto the desktop.

Navigating in Nautilus

Nautilus navigation is similar to most existing web browsers. To open a new window, right-click an empty space on the desktop and select 'New Window'. The default opening location for Nautilus is your home directory. This can be changed.

The default window layout is shown in Figure 7.2 on the facing page. The toolbar has icons for going forward and back, up a directory level, stopping, reloading, and returning to the home page. The path to the currently displayed directory or file is listed in 'Location'. A new path can be entered directly into this bar.

The left pane shows the current item being viewed and some information about that item. The bottom of the pane has 'History' and 'Notes' tabs.

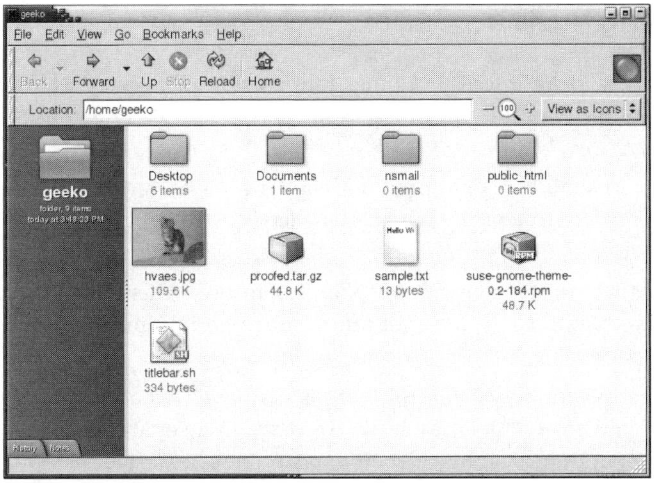

Figure 7.2: Nautilus Showing Home Directory

'Notes' can be used to make notes about an item. They are stored with the item. 'History' shows items you have accessed. To return to the default view, click the tab at the top.

Nautilus attempts to select appropriate icons for items based on what it can determine about the file type. A small preview is displayed for image and text files. Double-clicking a file opens the file in a viewer. The left tab will then display a list of possible applications with which to open the file. The file in the viewer cannot be edited within Nautilus.

You can also store bookmarks in Nautilus. Use 'Bookmarks' to add, edit, or access your bookmarks.

Managing Files

Files can be managed in Nautilus with drag and drop. To move files from one directory to another, use 'New Window' from the right-click menu or the 'File' menu in Nautilus to open two windows. In one window, open to the items to move. In the other, open to the destination. To move a file, just drag it to the new location and drop it. Copying is slightly more complicated. Right-click the item to copy and select 'Duplicate'. Then drag the copy to the new location. The menu displayed when an item is right-clicked has items for renaming files and editing other properties.

Configuring Nautilus

Nautilus takes its base font and other information from the desktop configuration. To make Nautilus-specific settings, use 'Edit' → 'Preferences' from a Nautilus window.

Under 'View Defaults', configure the defaults for viewing. Select if folders should be shown in 'Icon View' or 'List View'. Also set the sort order for both view styles.

In 'Appearance', select a theme for Nautilus to use. This theme controls the colors inside Nautilus. It does not affect your window manager or Gtk+ theme selections.

The settings in 'Windows' control what is displayed when a new window is opened. If you select 'Open each file or folder in a separate window', Nautilus will open a new window when you double-click a file or folder. Each item will have its own window. The sidebar is the left pane.

'Desktop & Trash' has options for the Nautilus desktop, the desktop directory, and the trash. Using the trash helps protect items from being accidentally deleted.

'Icon & List Views' has settings that control click behavior and sort order. Under 'Executable Text Files', set whether scripts should be run or displayed when clicked or if you should be asked each time. 'Show/Hide Options' controls listing of special file types.

'Icon Captions' controls the information available under icons. 'Sidebar Panels' controls what is available in the sidebar.

'Speed Tradeoffs' is useful for balancing between speed and display. Adjust the various settings to meet your needs.

Useful GNOME Applets and Applications

GNOME2 includes a variety of applets and applications. This is just an introduction to some of the most useful or interesting ones. These are all compliant with the GNOME2 configuration scheme.

Panel Applets

Dictionary

Dictionary is a useful applet for looking up the spellings and meanings of words. It accesses an online dictionary, so an Internet connection is required. Add it to a panel with 'Add to Panel' → 'Accessories' → 'Dictionary Lookup'.

Inbox Monitor

Inbox Monitor is a nice applet for checking if new mail has arrived. It can play a sound on arrival and can be configured to check a range of mailbox types and locations. Add it with 'Add to Panel' → 'Internet' → 'Inbox Monitor'.

Disk Mounter

This convenient applet is useful for mounting and unmounting drives. It can be configured to any mount point and offers a range of icons. Add it with 'Add to Panel' → 'Utility' 'Disk Mounter'.

Fish

For those who like silly amusements in the panel, try the GNOME fish. Historically named Wanda, the fish is fully configurable offering several animations and customized naming. By default, Wanda the fish offers a fortune when clicked. Add a fish (or snarling monkey) with 'Add to Panel' → 'Amusements' → 'Fish'.

GNOME Terminal

Use GNOME Terminal to access the command line. Start it with 'Applications' → 'System Tools' → 'Terminal'. The default font is based on your font preferences. A new feature of this version of GNOME Terminal is profiles. Using these profiles, make a variety of setting options for different purposes and easily switch profiles. For example, if you connect to different machines, you may want to use different terminal settings for each machine.

To create, edit, or manage profiles, select 'Edit' → 'Profiles'. Set the default profile used for new terminals in this dialog. To create a new terminal, click 'New'. Enter a name for the profile and select the existing profile on which to base the settings. Click 'Create'. Select the new profile from the list and click 'Edit'. Also use this to edit an existing profile. Under the various tabs, make settings for the new profile.

To switch profiles in an open terminal window, select 'Terminal' → 'Profile' then select the desired profile. This change takes effect immediately. Additional terminals can be opened as new windows or tabs from the 'File' menu. Keyboard shortcuts for the application can be configured under 'Edit' → 'Keybindings'.

File Roller

File Roller is a convenient user interface for creating a variety of archived files. It can create and extract archives as well as add or extract items from an archive. In addition to using the menu items and buttons for adding items, you can add items by dragging them from a Nautilus window and dropping them into File Roller. Start File Roller with 'Applications' → 'Accessories' → 'File Roller'.

Games

GNOME2 includes a wide selection of games in the menu under 'Games'. Aisleriot is a card solitaire game including several different solitaire layouts. Iagno is a similar to Othello. Tangrams is a game in which you use geometrically-shaped pieces to form a predetemined shape, such as a chicken.

For More Information

To find out more about the GNOME desktop, check the following links:

`http://www.gnome.org` The GNOME project home page.

`http://www.gtk.org` GIMP Toolkit (GTK) home page.

`http://www.sunshineinabag.co.uk` A Resource for GNOME2 Themes.

`http://www.gnome.org/faqs/` Frequently Answered Questions and Answers.

Ergonomics in the Workplace

This chapter is a short discussion of the ergonomic issues involved in the layout of computer workplaces. This text should not be seen as a substitute for studying the respective standards. No citations from these are included here and footnotes with references to other literature are completely omitted to preserve readability. It attempts to summarize the latest research findings in a short and concise manner, however, much will remain unmentioned. The items referred to in each section are mostly gathered from German literature and are almost always based on regulations and policies in the Federal Republic of Germany. This information is still useful in designing an ergonomic work area.

The Working Environment

If ergonomics specialists examined the home workstations of computer users systematically, they would find many problems. Unfortunately, no standard has yet prevented individual users from buying so-called "special computer tables". The low-priced metal-tube frames with "practical rollers" (little stability), "ergonomically retractable keyboard tray" (no wrist pad), "integrated PC case holder and printer stand with paper shelf" (little stacking space and sometimes little legroom), "swiveling mouse pad" (unstable and insufficient working space), and "good view of the screen" (too close, too high) allow you to use a computer for a short time only. They should not be used at professional terminal workstations as they hardly meet any criteria of the corresponding standards. You will not find much of this kind of computer furniture in professional computer equipment catalogs, because manufacturers indirectly keep an eye on the employees' health by observing the minimum standards of computer workstations. Even these minimum standards should be improved.

The Right Desk

A table at the wrong height strains arm and back muscles. The resulting cramped posture especially strains the spine. Too little leg room can force an unnatural body posture and cause disorders to the blood supply.

Choosing the right table is very easy. It should be as wide and deep as possible. An individual adjustment of the table height would be optimal. Working tables at which you can change between sitting and standing by turning the table into a writing stand, often just at the push of a button, are a luxury, but changing between a sitting and standing position brings relief.

- The flexible arrangement of working materials requires a table top of at least 160 x 80 cm.
- Workstations made of several interlinked boards are recommended.
- Tables that cannot be vertically adjusted must be 72 cm high. Tables that are vertically adjustable must be between 68 and 76 cm high.
- Even more width is needed for certain working tasks, such as CAD workstations. When changing between screen work and other kinds of work, at least 200 cm is required.
- There should be at least 60 cm leg room. Previous experience has shown, however, that this leg room is often too little.

- When using large screens, tables should be 100 or even 120 cm deep.
- The table surface should not be in bright colors and should have minimal reflection. A lot of office furniture is available in a subdued grey only.

Sitting Correctly on the Right Working Chair

Sitting in a working chair makes you sit in the same posture for a long time, unlike in an easy chair where you can move around easily. Constant sitting in the wrong position, such as bending forward or twisting to the side, can harm the respiratory and digestive organs. This leads to premature fatigue, circulatory disturbances, and backache resulting from overstraining the spine and the vertebrate disks. In extreme cases, years of sitting in the wrong position can lead to muscular and skeletal illnesses.

Correct sitting means a frequent change of posture. Different parts of the body are then constantly being used. Basically, it is a question of the correct adjustment. The height of your working chair is best when your forearms lying on the table are at right angles to your upper arms. You should be able to place your feet completely on the floor and your thighs and lower legs should also be at right angles. Gymnastic balls and balancing chairs offer an alternative to conventional seating arrangements.

Unfortunately, a good chair, constructed according to ergonomic criteria, is relatively expensive, but the investment in your health is worth it.

Important features of a good chair include:

- a backrest reaching to the shoulder blades and with an adjustable kinetic resistance
- support for the lumbar spinal column
- a seat that is also adjustable and can be tilted forwards or backwards
- automatic regulation of backrest and seat to retain an ideal angle
- springs that softly cushion the weight when sitting down
- stability provided with the help of at least five foot legs with rollers that are restrained when you stand
- adjustable height of the seat (according to standards, 42 to 53 cm) and backrest
- individual adjustment of arm rests, if there are any (luxury)
- a footrest if your feet do not reach the floor

Good Lighting for Productive Work

Generally speaking, workplace lighting does not come close to the intensity of light outdoors. This difference is unnoticed because the human faculty of perception is very flexible. The influence of lighting conditions on our own efficiency is often underestimated. If the light is too bright, you cannot see what is on the screen. If it is too dark, sharpness of vision decreases. The wrong lighting overstrains the visual system and, eventually, causes symptoms of fatigue and stress.

It is assumed that a combination of general lighting and individual workstation lighting is best. For the workstation at home, the combination of a high-powered ceiling lamp (500 watts, preferably with a dimmer) and one or two workplace lamps is recommended. The fluorescent lamps usually found in offices for general lighting should be supplemented by individual workstation lamps. The lighting should, however, not be too intense and be individually adjustable. Stark contrasts should be avoided. Be careful with strong desk lamps. Good illumination is, unfortunately, very expensive and the minimum requirements of lighting can also be fulfilled with cheaper illumination layouts.

- It is important that you are exposed to daylight. A view outside is important.
- General lighting is considered pleasant if it is not below 250 lx (usually 500 lx is required, 1000 lx for an open plan office).
- 500–750 lx should be emitted by the individual workstation lighting. However, individual lamps are often problematic. If they are too strong, the contrast to the general lighting is too great. Harmonic, soft transitions are considered more pleasant.
- The lighting should not flicker. In the case of worn-out fluorescent lamps, a flickering can sometimes be noticed from the corner of the eye.
- Avoid dark shadows.
- Ceiling lights should emit light diagonally from above. Lighting strips should be set perpendicular to the screen table. The line of sight at the screen table should thus run parallel to the lighting strips.
- Whether the lighting is considered to be pleasant depends on the color temperature and light color of the lamp type. Warm white or neutral white is recommended.

- The light requirement depends not only on the working task, but also on age: older people need more light. The fact that older people often have only a small lamp in their homes has nothing to do with their light requirement, but rather with the fact that they want to save electricity.
- A screen workstation near daylight requires optimum shielding against direct and reflex glare, especially when the line of sight is directly out the window or at a 45 degree angle to it. The built-in antiglare facilities should be variable. Under no circumstances should artificial illumination cause reflex glare on the screen.

Optimum Climate

The room climate determines our well-being to a great extent. Problems arise more often if it is too cold, too warm, too drafty, or too dry. Low relative humidity can lead to burning eyes, dry mucous membranes, skin irritations, and increased susceptibility to colds. Things get complicated when people who work in the same room are accustomed to different base temperatures. For your well-being, it is important to observe the recommended basic values for temperature and humidity and to avoid strong air movement. The working material itself should not contribute to the increase of temperature.

- For activities in a sitting position or simple work, a room temperature of 20 to 22 °C is recommended. In summer, the temperature should be 26 °C at the most. This value should only be exceeded for a short time when the outdoor temperature is higher.
- A lot of equipment, as well as people, emit heat and influence room air conditions. This should be reduced as much as possible.
- The air humidity should be between 40 (sometimes 50) and 65 percent and should be checked. This value is especially affected by heating systems.
- Draft (possibly from open windows and doors or air conditioning) should not exceed 0.1 to 0.15 m/s. Draft on individual parts of the body should be avoided.
- An air conditioner should be individually adjustable. It should be serviced regularly.

- The windows should be able to be opened and have sunshades to avoid glare effects. Sunlight can increase the room temperature considerably. Sunshades attached to the outside of the building provide the best protection.

- Plants can improve room conditions and are therefore recommended in all cases. They increase the relative humidity and filter pollutants from the air.

Too Much Noise Causes Stress

Noise is a physically powerful stress factor. Although it is often played down, too much noise makes you ill. Apart from health impairments, such as defective hearing, vegetative disorders, and psychic changes, noise affects our efficiency by impairing our ability to concentrate. Furthermore, discontent can reduce working motivation. The fact that proper noise abatement can possibly cost a lot of money is also problematic.

A calm working environment improves efficiency. Work at terminal workstations is often characterized as "mental activity". Therefore the maximum load value for scientific work or programming is 55 dB (A). The dB (A) represent a weighted evaluation of the acoustic pressure. The A-filter curve most resembles human perception. An increase of the sound level by 10 dB (A) is normally perceived as a duplication of volume.

- Because mainly mental work is done at terminal workstations, quiet working materials should be used from the start.

- The maximum limiting value for office work is 55 dB (A). With especially high mental demands or necessary communication of language, as low as 35–45 dB (A) is required. This is the case, for instance, for specialized work, scientific work, or programming.

- Furthermore, the evaluation level of a maximum of 55 dB (A) is important. If 70 dB (A) is measured for a quarter of an hour, the noise in the remaining time should be less than or equal to 55 dB (A).

- Workstations can be equipped with partitions, sound-absorbing floors, appropriately wallpapered walls, curtains, and other sound-reducing features.

- Loud working equipment, such as matrix printers, should be installed in sound-absorbing cases. The permissible noise levels for office equipment are determined in the DIN standards.

- An air conditioner should not increase the normal noise level.
- Strain caused by excessive noise can also be reduced by an organizational restructuring of work.

Office Equipment

Buying a Screen

If you already have poor sharpness of vision, low-quality screens can make things even worse. Apart from eye problems, tenseness, fatigue, and many other disorders can be caused.

The latest technological developments are triniton, or black-matrix, screens and TFT flat screens. Unfortunately, flat screens are still relatively expensive. There are extensive standards that regulate the readability of the depicted information. When buying a screen, it is recommended to study the extensive standards to avoid a wrong purchase. One thing is certain: a good screen is usually expensive. The normal tube screens do not last forever. They only retain their focus and contrast for a few years.

- All depicted characters should be sharply defined and clearly legible up to the edges of the screen. A positive representation (dark characters on a light background, such as in a book) is recommended.
- As the depicted characters must be large enough, a 17-inch monitor is recommended, at least for graphical user interfaces (like KDE). For the processing of CAD, layout, and graphics, it should be 21 inches.
- It is especially important that the screen does not flicker. In concrete terms, the minimum sync frequency with 15-inch monitors should be at least 73 Hz. However, 85 Hz is recommended. For larger screens, such as 21-inch, 100 Hz is a good value.
- Luminosity and contrast should be variable. The focus of the characters should not differ with adjustments of brightness or contrast.
- The image should be free from distortion and show no color errors.
- To avoid reflex glare, a good antireflective coating of the screen surface is recommended.
- The screen should be rotatable and inclinable. A vertical adjustment is recommended.

- Colors make the displayed information easier to comprehend. However, the display of colors can also be straining for the eyes because different colors are refracted differently by the lenses. For red colors, people are farsighted, but for blue colors people are nearsighted. Older screens often have convergence errors — the three beams of the screen tube are no longer aligned precisely, so colored borders appear around letters, for example.
- Electromagnetic radiation emitting from the screen should be kept to a minimum.
-

Screen Location

A screen put in the wrong place leads to a cramped posture at work, which can cause illnesses. A work table that has insufficient depth often prevents the screen from being placed reasonably. The natural position of the head and arms is designed for work that lies in front of the body.

A screen put in the wrong place leads to a cramped posture at work, which can cause illnesses. A work table that has insufficient depth often prevents the screen from being placed reasonably. The natural position of the head and arms is designed for work that lies in front of the body.

Ergonomics specialists have developed their own guidelines for the "vision and gripping area." These reject placing the screen to the side. An exception is only when the screen is rarely used. A reason for this placement is the fact that even the required minimum 80 cm worktable depth is insufficient with a large screen and the use of working documents. Often the screen is placed — as shown in many PC manual pictures — on top of the computer case. This also leads to an unnatural posture. Observe yourself while you are reading. Are you looking straight ahead or slightly down?

- Shoulder, keyboard, and screen should be in one line so you always look directly at the screen. This rule does not necessarily need to be observed all the time
- Ultimately, the workstation should be individually adapted to the person and the working task. Flexibility is the key. Easily movable, rotatable, and, ideally, screens that retract into the table are encouraged.
- A comfortable visual distance varies individually. At least 50 cm is required. Some people need considerably more.

- It is a good idea for users to look away from the screen from time to time. In this way, their eyes can adapt to a different distance.
- If a document is being copied, it should be at the same distance as the screen to avoid frequent changes of focus.
- The difference in luminance between the direct working area, the screen, and the immediately surrounding areas, such as the screen case, should not be more than three to one. For this reason, computer cases in offices are not black. The difference between the working area and the surroundings should not be more than ten to one.
- Shiny areas create large differences of luminance. This is why office furniture is not available in bright colors and has a matt surface.
- To minimize the reflex glare on the screen, the screen and the keyboard should be arranged so the line of vision is parallel to window panes. The further the screen is away from the window, the better.
- The screen should not be directly under a lighting strip, but to the side of it. The line of vision should be parallel to the lighting strip.

The Keyboard and the Wrists

It is well-known that the keyboard arrangement derived from the typewriter is not necessarily ergonomic. During typing, the fingers, hands, arms, and shoulders are strained. This leads to tense muscles. The strain caused by a keyboard of inferior quality adds up over time. Unfortunately, the tiny movements produced while typing are very difficult to measure. Risk factors include the RSI syndrome.

The keyboard is, without doubt, the most frequently-used input computer input device. Therefore, it must be especially well-designed. Ergonomic specialists often criticize the fact that the ⇑ Shift and Enter keys are too small. Another basic problem is the cable, which is often too short, preventing a comfortable individual placement. Consider buying a wireless keyboard or an extension for the cable.

- The keyboard should be separate from the screen. It should also be inclinable, but set in a stable position (sufficiently large, rubber-coated feet).
- The middle key row should not be more than 30 mm above the surface of the table.

- There should be room to rest your hands in front of the keyboard. If there is no built-in wrist pad, get one.
- The marking must contrast with the color of the plastic and be easy to read. The keyboard should have no intense color and a satin-matt finish.
- For the keyboard legend, a dark script on a light background is recommended. Black keys are not ergonomic.
- The form of the keys should enable light and accurate typing. The lift of key should be 2–4 mm and the working point should be distinctly felt. Here 50–80 g is recommended as the force of the key depression stroke.
- Those who type a lot should take regular breaks.
- Learning the touch system helps because the workload is distributed across all fingers.
- Split or individually separable keyboards are something to which you have to get accustomed, but nevertheless are an alternative worth considering. They have been constructed according to the latest ergonomic findings and are already recommended in some standards. They prevent wrist strain to the side.
- The keyboard of a notebook or laptop cannot correspond to the standards because of the crowded keys. A notebook should therefore not be used as workstation equipment unless it is linked to an external keyboard and mouse.

Liberating the Mouse

Due to the advance of graphical user interfaces, users are practically forced to use a mouse. The intensive use of the mouse can cause not only fatigue, but also disorders in the hands, arms, and shoulders. An example of this is RSI. The danger increases when a "bad" mouse is used. So far, there are no commonly accepted standards for an ergonomic mouse. Often a PC is sold with the standard mouse. This mouse should certainly be examined closely. Is the mouse really suitable or should it be replaced by a better one? Have the dealer unpack several mice for you to try. The cable is probably too short. Ask the dealer to give you an extension. Evaluate your own mouse use. Can you reduce the use of the mouse? Many professional programs with a lot of interaction do without any mouse clicks. Learn how to use shortcuts to operate programs. It takes time to learn, but you can work up to four times as fast. Often a combination of mouse and keyboard operation is recommended.

- The ergonomic mouse feels good in your hand. The keys should not be too close or too small. There are even mice for children's hands.
- Your fingers should be able to rest on the keys in a relaxed position.
- The mouse should be next to the keyboard. Left-handed users have an advantage because the keyboard has several function keys and the numerical key block between letter keys and a mouse on the right side. These extend the gripping distance. If you are left-handed, get a mouse for left-handers. Learning keyboard codes reduces the workload on the complete arm. An arm-shoulder area strengthened by the appropriate physical training can deal better with overstrain for a short time.
- The cable should be long enough. If necessary, purchase an extension. A wireless mouse is a luxury.
- The mouse needs a proper base to function well. Get a good mouse pad.
- Pay attention to the mouse driver. Good mice have mouse drivers with a multitude of functions. You can, for example, adjust the cursor movement exactly according to your requirements or assign special instructions to the different mouse buttons. The double-click might be placed on the middle button with the mouse driver.
- Make sure you adjust the acceleration and double-click adjustment of the mouse to your own preferences. Some people work with the mouse from the hand joint. Others prefer moving their complete forearm.
- An alternative to the mouse is a trackball. Here, you move a ball inside a stationary casing to control the mouse pointer. In contrast to the mouse, the trackball reduces the movements in the hand and arm area.

Links and Literature

A great manual for staff members and superiors with many checklists and questionnaires that also take the mental strain into account: Burmester, M., Görner, C., Hacker, W., Kärcher, M. and others (1997). The SANUS Manual. EU-compliant Screen Work (- research - FB 760). Berlin: Series of the Federal

Office for Work Protection and Work Medicine. [SANUS: Safety and health protection for terminal work on the basis of international standards]

A clear and well-structured guide for analysis and work protection tasks around the terminal workstation:

Richenhagen, G., Prümper, J. & Wagner, J. (1998, 2nd edition). Handbuch der Bildschirmarbeit (trans: Manual of terminal work). Neuwied: Luchterhand.

Information Network of the European Agency for Safety and Health at Work. Available in many languages, comprehensive information: `http://europe.osha.eu.int/`

Word Processing and More with OpenOffice.org

OpenOffice.org is an extensive and powerful office suite for Linux. It offers tools for all kinds of office tasks, such as writing texts, working with spreadsheets, creating impressive graphics, or designing complex presentations. Open, edit, and even save files in Microsoft Office formats. This chapter covers the basics for using OpenOffice.org.

Note

Because the name "OpenOffice" is a registered product of *Sun*, the Open Source office suite is not allowed to use this name. For this reason, it is called "OpenOffice.org".

Note

Recent Changes

Many comments and suggestions for improvement have reached us ever since OpenOffice.org replaced StarOffice as the most important office suite of the SuSE distribution in SuSE Linux 8.1. We have taken your criticism and feedback seriously and substantially improved the comprehensive open source office suite regarding stability, comfort, and speed. Here is a summary of only the more important improvements:

- SuSE again provides the state of the art of OpenOffice.org development. The new version 1.0.2 of the package eliminates a few bugs of the previous version and provides a much more stable working environment. A detailed account of the changes can be found on the web site of the OpenOffice.org project at `http://www.openoffice.org/dev_docs/source/1.0.2/release_notes_1.0.2.html`. Patches additionally integrated by SuSE ensure even more stability and user comfort.
- With SuSE Linux 8.2, the OpenOffice.org kickstarter is offered for the first time in the OpenOffice_org-Quickstarter package. This makes work with OpenOffice.org even more comfortable and faster. See *The OpenOffice Quickstarter* on the current page.
- The installation process of the most comprehensive office suite of the SuSE distribution was greatly simplified. The application no longer needs to be installed individually after the main SuSE package installation. This process now runs automatically in the background when the application is first started. One click and OpenOffice.org runs.

The OpenOffice Quickstarter

The Quickstarter provides a series of useful additional functions for OpenOffice.org. This application should be available under 'K Menu' → 'Office Applications' → 'Unspecified' → 'OpenOffice.org Quickstarter', if the 'Standard

System with Office' is installed. If not, the package can still be installed with YaST.

When started for the first time via the K Menu, the Quickstarter asks whether it should support the quickstart mode of the application. This function loads the complete OpenOffice.org suite in the background when KDE is started and brings it with lightning speed to the screen when the quickstart icon is double-clicked. You will quickly grow to like this option if you work with OpenOffice.org often and have enough RAM available.

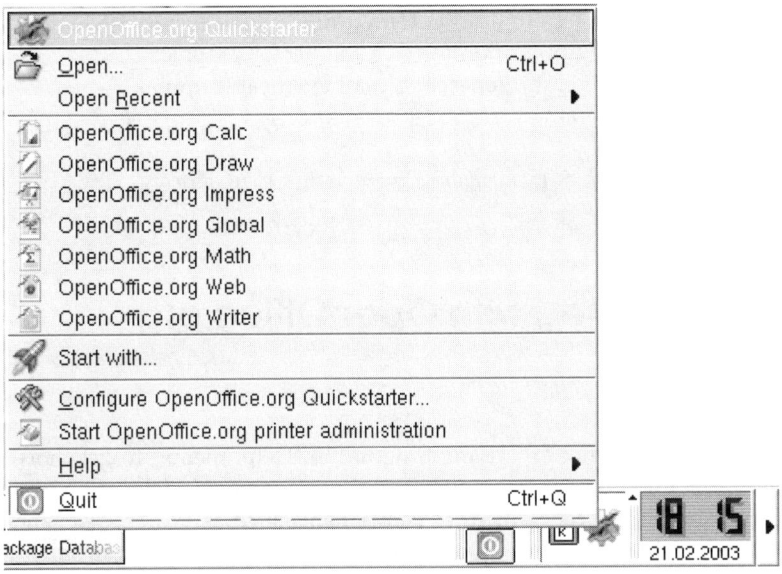

Figure 9.1: The OpenOffice.org Quickstarter

The quickstart icon appears at the lower right border of the screen after the application has been started. Right-clicking it with the mouse displays a menu like that shown in Figure 9.1. From it, the single modules of the OpenOffice.org office suite can be called directly. Quickstart also gives access to the documents opened most recently with it and to create a new document from a template. A series of preferences can be set for the application in 'OpenOffice.org Quickstart preferences...'.

Quickstart, once started, is activated automatically on your login to the graphical desktop. Clicking 'Close' in the quickstart menu, shown in Figure 9.1, stops the program from running in the future.

Overview of the Programs

OpenOffice.org consists of several programs that can interact. The programs are described in Table . The main focus here is on Writer and Calc. The other applications are only covered briefly. For more information, use the online help described in *Getting Help* on this page.

Writer	Powerful text processing application
Calc	Spreadsheet application with a utility for generating charts
Draw	Drawing application for creating vector graphics
Math	Application for generating mathematical formulas
Impress	Application for creating presentations

Table 9.1: *Available Programs in OpenOffice.org*

Getting Started with OpenOffice.org

Getting Help

Get help for OpenOffice.org at any time in the 'Help' menu. To get thoroughly acquainted with a topic, use 'Help' → 'Contents'. Help provides information about the OpenOffice.org components such as Writer, Calc, and Impress. The 'Help Agent' attempts to offer help information relevant to your current task. It updates its window when you perform different actions in OpenOffice.org and provides helpful hints. To use it, activate 'Help' → 'Help Agent'. 'Tips' or 'Extended Tips' display a help text when you point to an icon with the mouse. The text displayed by 'Extended Tips' is more detailed. At the outset, 'Tips' and 'Extended Tips' (both located in the 'Help' menu) are very useful. When more familiar with OpenOffice.org, easily deactivate them.

Tip

If you are not sure whether the features are active or not, click the 'Help' menu. Checked menu items are activated.

Tip

Converting Microsoft Office Documents

Easily edit Microsoft Office 97 or 2000 documents in OpenOffice.org by selecting 'File' → 'AutoPilot' → 'Document Converter…'. Choose the file format to convert. Various StarOffice and Microsoft Office formats are available for selection. Then click 'Next' and specify where OpenOffice.org should look for documents to convert and in which directory the converted files should be placed. Also review the other settings on this page.

Note

Documents from a Windows partition are usually in a subdirectory of `/windows/`

Note

Click 'Next' to proceed to a summary. Here, check your entries again. Click 'Convert' to start the conversion procedure.

Making and Changing Settings

All global settings can be accessed under 'Tools' → 'Options'. A window as shown in Figure 9.2 opens. The left side shows the various settings arranged in a tree structure.

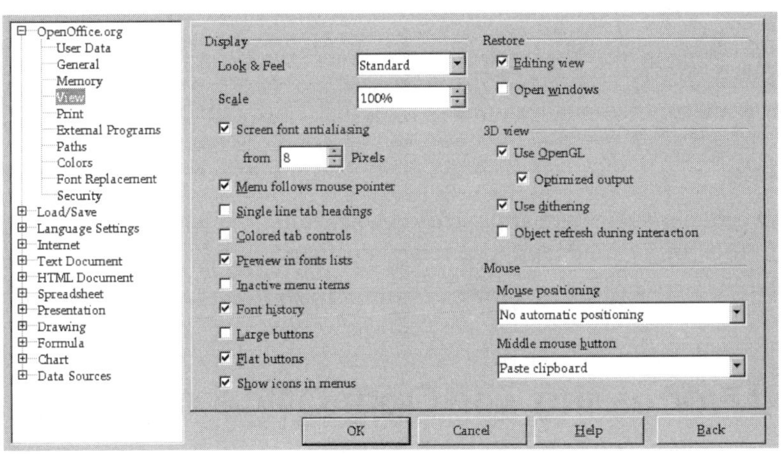

Figure 9.2: The Options Dialog

'OpenOffice.org' This structural unit contains various basic settings. Enter user data, such as the address and e-mail, and important paths and settings for printers and external programs.

'Load/Save' In this dialog, determine how files are opened and closed. A number of special parameters affect the handling of other formats.

'Language Settings' This menu contains various settings for the language and linguistics. Country-specific parameters and spell checker settings can also be adapted here. The support of Asian languages, which was improved considerably since StarOffice 5.2, can be activated here.

'Internet' Proxy and search engine settings.

'Text Documents' Global settings for Writer, such as default fonts and layout.

'HTML Document' All parameters affecting the Internet functionality of OpenOffice.org can be set in this menu.

'Spreadsheet' Various settings for Calc, such as sort lists, grid, and input.

'Presentation' Settings for all presentation documents. For example, specify the measurement units used for snapping to the grid.

'Drawing' Define the scale, grid, print options, and other settings.

'Formula' Print options and formats.

'Chart' Default colors for charts.

'Data Sources' Settings for access to external data sources.

Note

All settings made here apply *globally* — settings made in this dialog are used every time you open a new document.

Note

Text Processing with OpenOffice.org Writer

Creating Texts with the AutoPilot

The AutoPilot is a small utility that uses your entries to create a ready-to-use text from a template. For example, to write a business letter, select 'File' → 'AutoPilot' → 'Letter...'. A dialog as shown in Figure 9.3 opens.

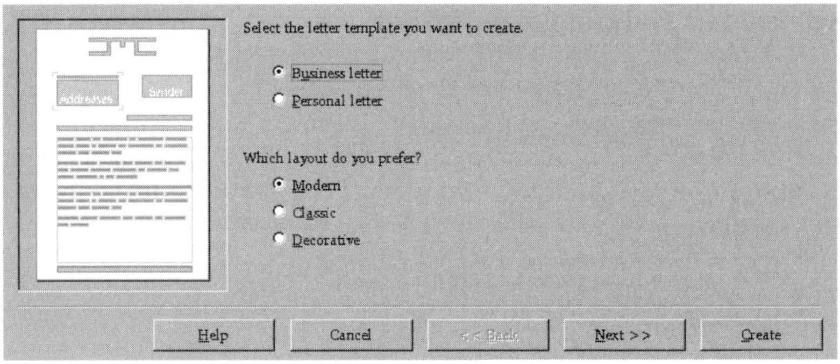

Figure 9.3: *The AutoPilot in OpenOffice.org*

Click 'Next' to proceed to the next page. To modify previous entries, use 'Back'. Click 'Create' to generate the letter according to your specifications. 'Cancel' exits the dialog. 'Help' displays a help text in the Help Agent.

The following list shows the individual pages and their entries. You do not need to enter all details. Generate your letter at any time with 'Create'.

1. Decide whether to write a business letter or a personal letter. Three styles are offered: modern, classic, or decorative.
2. Add and position graphics.
3. Enter your sender address and specify the position and size of the sender field.
4. Enter the details of the addressee.
5. Add elements, such as the date, subject line, and page numbers.
6. Define footers and the size of the margins.
7. Enter information for additional pages of your letter.
8. Enter document information and the file name.
9. Select the paper tray and when to print your logo and sender data.

Now, all you need to do is compose the letter text. There are other useful AutoPilots for creating documents like fax messages, agendas, memos, and presentations.

Creating Texts without the AutoPilot

Create a new text document by simply clicking 'File' → 'New' → 'Text Document'. You can now start writing. When opening a new document, a second bar (the object bar) is displayed below the standard function bar. Use these buttons to format your text. Documents can also be formatted with the Stylist, described in *Working with the Stylist* on page 170.

Selecting Text

To select text, click and hold at the beginning of the desired range and move the cursor to the end of the range. Selected text appears inverted. After selecting the desired text, release the mouse button. Clicking the right mouse button opens a context menu.

The context menu allows the modification of the font type, the font style, and other settings. Undesired changes can easily be undone immediately.

The Navigator not only displays lots of information about the content of a document but also allows to precise navigation to various locations within the document. As an example, the Navigator in Writer provides a quick overview of the available chapters. It also provides information about included images. Figure 9.4 on the next page shows the Navigator in Writer.

The content of the Navigator varies depending on the type of the document. Open it by clicking 'Navigator' in the 'Edit' menu.

Working with the Stylist

The Stylist enables you to format texts comfortably and quickly. Open or close it at any time with 'Format' → 'Stylist' or by pressing F11. Figure 9.5 on page 172 shows the dialog window of the Stylist.

A style is a designated assignment of predefined formatting, such as paragraph indents, text style, text color, and font size.

Tip

If the box in the lower part of the Stylist is set to 'Automatic', OpenOf fice.org tries to "guess" which styles could be useful for the current context. If 'All' is set, all styles of this group are listed.

Tip

Text can be *hard-formatted* or *soft-formatted*:

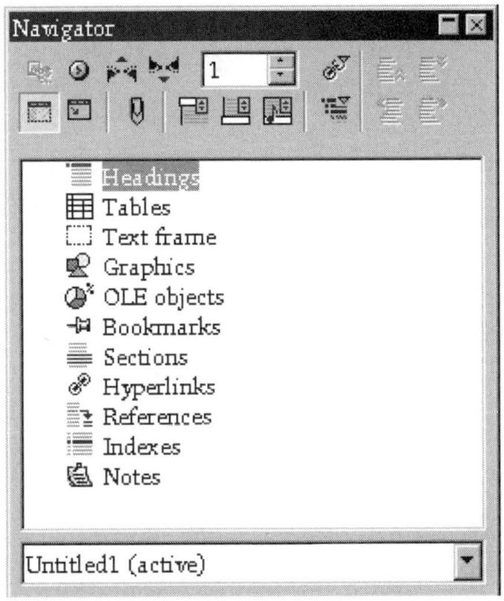

Figure 9.4: The Navigator in Writer

Hard formatting A text attribute is *directly* assigned to a text area. It is called hard because it is *hard* work to change.

This procedure is only useful for short texts (short letters, articles, and the like), but is a quick and intuitive method.

Soft Formatting The text is not formatted directly, but is assigned a style, which can be modified easily. A change of the style automatically results in an update of the text to which it is assigned.

This approach is useful for larger texts (theses, books, and the like). Although not as intuitive, it is very effective and fast if the formatting is changed extensively. It provides a substantial advantage for trying different layouts.

The Stylist offers various styles for diverse formatting needs:

Paragraph Styles Indents, spacing, hyphenation, tabs, alignment, fonts, initials

Character Styles Font, font size, language

Frame Styles Position, anchoring, frame

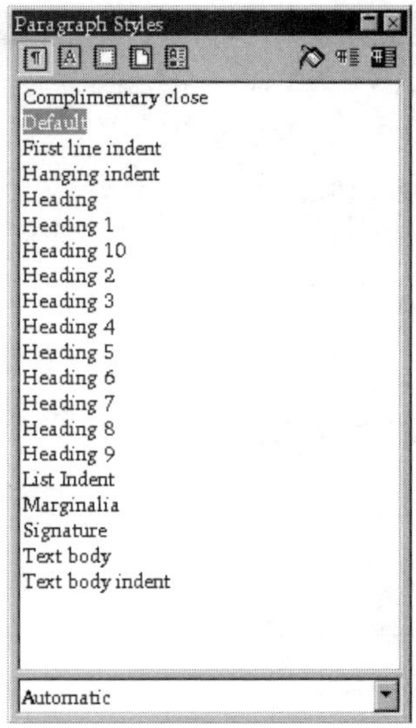

Figure 9.5: The Stylist for Writer

Page Styles Header, footer, margins, columns

Numbering Styles Bullet or numbering type, structure, graphics, position, options

Assigning Paragraph Styles with the Stylist

The Stylist can spare the user a lot of work when a style should be assigned to a paragraph:

1. Select the style to use from the Stylist.
2. Click the paintbucket icon in the Stylist. 
3. Click the paragraphs to which to assign the style.
4. Pressing (Esc) or clicking the paintbucket icon again turns the function off.

Creating a New Style

Easily create your own styles as follows:

1. Format a paragraph or a character as desired. Use the toolbar or the 'Format' menu.
2. In the Stylist, left-click 'New Style from Selection' (to the right of the bucket symbol) with the left mouse button.
3. Enter a name for your style and click OK.

Use the newly created style for other paragraphs. Easily change details of the style by right-clicking the name and selecting 'Modify…'. All modifications can be made in the dialog that opens.

Inserting a Table

Create a table by clicking the 'Insert' icon in the toolbar and keeping it pressed for a few seconds. Another toolbar appears in which to specify your selection. If you touch the third icon with the mouse, a grid as shown in Figure 9.6 opens.

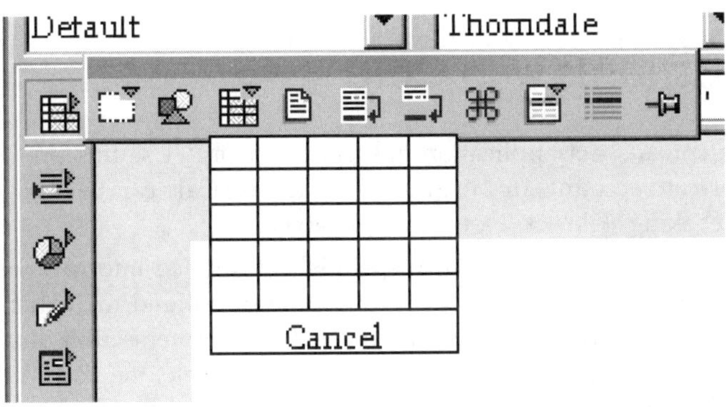

Figure 9.6: Inserting a Table Using the Toolbar

Run the mouse over the grid. The grid automatically turns black when you move over it and shows the current selection of lines and columns. Insert the table in the current text at the current cursor position with a click.

Tip

The 'Insert' icon changes depending on what was last inserted.

Tip

Inserting Graphics

Graphics can be inserted, as described in the preceding section, with the vertical toolbar (second icon from the left). Alternatively, select 'Insert' → 'Graphics' → 'From file...'.

A dialog window opens. Select the desired file. If you click 'Preview', the contents of the file are displayed on the right-hand side. This procedure may take some time with larger images. After confirming your choice, the inserted image appears at the cursor position. Activate the image (shown by the eight squares surrounding the image). Now, select 'Graphics...' in the context menu. The dialog offers various settings, such as wrapping and borders.

To modify the size of the image, click it to activate it. Click one of the "handles", keep it pressed, and drag in the desired direction. A dashed frame shows the new dimensions. Release to scale the image.

To change the position of the image instead of its size, click the image and keep the mouse button pressed. Move the image to the desired position. Release the mouse button.

Spreadsheets with Calc

Calc is the spreadsheet application in OpenOffice.org. Use this program for your private accounts or business calculations. Calc can be started from Writer by clicking 'File' → 'New' → 'Spreadsheet'.

At start-up, Calc presents an empty spreadsheet divided into rows and columns. The rows are numbered from top to bottom and the columns are lettered from left to right. "Cells" are located at the intersection of a row and a column. Each cell has a unique address. For example, the address `B3` refers to the cell located in the second column (`B`) and the third row. This is also indicated at the top left next to the entry line.

Possible contents for cells include numbers, text, dates, times, currencies, and formulas. A cell may be active or inactive. There can only be one active cell at a time. The active cell has a thick black frame. Move the activation with the cursor keys or by clicking another cell with the mouse. An active cell can be edited.

Changing Cell Attributes

To enter something in a cell, simply write in the cell. By default, texts are aligned to the left and numbers to the right. Confirm your entry with ↵.

To change the formatting of your cells, select the cells to modify then right-click to open a context menu. Select 'Format Cells. . . ' to open a dialog in which to adjust the settings. The dialog, as shown in Figure 9.7, has the tabs 'Numbers', 'Font', 'Font Effects', 'Alignment', 'Borders', 'Background', and 'Cell Protection'.

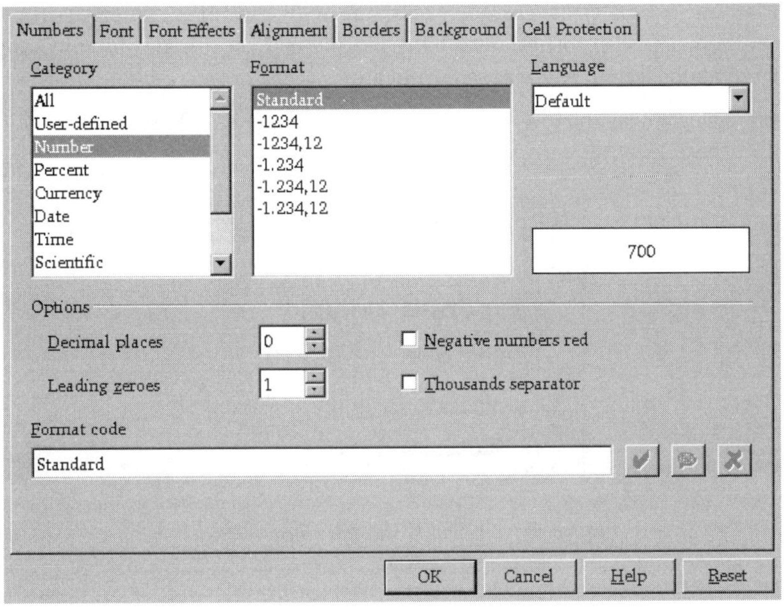

Figure 9.7: Setting Cell Attributes

'Numbers' Choose a category, such as percent, currency, date, or time. The format determines the decimal digits and leading zeros.

'Font' Set the font face and style.

'Font Effects' Set additional font effects including underlining, strikethrough, relief, outline, and shadow.

'Alignment' Determine the horizontal and vertical position of the contents of the cell. The direction of the text can also be set here.

'Borders' Add borders to a cell. All kinds of shadows and line styles can be adjusted here.

'Background' Determines the color of the cell background.

'Cell Protection' Prevent changes to the cell by activating 'Protected'.

A Practical Example: Monthly Expenses

Calculations in OpenOffice.org can be made with formulas. Enter your numbers in the cells. Use formulas and the unique cell coordinates to calculate other values based on the entered values.

For example, you want to check your monthly expenses. You can see the items in the following (simplified) spreadsheet:

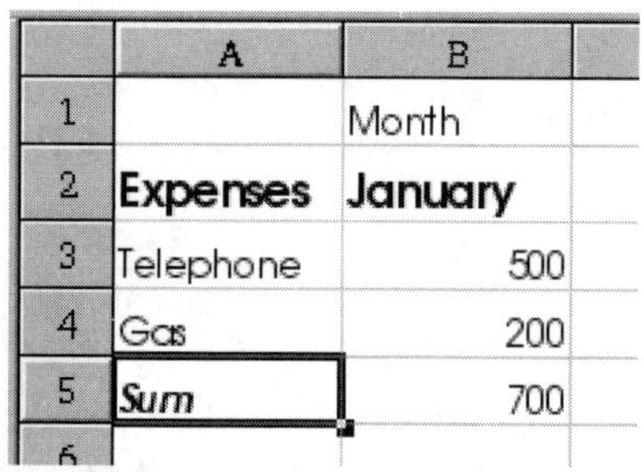

Figure 9.8: A Spreadsheet Example for Calc

The cell `B3` contains the phone bill for January and `B4` contains the fuel expenses. To add both amounts, enter the formula `= B3+B4` in `B5`. The result is displayed in `B5`. If you have mistyped the numbers (or estimated your phone bill inaccurately), reenter the amount. The sum is updated automatically.

Calc offers many functions beyond the four basic mathematical operations. An extensive list arranged in categories is available under 'Insert' → 'Function...'. The spreadsheet can be extended easily. To insert another entry between `Fuel` and `Sum`, right-click the adjacent `5`. Select 'Insert Row' from the context menu. A new row is inserted in row `5`.

Entering formulas becomes rather burdensome for larger numbers of cells. If you have several items in your `A` column and want to add them, try the `SUM` function.

To do this, enter

in the field `B6`. An alternative possibility is to click the Sigma (Σ) icon next to the input line and enter the range manually.

This formula adds all numbers from `B3` to `B5`. You can also specify several ranges.

As shown in the above formula, a range is defined by two cell addresses separated by a colon. Several ranges can be separated by semicolons. Accordingly, the formula

adds everything from `B3` to `B5` *and* from `D3` to `D5`.

Creating Charts

Add some more entries to the spreadsheet. Write a few more months in row `2` so it looks like Figure 9.9.

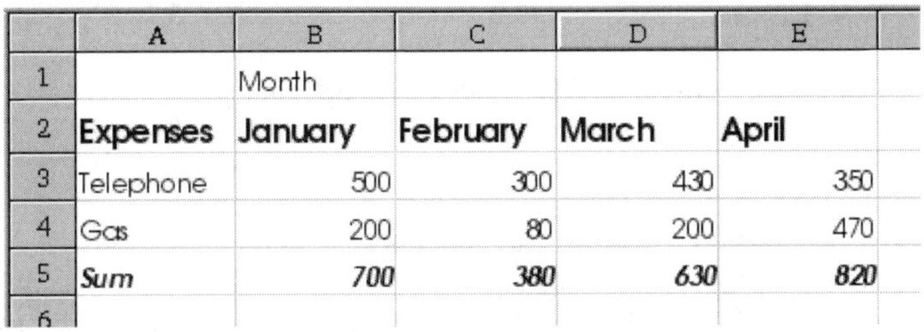

	A	B	C	D	E
1		Month			
2	**Expenses**	**January**	**February**	**March**	**April**
3	Telephone	500	300	430	350
4	Gas	200	80	200	470
5	***Sum***	***700***	***380***	***630***	***820***
6					

Figure 9.9: Expanded Example Spreadsheet

Select the range from `A2` to `E5`. The text appears white on black.

To create a chart, click 'Insert' → 'Chart...'. A dialog window appears. Optionally, modify the selection or use the first row or column as a label. Usually, the offered settings can be accepted. Click 'Next'.

The dialog window has four pages. The most interesting and important page is shown in Figure 9.10 on the next page.

The available chart types are displayed in the center. Options include line, area, column, and bar. To the left, see a preview of your data presentation.

The line chart is best suited for our example. Click 'Next' to proceed to different variants of line charts: with or without symbols, stacked, percent, or cubic spline. Select, for example, 'Symbols'. If you activate 'Show text elements in preview', the designations (like `January` and `February`) are displayed on the X axis and the values on the Y axis. A legend is added on the right-hand side.

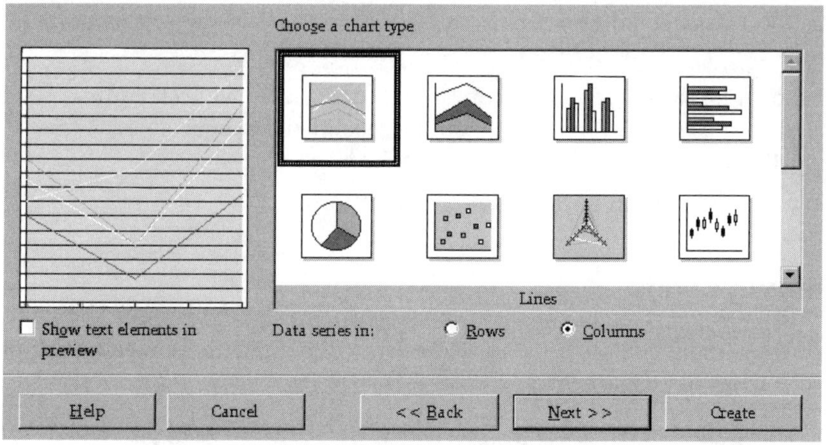

Figure 9.10: Choice of Chart Types

In the next page, assign a title to the chart and to the X axis and the Y axis. By default, the X axis is deactivated. After you click 'Create', the chart appears in your spreadsheet. Figure 9.11 on the facing page shows the example chart.

Importing Spreadsheet Tables

From time to time, you may need to import information in tabular form to a Calc table, such as stock exchange data, phone rates, or lists. There are two ways to import this information to Calc.

Method 1: Importing from the clipboard

Suppose you want to import stock exchange information. To do this, enter the address of your favorite stock exchange page in a web browser. When the table appears, select it with the mouse button. Depending on the browser, you may need to press 'Copy'. The selected range is copied to the clipboard.

In OpenOffice.org, open a new document with 'File' → 'New' → 'Spreadsheet'. Select the cell from which to begin the inserted table. Select 'Edit' → 'Paste'. The table is pasted to the document together with all formatting specifications, hyperlinks, and other information.

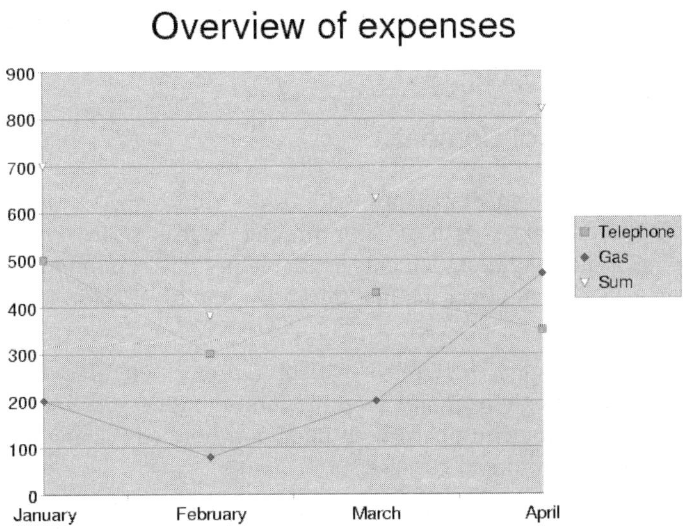

Figure 9.11: A Chart in Calc

Method 2: Importing with a filter
To import an existing HTML file to Calc, select 'File' → 'Open'. A dialog window opens. Now select 'File type' → 'HTML (OpenOffice.org Calc)'. Use the arrow keys to navigate in the list. Select the file name and click 'Open' to import the table.

Drawing with OpenOffice.org Draw

Draw can be used to create vector graphics. A line can be described in two ways:

First, by means of many dots that combine to form a line. This is the "classic" variety, also referred to as bitmap image. Common bitmap formats include GIF, JPEG, and PNG. However, this solution is only a rough approximation that depends on the number of dots.

A line can instead be described by defining the two end points. This saves a lot of memory, but requires a description of the line thickness, color, and other details. Common formats include EPS and AI. This method of representation is referred to as vector graphics. They are a *mathematical* description of the picture.

Drawing Graphical Elements

To create a new drawing, start Draw with 'K' → 'Office' → 'OpenOffice.org' → 'Draw'. If OpenOffice.org is already running, instead select 'File' → 'New' → 'Drawing'. The graphical elements available in Draw can be modified with various operations that affect the line thickness, line type, color, fill, and other parameters.

Try to draw a rectangle. The toolbar is displayed on the left-hand side. Click the filled rectangle icon and keep the mouse button pressed for a few seconds. A small submenu opens with filled and unfilled rectangles and squares, some with rounded corners.

Select a filled rectangle. The shape of the mouse pointer will change to a crosshair. Click the document to set a corner and drag the mouse down to the right. A rectangle appears and scales to the mouse movements. Release the mouse button when the desired size is reached.

To change the fill color, activate the rectangle with a mouse click. Green handles, which can be used to modify the size, appear at the four corners and the four edges.

If you press the right mouse button, the context menu opens. Select 'Area...' to access a dialog box for various settings. Click 'OK' when satisfied with the result. Alternatively, change the color using the toolbar.

The toolbar contains even more useful graphical elements, such as circles, ellipses, lines, and even 3-D elements. For more information and assistance, use the help function.

Creating Presentations with OpenOffice.org Impress

Presentations are used for the logical structuring of concepts and their visually appealing presentation.

Creating Presentations with the AutoPilot

If you have difficulties putting your ideas on "virtual paper", try using the AutoPilot. Select 'File' → 'AutoPilot' → 'Presentation...'. With the AutoPilot, define the basic structure of your presentation in three brief steps. Configure backgrounds, the output medium, and various effects. Also import information from an existing presentation with the help of the assistants.

After you have terminated the AutoPilot with 'Create', Impress offers a number of templates for the page layout. Select one that suits your purposes and enter a title for the first page. Click 'OK' to generate the first page of the newly created presentation.

To complete your presentation, enter headers and texts. With 'Presentation' → 'Slide Show', view the presentation immediately. Advance page by page by pressing the left mouse button. Exit presentation mode with (Esc).

Turn to the help system of OpenOffice.org for information about the range of modification options.

Adding a Slide

To add a slide to your presentation, use 'Slide' → 'Insert'. A dialog window opens as in Figure 9.12.

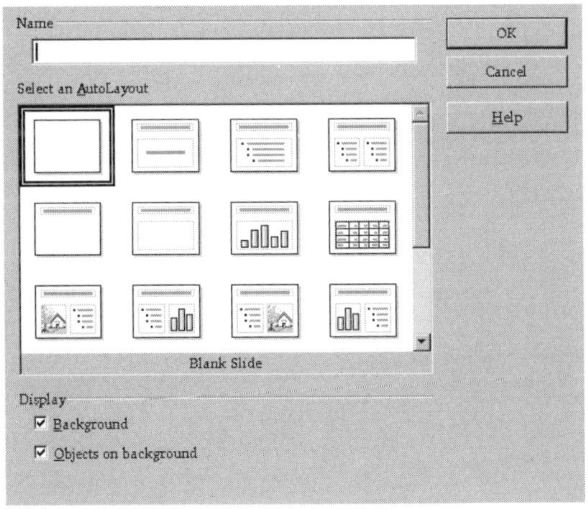

Figure 9.12: Inserting Slides in Impress

Enter a name for the slide and determine which AutoLayout to use. Click 'Ok' to insert the slide or 'Cancel' to abort the procedure.

Use templates with 'File' → 'New' → 'From Template...'.

For More Information

To track or support the ongoing development of OpenOffice.org or get more information on this important project, visit the OpenOffice.org home page at `http://www.openoffice.org`.

Adobe Acrobat Reader — The PDF Viewer

The Acrobat Reader from Adobe is a program for viewing and printing PDF files (Portable Document Format). Acrobat Reader can be used as a standalone application or as a Netscape plug-in. The comfortable user interface allows quick and easy navigation even in complex documents. In Linux, the program is called `acroread` and is included in the standard installation.

The developers' goal was to make paperless information management possible for computer users. Electronic documents of a visionary paperless office theoretically have several advantages. These range from easy e-mail sending to space-saving archiving of larger amounts of data.

Viewed globally, the PDF format is only one of the many possible core image formats for text. Acrobat Reader is a viewer for this file format. The program and the file format have several useful features. Figure 10.1 shows the screen displaying the help document.

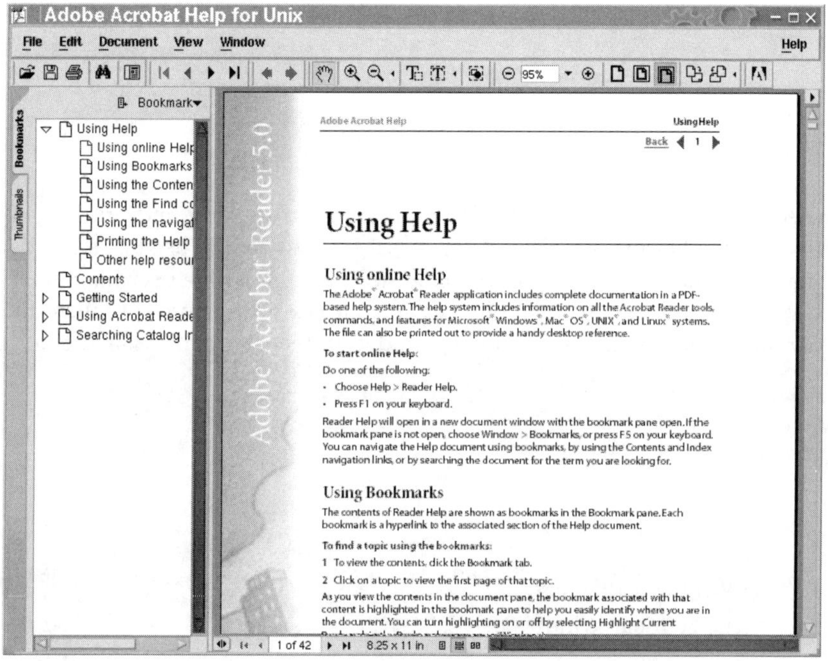

Figure 10.1: *Adobe Acrobat Reader*

The PDF format has been highly optimized for its intended use and is now regarded as the standard format for portable documents. Adobe Acrobat Reader takes full advantage of all PDF features. It is available for Macintosh and Windows as well as Unix and Linux. This provides users with a standard interface to go with their standard documents, giving standardized viewing and printing. Acrobat Reader can be integrated in Netscape in the form of a plug-in (a special program that performs services for another program). When you click a PDF file on the web,

Acrobat Reader is started automatically and the selected document is displayed.

PDF documents can contain links and bookmarks pointing to other parts of a document or to other documents. These are displayed in a separate window to the left of the text when the 'Bookmarks' tab is active. They are also shown in the text. Clicking a link immediately opens the appropriate page. PDF files can also contain preview images, often called thumbnails. These miniature images, which represent one entire page, are also displayed in the left window. Thumbnails provide a quick overview of the document and can be used to locate specific sections or passages.

Note

With Acrobat Reader, PDF documents cannot be created, only viewed. Unfortunately, Adobe currently provides Acrobat (the full text processing application) only for Windows and Macintosh. In SuSE Linux, you can use various programs to create your own PDF documents. For example, ps2pdf is a widely-used utility for generating PDF files from PostScript files.

Note

Opening a PDF File

Start Acrobat Reader with 'SuSE Menu' → 'Office' → 'Viewer' → 'Acrobat Reader'. Alternatively, start Acrobat Reader from a terminal with `acroread`. Open a file in Acrobat Reader with 'File' → 'Open', Ctrl + O, or the respective icon.

If you click any file with the `.pdf` extension in the KDE file manager and have the basic SuSE Linux system, the file is opened with KGhostView instead of Acrobat Reader. Because PDF files are based on the PostScript format, KGhostView can display and print them. However, KGhostview lacks the link and search functionality of Acrobat Reader. Manually configure KDE to use Acrobat Reader instead, if desired.

This can be done with the 'File Associations' dialog, shown in Figure 10.1 on the preceding page, accessed from 'Settings' → 'Configure Konqeror'. In the tree, look for the extension pdf under 'application'. In 'Application Preference Order', move 'Acrobat Reader' to the top. Following a restart of the file manager, PDF files should automatically be opened with Acrobat Reader.

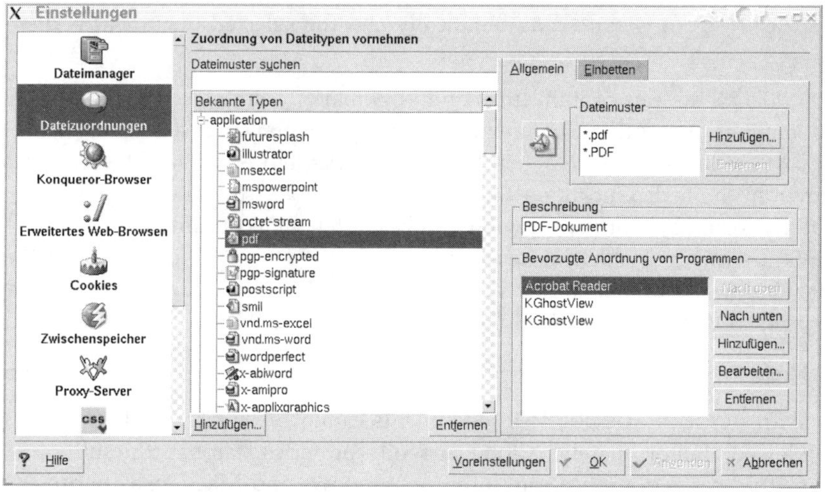

Figure 10.2: File Type Association in Konqueror

The Acrobat Window

If the default settings are used, Acrobat Reader appears as shown in Figure 10.3. The first line with control components is the menu bar. The menus contain all the control commands for Acrobat Reader. Familiarize yourself with the keyboard shortcuts to use the program more efficiently.

Figure 10.3: The Menu Bar and Toolbar of Acrobat Reader with Bookmarks

The toolbar is under the menu bar. Use the toolbar icons to access the most important functions. The icons are structured in groups that can be arranged according to your own preferences or moved to other sides of the application window. It is even possible to move the icons to a separate application window or hide some of them.

The window on the left-hand side below the toolbar contains the links (referred to as bookmarks) or the preview images (thumbnails). If a document does not have these functions, the window is not shown.

The selected document is displayed on the right-hand side. Normally, this window takes up most of the space in the program window.

The status bar below the document includes more information and additional tools (Figure 10.4). Use the tools for navigating in the document and toggling the page display modes 'Single Page', 'Continuous', and 'Continuous – Facing'.

Figure 10.4: Acrobat Reader Status Bar

Readability

Sometimes the document text is shown too small to read. Acrobat Reader has several ways to enlarge the text. The easiest way is to click the paper icons in the toolbar. This way, change the size of presentation to '100 %', 'Full page', or 'Width of page'. Click the magnifying glass in the toolbar to activate its function. A left-click in the document enlarges. Ctrl-click reduces the display size. Alternatively, click the percent display and directly enter your own zoom factor (see Figure 10.3 on the facing page).

Navigating Documents

To change pages, use the mouse or the keyboard. Use the mouse to control the vertical and horizontal scroll bars. Alternatively, click the arrow icons in the toolbar or status bar. To move to a specific page, click the page number in the status bar and type in the page number. The arrow keys of the keyboard move the page up or down in small steps. PgUp and PgDn change to the previous or next page.

Tip

Use (F6) to turn the link window off and on. (F7) and (F8) tell the program to show or hide the menu and toolbar, respectively. (Ctrl) + (F) opens the search dialog.

Tip

Finding Specific Information

Acrobat Reader has an easy to use search function for finding text strings. To use it, click the icon with the binoculars or select 'Edit' → 'Find'. Enter a search string in the dialog then click 'Find'. Acrobat Reader displays the first match found in the document. To find the next match, click 'Find Again'.

Printing

In the printer menu, the following options are important:

Printer selection: With 'Printer command', specify the print queue. `lpr` is the default.

Reverse printing: Use this to print the document last page first.

Enlargement of the pages: Use 'Fit to page' if the page size of the document is larger or smaller than the paper.

Help

Clicking 'Help' opens a PDF file with a detailed help text. Use Acrobat's search, link, and scrolling functions to find the information needed.

Opening PDF files in Netscape

If PDF documents cannot be opened automatically, it may be due to an incorrect Netscape configuration. Netscape must be instructed what to do with a PDF file. To access these settings, open 'Edit' → 'Preferences' → 'Navigator' → 'Applications'. The MIME type is *application/pdf* and the file extension is *pdf*. If you have an entry for this MIME type, click 'Edit'. Otherwise, click 'New'. *nppdf.so* should be available for selection. This dialog is shown in Figure 10.5.

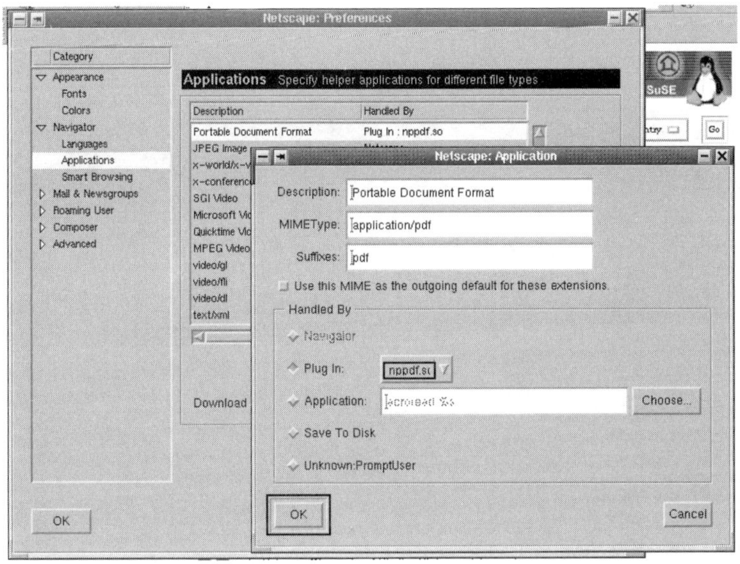

Figure 10.5: Netscape Settings

If, for some reason, the plug-in module is not available, enter `acroread %s` under the 'Application' column. In this case, Acrobat Reader will not be opened in Netscape as a plug-in, but instead started as an independent application in its own window. Acrobat Reader must be installed on your system first.

Konqueror — The KDE File Manager and Web Browser

Konqueror is a combined web browser, file manager, and document viewer. This chapter provides information about Konqueror's uses. It also explains how to use it.

Starting Konqueror

Konqueror can be started in several ways. In KDE, click the house icon in the panel to the start Konqueror. Alternatively, press the key combination Alt + F2 and enter `konqueror`. Figure 11.1 shows a Konqueror window.

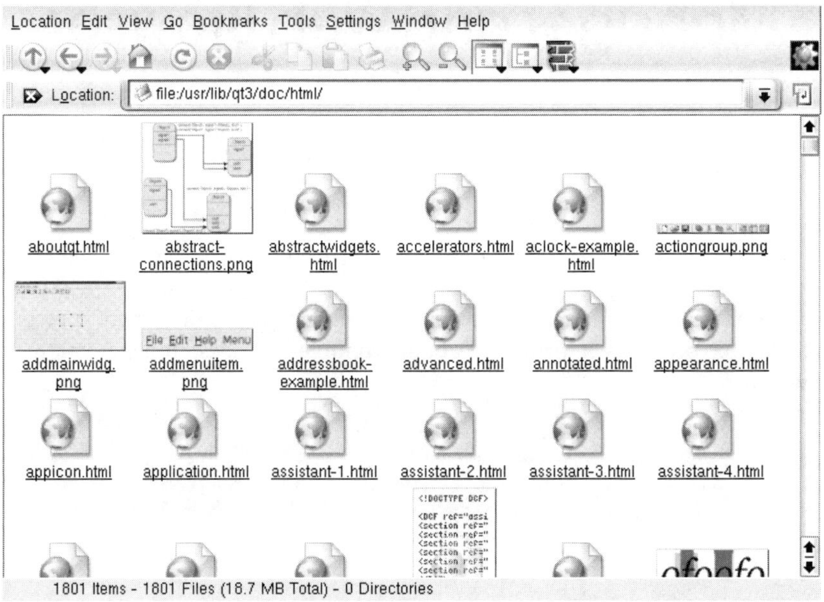

***Figure 11.1:** The Konqueror Window*

The Konqueror Window

The Konqueror window is divided into several parts. The title bar is the strip at the top of the window. It displays the path of the current directory, document, or web page.

Below the title bar is the menu bar. Depending on whether Konqueror is running as a web browser or as a file manager, you can only select certain items. The toolbar shows icons frequently needed for navigation in Konqueror. If you leave the mouse cursor over an icon for a few seconds, a small help text appears.

Beneath the toolbar is an entry line in which to enter URLs. A URL is a general address for one of many different objects. These locations can be on the Internet or a local hard disk. Enter a URL and press ⏎.

A URL consists of a transmission protocol and an address. The most common protocols are:

`http`	web pages
`file`	local files
`ftp`	files on an ftp server
`smb`	shares on a Samba computer
`man`	man pages
`info`	info pages
`tar`	compressed files in tar format
`audiocd`	audio CDs in Konqueror
`floppy`	browse floppies

There are a number of other protocols. Valid URLs are, for example, `http://www.suse.de` and `file://localhost/opt/kde2` or, in abbreviated form, `file:/opt/kde2`.

Tip

Clicking the × icon (located left of the input box) deletes the entire contents of the box.

Tip

To return to previous entries, click the down arrow on the right end of the box. This opens a list of all previous entries. Select the desired entry. You can also have a bookmark panel displayed. 'Settings' → 'Display bookmark toolbar' activates or deactivates this.

Below the URL line is the main window. It displays the contents of directories, web pages, or documents. This window can be split in two, if two documents or web pages need to be displayed at the same time.

If you divided the window (see *Different Display Modes*), a status line is available for each view. A small LED on the left side indicates the active view.

Konqueror Basics

Help

There are several options to get help for Konqueror. The usual way is to select 'Help' → 'Konqueror Manual' from the menu. The KDE help center starts and displays the full documentation for Konqueror plus references to further sources of information.

There are many ways of getting help in Konqueror. Normally, select 'Help' → 'Konqueror manual'. The KDE help system starts, showing documentation for Konqueror with numerous additional references. For information about an icon, just hover the mouse over it. For more information, press ⇑ Shift + F1 or choose 'Help' → 'What's This?' then click the icon. A small window opens giving more detailed information. Left-click to close it again.

Different Display Modes

In 'View' → 'View Mode', select the icon view, multicolumn view (the file name appears to the left of the icon), tree view, detailed list view, or text view. Figure 11.2 shows, from left to right, icon view, tree view, multicolumn view.

At first glance, the tree view and the detailed list view both look the same. You can, however, examine the directories more closely by enabling the tree view — several directories can be opened at the same time. The tree view is denoted by a '+' or '-' before the folder name. The detailed list view does not provide this option. It is used to navigate quickly across directory.

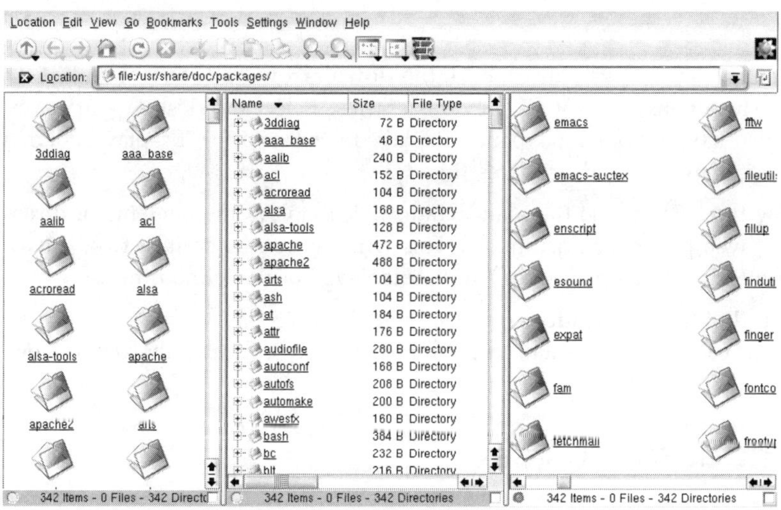

Figure 11.2: Divided Konqueror Window with Various Views

Dividing Windows and Saving this Configuration

To customize the overview of files and directories, Konqueror offers several views. See Figure 11.2 on the facing page for examples.

Konqueror can divide the window horizontally or vertically. To do this, just click, in the 'Window' menu, 'Split View Left/Right' or 'Split View Top/Bottom'. The active display shows a green dot in the status bar.

You can even activate a terminal window. If the check mark in front of 'Show Terminal Emulator' is activated, a terminal window is opened in which to enter and run commands as usual. This makes it easy to combine both preferences — graphical and command-line oriented — in one window.

Once you have assembled a display, save it under 'Window' → 'Configure View Profiles…'. Give your profile a name with which to load it again in the future. In addition, decide if the window size should be saved. If the space is too small, move your Konqueror window to its own desktop and choose 'Fullscreen Mode'.

Tabbed Browsing

Konqueror has inherited another useful characteristic from Mozilla: tabbed browsing. The advantage of tabs is that you only have one Konqueror window with several subareas, such as web pages or a view of your file system.

To create a tab, select 'Window' → 'New Subwindow'. Right-clicking the tab opens a pop-up menu. In this menu, decide what to do with the tab: create a new one, duplicate an existing one, separate one (which will then appear in a separate window), or close one or all tabs.

Konqueror as a File Manager

Navigating in Konqueror

As a file manager, Konqueror enables navigation through various directory levels with ease. Enter your home directory in the URL entry line, for example, or click the icon with the house.

Switch directories or open files with the mouse as usual. A single-click is usually sufficient for changing directories or opening files. You can also move around in Konqueror using the arrow keys. Use any of the arrow keys to highlight an item (the background of the selected icon is shown in a different color). Pressing (↵) opens the file or changes to the directory.

To select a number of files, press (Alt). To return to the previous directory, click the left arrow in the toolbar.

Navigating with the Sidebar

Konqueror offers a sidebar. This is a window that can be displayed or hidden in Konqueror, providing several options: display your bookmarks, recently visited URLs, home directory, and much more. Activate the sidebar via 'Windows' → 'Display extended sidebar' or press (F9).

Deleting Files and Directories

In KDE, there are two methods to delete files and directories. Each method has different advantages. In the first method, the highlighted files are moved to the `Trash` directory when you choose 'Edit' → 'Delete'. They are stored there and can be retrieved until the trash can is emptied. Of all the deleting methods, this is the safest. Delete the contents of the trash by right-clicking the trash icon on the desktop. In the pop-up menu that appears, choose 'Empty Trash Bin'.

The second method deletes the file by marking the file system objects as "free". These deleted files can only be restored with special tools, if at all.

Selecting Several Files

To select several files in Konqueror, drag a frame around the files required. Click a free area in the window, keep the mouse button pressed, and move the mouse. A dotted frame surrounds the selected files and the background color changes. Add individual files to the selection by clicking them while keeping (Ctrl) pressed.

Now, release the mouse button and start the desired action (copy, move, delete, etc.). For a more exact selection, such as all PNG files, choose 'Edit' → 'Select'. In the dialog box that appears, enter an expression like `*.png`. Now all PNG files in the currently displayed directory will be selected. To add additional files to your selection, open the dialog box again and repeat the individual steps.

Finding Files

To search for files, go to 'Extras' → 'Find file...'. Specify the name or pattern along with the path and click 'Find'. Konqueror will search the specified directory and show the results below. Conduct a more precise search by selecting 'Date Range' (from when to when) or 'Advanced' (type, text, or size). The program can be run separately by pressing Alt + F2 and entering 'kfind'.

Renaming Files

To rename files, right-click the respective file. A pop-up window opens. Select 'Rename'. Give your file a new name and complete this action with ↵.

Using Filters

If your directories show more files than desired, try using filters. Filters can limit the display to just the files needed. To do this, select 'Extras' → 'View Filter'. It lists the currently recognized file types. If you click an entry, only this file type is displayed in the Konqueror window. With 'Use multiple filters', designate several filters. To view all files, select 'Reset'.

Browsing Compressed Files

Konqueror has another interesting feature: it can browse compressed files. If you have a tar.gz file, click it and Konqueror shows the contents as if it were a directory.

You can also copy individual files from it. Copying files into an archive is not yet supported, but this feature may be included in one of the next versions. If the input field in the URL bar begins with `tar:/` or `zip:/`, this indicates that you are surfing a compressed file.

Converting Audio CDs

Using `audiocd:/`, Konqueror can be used to convert the contents of audio CDs to various formats and save them to the hard disk. The exact procedure is described in *Reading Audio CDs* on page 251.

Creating an Image Gallery

If a directory contains an extensive collection of images, it might be difficult to keep track. Konqueror can help you by creating an HTML file with thumbnail images. Open the respective directory in Konqueror and select 'Extras' → 'Create Image Gallery'. A window opens in which to specify the background and foreground colors, the title, and where to save it. Launch the action by clicking 'Ok'. By default, a file called `index.html` is created. Open it with Konqueror to see your images displayed in thumbnail format in a clear overview.

Pop-up Menus with the Right Mouse Button

If you have a directory displayed in an open Konqueror window, open a pop-up menu with the right mouse button at any time. Depending on the file type, you can start various actions here. If you click a file or directory, entries appear as in the 'Edit' menu.

Konqueror as a Web Browser

Konqueror is more than a file manager. It is also an effective web browser.

Opening Web Pages

Simply enter a web address in the URL line, for example, `www.suse.de`. Konqueror displays the address. You do not even need to write the protocol (`http://`) at the beginning, as it is recognized automatically by the program. This feature only works properly with web addresses, however. For FTP servers, you must enter `ftp://` at the beginning of the entry line.

Saving Web Pages and Graphics — Web Archives

As in other browsers, you can save web pages. To do this, select 'Address' → 'Save as ...' and provide a name for your HTML file. However, this will not save any images. To archive an entire web page, including the images, select 'Extras' → 'Archive Web Page'. Konqueror suggests a file name that you can usually accept. The file name ends with `.war`, the suffix for web archives. To view the saved web archive later, simply click the respective file and the web page is then displayed in Konqueror along with its images.

Enhanced Web Browsing (Internet Keywords)

Searching the web using Konqueror is very practical. Konqueror defines a number of search engines for you, all with a specific shortcut. To search for a certain topic on the Internet, enter the shortcut and the keyword, separated by a colon. The relevant page containing the search results is then displayed.

You can also define your own shortcuts. Simply select 'Settings' → 'Configure Konqueror' → 'Web Shortcuts'. A dialog appears in which to define your own abbreviations.

Translating Web Pages

Konqueror cannot translate web pages directly, but requires an external Internet source. To translate a web page, enter the address then select 'Tools' → 'Translate Web Page'. A dialog opens in which to choose the source language and the target language. After the selection has been made, it will take a few seconds until the translated page appears.

Bookmarks

If you frequently visit certain pages, it is often a hassle to type in the same address repeatedly. Konqueror helps you set up a bookmark list. For this, use the 'Bookmark' menu. Here, save all your bookmarks, from web pages to directory links, on your local hard disk.

To create a new bookmark in Konqueror, click 'Bookmarks' → 'Add Bookmark'. If you have already added some bookmarks, you will also see them in this menu. It is recommended to arrange your collection by subjects, grouped hierarchically. 'New Directory' creates folders in which bookmarks can be grouped. Open the bookmark editor by selecting 'Bookmarks' → 'Edit Bookmarks …'. Using this program, organize, rearrange, add, and delete bookmarks.

If you are using Netscape or Mozilla as additional browsers, you do not need to set up your bookmark folders again. The bookmark editor includes 'File' → 'Import Netscape Bookmarks' with which to integrate your Netscape and Mozilla bookmarks into your most current collection. The reverse is also possible via 'Export as Netscape Bookmark'.

Change your bookmarks by right-clicking the entry. A pop-up menu appears in which to select the desired action (cut, copy, delete, etc.). When you achieve the desired results, save it with 'File' → 'Save'.

To save your bookmark list and have instant access to it, make your bookmarks visible in Konqueror. Select 'Settings' → 'Show Bookmark Toolbar'. A bookmark panel is automatically displayed in the current Konqueror window.

Java and JavaScript

Do not confuse these two languages. Java is an object-oriented, platform-independent programming language from Sun Microsystems. It is frequently used for small programs (applets), which are executed over the Internet for things like online banking, chatting, and electronic shopping systems. JavaScript is an interpreted scripting language mainly used for the dynamic structuring of web pages (e.g., for menus and other effects). Konqueror enables the activation or deactivation of these two languages. This is even possible for specific domains, which means that the access can be permitted for some hosts and blocked for others.

Note

For applets to run correctly, at least a "Java Runtime Environment" must be installed. The minimum solution can be found in the package `javarunt` package. If you need to compile Java source code, install the Java Development Kit (package `java`) instead.

Note

If you have high system security requirements, completely deactivate Java and JavaScript. Unfortunately, some web pages require JavaScript.

Proxies

If your provider allows access to a proxy server, enter it for KDE. The advantage is that your pages may be available faster if several users access them simultaneously.

In 'Settings' → 'Configure Konqueror...', select 'Proxy Server'. Enter the proxy for HTTP and FTP along with their respective ports. Under 'No proxy for:', exclude specific servers. Normally, enter `localhost` here or the name of your Linux computer.

Konqueror as File Viewer

In Konqueror, view different files as well as directories and web pages. If you click a text file, for example, the program belonging to this will not be started. Instead, the text will be "embedded" into the Konqueror window.

To edit the files, start the corresponding program separately. Right-click the file type. A pop-up menu is displayed. Use 'Open with' to start other programs that can handle this file type for editing.

For More Information

More information about Konqueror can be found on its home page at `http://www.konqueror.org`.

The Web Browser Galeon

Recently, the widely-used web browser has been transformed into a real "jack of all trades". The fact that today's Internet applications feature such depth in integration and are heavily integrated into their corresponding desktop environments is almost taken for granted. Users of outdated machines soon feel the effects of this development. All-around browsers are often memory-eaters, sluggish in their operation, and occupy thirty megabytes on the hard disk.

That is why the idea behind Galeon is to devote itself just to one assignment: the web and only the web. Galeon implements the speedy "Gecko" engine of the Mozilla browser and integrates this into a slick, extremely functional user interface. The application loads quicky and is one of the fastest browsers available.

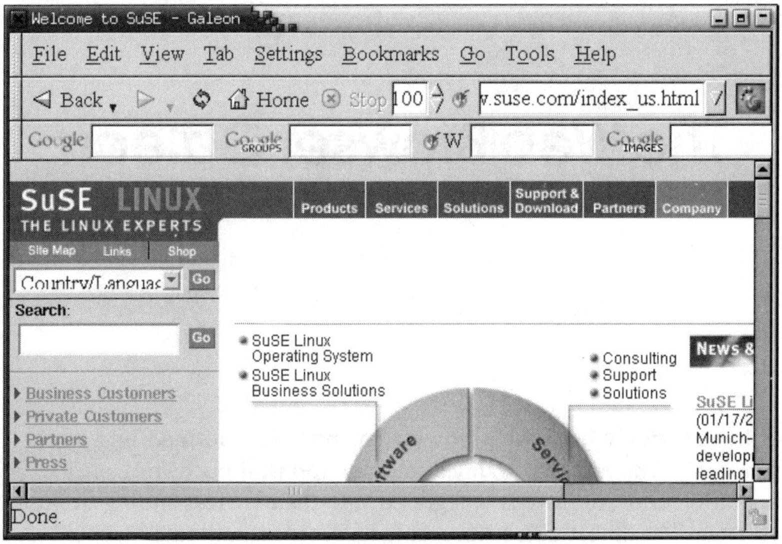

Figure 12.1: The Main Window in Galeon

With Galeon on the Internet

Galeon's most essential navigation tools can be found in the first toolbar. 'Next' and 'Back' offer the feature of flipping through Internet sites, just as in other browsers. To the the right of those buttons is 'Reload', which updates the contents of a site. 'Cancel', which stops a connection or transfer from taking place, follows. A useful function is zoom, usually scaled to 100% a 1:1 display of the document. To the right of it, both the up and the down arrows can be used to set the zoom levels in intervals of ten. Enter Internet (URLs) addresses in the following entry box. To the far right is the GNOME foot, which shows Galeon's progress. If the icon is animated, Galeon is working and transferring data.

Optimized for the Web

Galeon is primarily designed to make surfing the Internet as convenient as possible. In the default configuration, Galeon presents a second toolbar, enabling quick access to the popular Google search engine as well as its news and image search function. It can also offer access to an online dictionary and use the "bookmarklets". This is made possible by small JavaScript functions built into Galeon. You can, for example, find out how current a page you is, or allow the Internet site to slowly scroll down the screen. This provides a lot of practical functionality.

Efficient Surfing with Tabs

Galeon can display multiple WWW documents in a single application window. Such a procedure is often more practical than opening a new window for each Internet document. To open a link in a web site in the form of a new tab, right-click that link. Select 'Open in new tab' in the emerging pop-up menu. Now, Galeon will divide its application window into "index cards", so you can maintain easy access to the documents. Create a fresh Galeon tab by clicking 'File' → 'Open New Tab'.

Settings and Controls

All settings characteristic of other web browsers can be also be accessed here via 'Settings' → 'Preferences'. With this dialog's user-friendly layout, the key selection options are quite self-explanatory. Galeon's appearance can also be changed with these options.

Galeon features built-in password management and cookie controls. It also has options that specify the web sites from which images may be downloaded. All these options can be accessed through a single dialog via 'Tools' → 'Cookies' → 'View Cookies'.

After the brief period of initial adjustment, you will find that Galeon is optimized for its single important task. The breathtaking speed of the Mozilla HTML engine does its part as well. Have fun!

For More Information

For more information see the Galeon `http://galeon.sourceforge.net` and GNOME home page `http://www.gnome.org`.

KMail — The KDE Mail Application

KMail is the KDE mail application. In addition to the usual features, like sending and receiving e-mail and multiple mail protocols, it offers several custom-definable filters for sorting e-mails into individual folders. This is useful for separating important business correspondence from less important e-mails from mailing lists, for example. Mails can be either read at leisure or briefly skimmed over and safely deleted.

Configuring KMail

A `Mail` folder is added to your home directory when running KMail for the first time. This folder contains the initial mail directories (inbox, outbox, sent, and trash). Use 'Settings' → 'Configure KMail...' to enter the information needed for KMail to send and receive your messages.

Defining Your User Identity

The settings in 'Identity' are organized into three tabs — 'General', 'Advanced', and 'Signature'. To create a new identity profile, select 'New...' and enter a name for the profile in the dialog that opens.

Clicking 'OK' opens a new dialog box in which to set a few more options. Name, organization, and e-mail address can be entered and modified in the 'General' tab. The 'Advanced' tab is provided for entering an OpenPGP key, a possible BCC or reply-to address, and the location for e-mail storage. 'Signature' allows the definition of a signature footer to every message. This still requires the switching 'activate signature'. Choose whether the signature should be read from a file, taken from the input box, or inserted from some application output.

Confirm your profile settings with 'OK'. Select one of defined identities when writing an e-mail. This allows the handling of more than one e-mail address.

Setting up Network Connections

The settings in the 'Network' icon panel tell KMail how to receive and send e-mails. There are two tabs, one each for sending and for receiving messages.

Many of these settings vary depending on the system and network where your mail server is located. If you are unsure about the settings or which items to select, consult your Internet service provider or system administrator.

Sending Create outgoing mail boxes under the 'Send' tab. 'Add' gives the choice of either SMTP or sendmail. For most purposes, select SMTP here. After making this selection, a window appears in which to enter SMTP server data, such as 'Name', 'Server', and, if needed, the required authorization. A preprocessing command that is run before the sending of each message can be entered in the corresponding field.

Security settings are under the 'Security' tab. Specify your preferred encryption method here. If uncertain about which to choose, click 'Test server capacity'. The corresponding settings are then tested and applied.

Receiving Everything regarding receiving e-mails can be found under the 'Receiving' tab. Under 'Add' select the desired format: local (Mbox format), POP3, IMAP, or local (maildir format). POP3 is usually used when accessing remote servers.

After making your selection, a window appears in which to enter the POP3 server data. Give the server a unique name. Enter the values provided by your Internet Service Provider or your system administrator in the corresponding fields. The fields that need to be filled out here are 'User', 'Server', and 'Password'.

The 'Extras' tab offers several methods of encryption and authorization. If you are uncertain about which options your server provides, try 'Test server capabilities'.

Changing the Appearance of KMail

'Appearance' adjusts KMail to your preferences. Use 'Fonts' to configure the fonts for the various displays, like the message text, first-level quoted text, and so on. Activate 'Use custom fonts' before configuring it.

To customize the colors, activate 'Use custom colors' in the 'Colors' tab. Double-clicking an entry opens a dialog box with a color picker.

The 'Layout' tab offers options for splitting the KMail window and for displaying a MIME tree. A MIME tree shows all the attachments to a message. It also has options for general settings, like customizing the date display and message grouping.

'Profiles' is responsible for the administration of default appearance presets. Some standard profiles are provided already, like for users who prefer high constrast or for purists.

Caution

Selecting a profile overwrites the current layout settings.

Caution

Using KMail

Main Window

The main window appears when KMail is started. It is divided into three sections in its default setting.

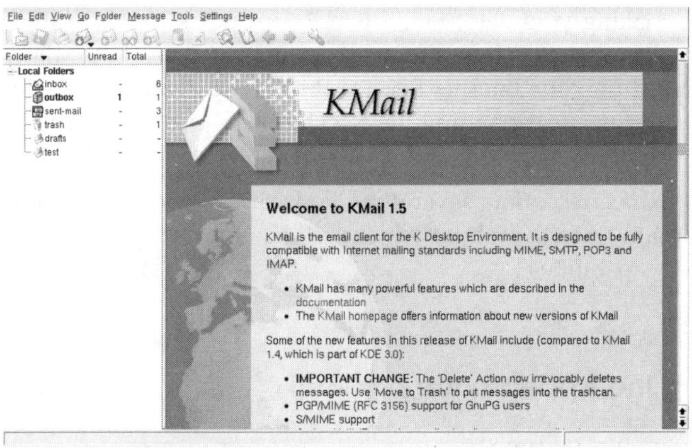

Figure 13.1: Main Window in KMail after Start-Up

- Folder area (left)
  This section contains a list of your mail folders (also known as mail boxes). The columns next to the folder name indicate the total number of messages and how many many are still unread. Select folders by simply clicking them. The messages they contain then appear in the top right frame. The total number of messages is also displayed in the status bar at the bottom of the application window.

- Header area (right)
  In this window panel, the header information (from left to right: subject, sender, and time of reception) is listed for messages in the currently selected folder. Clicking the header selects the message, which is then displayed in the message window. The messages can be sorted by clicking the desired column (subject, sender, date, etc.).

- Message area (below)

  The header and contents of the currently selected message are displayed in this frame. Attachments are depicted as icons at the lower end of the message, based on the MIME type of the attachment. Use (PgUp) and (PgDn) to scroll through the pages of the message or use (↑) and (↓) to scroll line-by-line. The shortcut keys can be found in the main window.

Messages can be marked with different status flags. The status can be changed in 'Message' → 'Highlight as'.

'New' (red dot, header in red print): The message is new and has not yet been read.

'Unread' (green dot, header in blue print): a message changes its status from 'New' to 'Unread' after the folder containing it is reopened.

'Read' (–): The message has been read.

'Replied' (blue, U-shaped arrow): The message has been answered.

'Waiting' (envelope): The message has been placed in the outbox to send later.

'Sent' (slanted envelope): The message was sent.

'Important' Label for important messages.

Creating a New Message

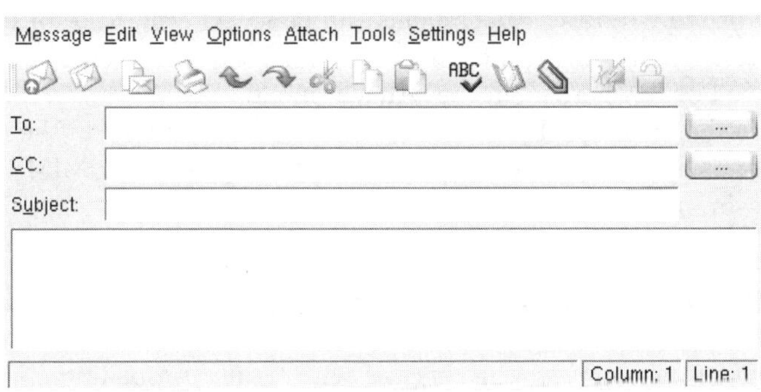

Figure 13.2:

Select 'Message' → 'New Message' or press Ctrl + N to compose a new message. Fill in the respective fields in the 'New Message' window. There are various key shortcuts that assist in composing the message. To send messages from different e-mail accounts, select an identity configured in *Defining Your User Identity*. The buttons next to 'To:' and 'CC:' (and possibly 'blind copy (Bcc):') open the address book, allowing selection of an address instead of entering it manually. Pressing Ctrl + T after typing the first few characters of the address returns a list of possible completions. When the message is completed, click 'Send'. Use 'View' to set up various headers.

Attachments

One of the following methods for attaching files to messages is recommended:

- Click the paper clip icon and select the file to attach.
- Use the mouse to drag a file from the desktop or another folder into the 'New Message' window.
- Select one of the options in the 'Attach' menu.

The MIME type of a file is usually recognized properly, but can be selected from a list in the case of an error. The 'description' field takes a short explanatory text. An encoding for the attached file should then be selected from the options list (the default values usually work well). When a file is attached to your message, it appears in the list of attachments in the lower part of the window. Attachments can be saved, removed, or opened by selecting the name of the attachment then subsequently clicking 'Remove', 'Save', or 'Properties' in the 'Attach' menu. PGP keys can likewise be added to the messages by choosing the respective options in the 'Attach' menu. PGP keys are treated like file attachments. Their MIME type is `application/pgp-keys`.

Check Message for Spelling Errors

The spelling of messages can be checked with 'Edit' → 'Spelling...'. KMail uses KSpell to check the spelling. KSpell is the KDE front-end for the ispell and aspell spell checking programs. The spell checker must be configured via 'Settings' → 'Spellchecker...'.

Message Folders

Message folders serve as an organizing tool for your messages. By default, all the message folders are stored in the `Mail` folder in your home directory. The `Inbox`, `Outbox`, `SentMessages`, and `Trash` folders are created when KMail is first run. These folders have the following functions:

- Inbox: New messages are stored here (unless a filter has been defined).
- Outbox: Messages to send are stored here.
- Sent: Copies of all e-mails sent are stored here.
- Trash: Stores deleted e-mails.

If the standard folders, though sufficient for the needs of the casual user, are not sufficient for organizing your e-mail, create additional folders. Select 'Folder' → 'Create' to add a new folder. In the dialog that opens, enter a name for the new folder (see Figure 13.3 on page 219). To create a subfolder, select the prospective parent folder (in the drop-down menu labeled 'Belongs to:'). In this window, specify the folder type, any mailing lists belonging to it, and an expiration date (the period after which the e-mails are marked for deletion).

Moving Messages

To move messages from one folder to another, highlight the message to move then press (M) or click 'Message' → 'Move to...'. In the list of folders that appears, select the folder to which to move your messages. Messages can also be moved from the upper window into the left window panel by dragging and dropping the message into the appropriate folder.

To remove all the messages from a folder, click 'Folder' → 'Empty'. All the messages located in the folder are then moved to Trash. The messages are not permanently deleted until you actually empty the trash.

The Address Book

The address book stores frequently used e-mail addresses. Access it from 'File' menu, with the open book icon in the main window, or in the 'New Message' window.

Create a new entry with 'File' → 'New contact...'. A window opens with a form for entering the personal contact data in the 'General' tab. Most entries are self-explanatory.

The 'View' menu allows creation of custom views of the contacts. The table view is the default setting. 'Add view' opens a dialog in which to name the view. 'View type' has options for whether the contacts should be displayed as icons, in a table, or as cards. 'OK' continues to the next dialog box in which to select the fields to include in the custom view. Filters and preferences can be set in the corresponding items. 'OK' activates the newly created view.

Filters

It can be difficult to keep track of all messages. Filters enable automatic processing of incoming messages and manual processing of selected messages in a folder. To filter selected messages to a specific folder, highlight the messages and enter Ctrl + J to activate already existing filter rules or select 'Message' → 'Create Filter' to create a new one. In doing so, *all* existing filter rules are applied to this message. There is no way to use only particular filters for one given message.

Filter Rules

A filter consists of one or several filter rules and filter actions. A filter rule can select messages according to criteria such as the sender, content, or recipient. The respective filter action can perform tasks such as moving, deleting, marking, or forwarding these messages.

Examples of Filters

Assume, for instance, you are subscribed to the KDE user list `kde-user@kde.org`. Whenever a message from the mailing list arrives, the mail is moved into another folder. The following steps are necessary for creating this filter.

1. Add a new folder as described in *Message Folders* on the page before. Assign a name such as kde-user.

2. First find a way of identifying messages to filter. The messages of the KDE user list described in our example can be identified by the `kde-user@kde.org` address, found in the 'To': or 'Cc': field.

3. Click 'Settings' → 'Configure Filters'. The left side of the window that opens displays the existing filters. The right side is composed of two panels: filter rules and filter actions.

4. Click the 'New' icon to create an empty filter. It appears as `unknown`.

5. Select 'To:' or 'Cc:' from the first drop-down menu and 'contains' from the second drop-down menu. Enter `kde-user@kde.org` in the text field.

6. In 'Filter actions', select 'Move to Folder' from the first drop-down menu. A second drop-down menu with the list of folders appears. Choose the folder to which the filtered messages should be moved if they meet the desired criteria. In this case, choose `kde-user` from the drop-down menu.

7. Confirm the changes with 'OK'.

You might need complex criteria to filter your messages. You may want to only save the messages from the KDE user list written by Fred Johnson (`fj@anywhere.com`). Here, the remaining filter criteria come into play:

1. Click 'Settings' → 'Configure Filters' and mark the newly created filter.

2. To filter all messages containing `kde-user@kde.org` in the 'To:' or 'Cc:' fields *and* originating from Fred, define a second filter under 'Filter Criteria' using the second row of drop-down menus. Select 'From' in the first menu and 'contains' in the second. Then enter the e-mail address to filter. Select the second pop-up menu inside the filter criteria from the drop-down menu and select 'From'. Next to it, select 'contains'. Enter Fred Johnson's, e-mail address (`fj@anywhere.com`). Activate 'Applies to all'.

3. Select the action to execute (move, delete, etc.).

You have now created a filter that transfers all mails from Fred Johnson on the KDE user list as specified.

Mail Encryption with PGP or GnuPG

The following section, which is mainly intended for newcomers, briefly describes the encryption of messages with KMail.

You can encrypt your e-mails handled by KMail. This does not mean, however, that the attachments will be encrypted. This must be taken care of in advance with a shell command or one of the other tools. Before you can implement PGP or GnuPG in KMail, the respective application must be installed and configured correctly. For details, refer to the man page for the man page for (`man`) or the man page for (`man`).

Requirements for PGP and GnuPG

KMail assumes that your PGP binary is called `pgp`. If you use GnuPG, KMail will expect a binary file named `gpg`. First, generate a key pair for your identity. This must be done in the command line (use `pgp -kg` or `gpg --gen-key`). KMail currently does not offer integrated support for generating a PGP or GnuPG key. The identity, usually your name and your e-mail address, for example, `JohnDoe<john@example.com>`, and your password are required for the interaction between KMail and PGP and GnuPG.

KMail Settings

Open the KMail settings dialog with 'Settings' → 'Configure KMail'. Click 'Security' → 'OpenPGP'. Specify the application to use for this purpose in 'Select encryption program'. The option 'Automatic recognition' is usually chosen.

Under the 'OpenPGP' tab, there are the following additional options:

- 'Keep passphrase in memory': If this option is disabled, KMail will ask for your password whenever you sign a message (before sending it) or when you decrypt a (received) message. If you enable this option, KMail will only ask you twice for your password then keep it in the memory. It will not be written to the hard disk. However, remember that a user with the respective permissions (e.g., `root`) might be able to read your password from the memory.
- 'Always encrypt to self': If this option is disabled and you want to send an encrypted e-mail, you will not be able to read this message yourself once it has been created and encrypted. Enable this option

when you still want to be able to read your encrypted messages yourself. You can read the pure text of the message in the `Sent` folder.

- 'Show ciphered/signed text after composing': Enable this option to have the text displayed after it is encrypted or signed.
- 'Always verify the encryption key': If you click this option, you will be asked each time which key to use for signing and encoding.

Once the preferences have been set, click 'Identities' (left border). Select the identity with which encrypted or signed messages should be sent and choose 'Change'. Select the 'Advanced' tab in the opened dialog box. Clicking 'Change' for the 'OpenPGP key' entry displays a selection box from which the keys can be chosen. The encryption system is now ready. Confirm with 'OK'.

The public key must be made available to recipients of a signed message to enable them to verify its authenticity and also needs to be publicly accessible to enable others to send encrypted messages to the owner of the key. Public keys can be stored on a public PGP key server, such as `www.pgp.net`.

Signing Messages

Create your messages as usual. Before sending the message, click the corresponding icon (second to last) in the toolbar of the window or choose 'Options' → 'sign message'. The message can then be sent. To sign it, KMail must know your PGP password. However, if you have already provided the password, KMail will sign the message without requesting any further information. The results of the PGP signing process can be reviewed in the `SentMessages` folder (or in the outbox if you did not use 'Send now'). There, your e-mail should be marked with the notice that it was signed by you.

Sending Public Keys

Create a message for the person who should receive your public key. Choose 'Attach Public Key' in the 'Attach' menu. The mail can then be sent. There is no guarantee that the recipient of a signed message will receive the correct key. It is possible that the mail is intercepted on the way to the recipient and gets signed with another key. Therefore, the recipient should check the attached key by comparing the finger print with a previously received value. Further information on this can be found in the PGP and GnuPG documentation.

Decoding Encrypted Messages

In KMail, you only need to select the message. Enter your password when prompted. KMail will attempt to decrypt the message if it was encrypted with your public key and display it in clear text. If not, you will not be able to read the e-mail. KMail saves the e-mails as encrypted messages to prevent anyone from reading them without your password.

Receiving a Public Key

You can receive a public key as attachment, over FTP, or on a floppy disk. Before using it to encrypt an e-mail, check the key (look over the fingerprint or look for a reliable signature).

Then you can add the key to your public key ring by entering the command `pgp -ka` ⟨*filename*⟩ or `gpg --import` ⟨*filename*⟩ in a command line. If the key does not have a trustworthy signature, you will not be able to use it to encrypt in KMail (use `pgp -ks` ⟨*identity*⟩).

Using Other People's Public Keys — Encoding Your Own Messages

To send an encrypted message to a recipient whose public key you have received, simply write the message in the 'Create Message' window. Before sending the message, click the red key icon in the window's toolbar. Now, the message can be sent. If KMail cannot find a key for the recipient, a list with all the available keys is shown. Select the appropriate one from the list or abort the process. KMail also informs you if errors occur during the encryption process. You cannot read encrypted mails if you did not click 'Always encrypt to self' in the 'Security' tab.

For More Information

More information can be found on KMail's web site at `http://kmail.kde.org`.

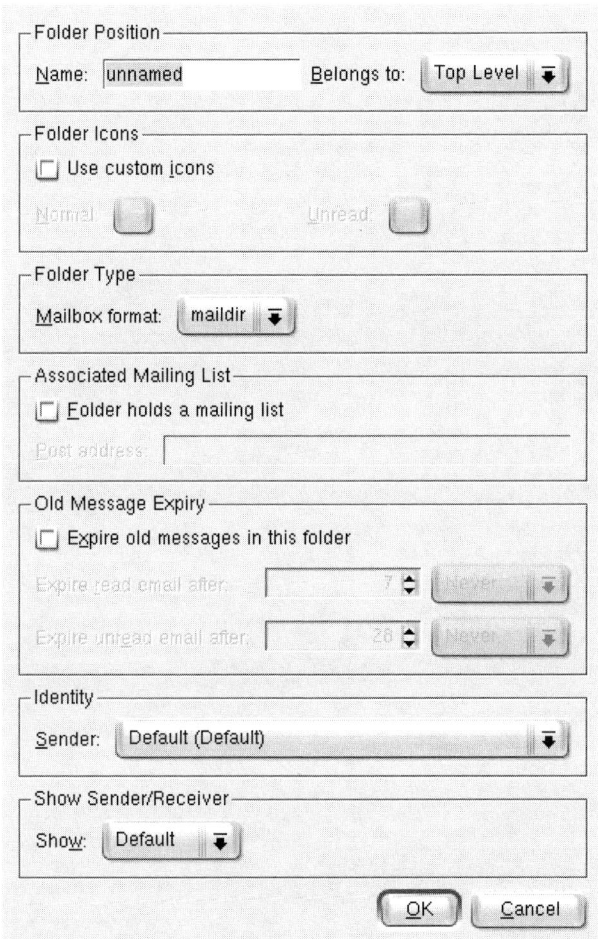

Figure 13.3: *Creating New Folders*

Evolution: An E-Mail and Calendar Program

Evolution is a groupware suite created by Ximian. It offers regular e-mail features along with extended features like task lists and a calendar. Use Evolution to make appointments with other users through the calendar features or just to check and sort your e-mail. It also provides a complete address book, including the ability to send your contact information as a vCard to others.

Starting Evolution

Evolution is not included in the default SuSE installations. To install Evolution, use YaST to install package `evolution` and all dependent packages automatically selected by YaST.

Evolution is a GNOME application. However, with the required libraries installed, it can be used from any window manager. To start Evolution from GNOME, select 'Programs' → 'Applications' → 'Evolution'. It can also be started from the SuSE menu under 'Internet' → 'Tools' → 'Evolution'. From a terminal, Evolution can be started with `evolution &`.

Evolution Setup Assistant

When started for the first time, Evolution opens a configuration tool to assist in initial setup. If it does not open automatically, access it from the Inbox view with 'Tools' → 'Mail Settings...' then clicking 'Add' in the 'Accounts' tab. Click 'Next' to use the assistant. Enter your name and e-mail address in the appropriate fields. If you have multiple e-mail addresses, use your preferred address here. Additional addresses can be configured later. Click 'Next'.

Select the appropriate incoming mail format for this address from the 'Server Type' drop-down box. 'POP' is the most common format for downloading mail from a remote server. 'IMAP' works with mail folders on a special server. Obtain this information from your ISP or server administrator. Complete the other relevant fields displayed when the server type is selected. Click 'Next' when finished.

The next set of information to enter is about mail delivery. This will be used for all the e-mail addresses configured. To use outgoing mail on the local system, select 'Sendmail'. For a remote server, select 'SMTP'. Get the details from your ISP or server administrator. For SMTP, complete the other fields displayed after selection. Click 'Next' when finished.

By default, the e-mail address is used as the name to identify the account. Enter another name if desired. The field 'Make this my default account' determines whether the account should be used as the default. The default account is the e-mail address initially selected for sending mail. Another account can be selected in the message composition window if desired. Click 'Next'.

The time zone information from the next window is used for the calendar functions. It is important to select the correct time zone for using the appointment scheduling functions. Click the dot on the map for a city in your time zone. Selection zooms the display to that area and a change can be made if desired. When the correct time zone is displayed under 'Selection', click 'Next'. In the next window, click 'Finish' to save the data entered. Use 'Back' to make changes.

Importing from Other Mail Programs

Evolution can import mail from other mail programs, such as Netscape or KMail. To import, select 'File' →'Import'. For KMail or mutt, use 'Import a single file'. For Netscape, select 'Import data and settings from older programs'. More information is available in the internal help.

The Evolution Window

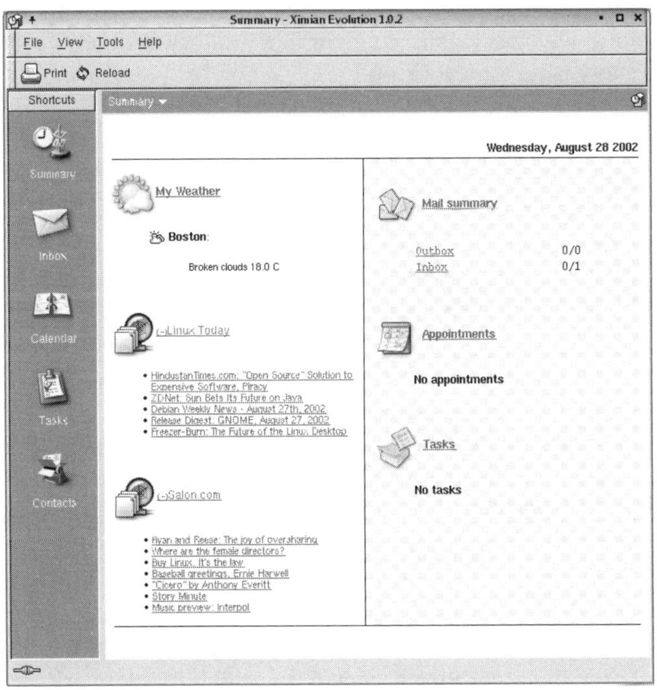

Figure 14.1: The Evolution Window with Shortcuts and Summary

The default window view is shown in Figure 14.1 on the preceding page. The menus and menu items available and the icons in the toolbar vary from window to window. Use the 'Shortcuts' pane to the left to select the information to display in the right pane. Adjust the size of any panes by dragging the dividing bars.

Tip

Right-clicking an item, such as a mail message or contact, opens a menu of actions relevant to that item.

Tip

Use 'View' to remove the 'Shortcuts Bar' or add a 'Folder Bar' at any time. The different items listed in the 'Shortcuts' are described in the following.

Summary

The 'Summary' provides some basic information about mail, appointments, and tasks along with personally configurable weather and news sources. This window is shown in Figure 14.1 on the page before. Use 'Tools' → 'Summary Settings' to configure the information displayed.

Inbox

In this view, the upper half of the window shows the contents of the folder Inbox. The lower half is a preview pane used to display the selected mail message. Disable the preview pane with 'View' → 'Preview Pane'.

To change the folder displayed, click the down arrow next to 'Inbox' and select another folder from the list. The search bar can be used to search the messages in a folder. The table headers for the message list can be clicked to sort the messages by that header. The sort can be either ascending or descending as shown by the arrow to the right. Click the header until the correct direction is displayed.

Calendar

The initial display shows a day view of the current day with the month and a task list shown in an additional pane to the right. Week, work week, and month views are also available from the toolbar or the 'View' menu. Use the search bar to find an entered appointment. Add appointments and tasks using the buttons in the toolbar. Also use the toolbar to page through the calendar or jump to a specific date.

Tasks

'Tasks' provides a list of tasks. Use the toolbar to add tasks. Search the tasks with the search bar.

Contacts

This view shows all the addresses in your address book. To locate a particular address, use the search bar or click the button to the right displaying the first letter of the contact's last name. Add contacts or lists with the toolbar.

Mail

To configure the mail settings in Evolution, switch to the 'Inbox' view with the 'Shortcuts'. Select 'Tools' → 'Mail Settings...'.

Configuring Accounts

Evolution is capable of fetching mail from multiple mail accounts. The account from which to send can be selected when composing a message. To edit a current account, select the account and click 'Edit'. To add a new account, click 'Add'. This opens the configuration assistant described under *Evolution Setup Assistant* on page 222. Delete a current account by selecting it then clicking 'Delete'

To make an account the default account used when sending mail, select the desired account then hit 'Default'. To disable fetching mail from an account, select the account then click 'Disable'. A disabled account can still be used as the address for sending, but that account will not be checked for incoming mail. Reactivate the account with 'Enable'.

Other Settings

Use 'Display' to select or disable the quote highlight color or after how long a message is marked as read after opening. Also make settings regarding how images in HTML mail messages are treated.

Use 'Composer' to make settings for your mail composer. 'Other' contains settings for PGP, character encoding, and other functions.

Writing Mail

Click 'New Message' to compose a new message. Replying or forwarding a message opens the same basic message editor. Next to 'From', select from which account to send the message. In the recipient fields, enter an e-mail address or part of a name or address in your address book. If Evolution can match what you enter to something in the address book, Evolution displays a list from which to select. Click the desired contact or continue entry if none match. To select directly from the address book, click 'To' or 'CC' instead.

Evolution can send regular text e-mail or HTML e-mail. Use the format toolbar to format HTML mail. Click 'Attach' or 'Insert' →'Attachment' to send a file along with the message. To protect your e-mail with PGP, make appropriate selections from the 'Security' menu.

To send your message, click 'Send'. If not ready to send it immediately, make another selection under 'File'. For example, save the message as a draft or send it later.

Folders

It is often convenient to sort e-mail messages into a variety of folders. Evolution also offers folders. To view your folder tree, select 'View' → 'Folder Bar'. If you are accessing mail over IMAP, the IMAP folders will also be shown in this folder bar. For POP and most other formats, your folders are stored locally, sorted under 'Local Folders'. Your 'Contacts', 'Calendar', and 'Tasks' are also treated as folders in this view, but should not be used for filing mail.

Several folders are included by default. 'Inbox' is where new messages fetched from a server are initially placed. 'Sent' is used for saving copies of mail you send. 'Outbox' is temporary storage for mail that has not yet been sent. It is useful for working offline or if the outgoing mail server is temporarily unreachable. 'Drafts' is used for saving unfinished e-mail messages. 'Trash' is temporary storage for deleted items. Configure automatic emptying of that folder under 'Tools' → 'Mail Settings...'.

New folders can be created under 'Local Folders' or as subfolders of existing folders. Create as complex a folder hierarchy as desired. To create a new folder while in 'Inbox' view, select 'File' → 'Folder' → 'New Folder'. In the dialog that opens, enter a name. Also select the folder for which the new folder will be a subfolder. Leave the 'Folder Type' as 'Mail' for a new mail storage folder. Click 'OK' to create the new folder.

To move a message into a folder, select the message to move. Right-click to open the context menu. Select 'Move to Folder...' and, in the dialog that opens, the destination folder. Click 'OK' to move the message. The message header in the original folder will be shown with a line through it, meaning it is marked for deletion in that folder. The message is stored in the new folder. Messages can be copied in a similar manner.

Manually moving a number of messages into different folders can be time-consuming. Filters can be used to automate this procedure.

Filters

Evolution has a number of options available for filtering. Filters can be used to move a message into a specific folder or to delete a message. Messages can also be moved directly to the trash with a filter. There are two options for creating a new filter: creating a filter from scratch or creating a filter based on a message to filter. The latter is extremely useful for filtering messages sent to a mailing list.

Creating a Filter from Scratch

Select 'Tools' → 'Filters'. This dialog lists your existing filters, which can be edited, and allows for deletion or addition. Click 'Add' to create a new filter.

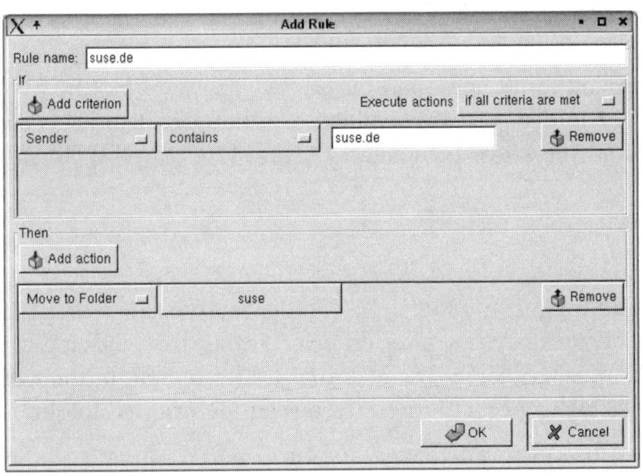

Figure 14.2: Creating a Filter

Enter a name for the new filter in 'Rule Name'. Select the criteria to use for the filter. Options include sender, recipients, source account, subject, date, and status. The drop-box showing 'Contains' provides a variety of options, such as "contains," "is," and "is not." Select the appropriate condition. Enter the text for which to search. Click 'Add criterion' to add more filter criteria. Use 'Execute actions' to determine if all or only some of the criteria must be met to apply the filter.

In the lower part of the window, determine the action to be taken when the filter criteria are met. Messages can, for example, be moved or copied to a folder or assigned a special color. When moving or copying, select the destination folder by clicking. In the folder list that appears, select the folder. Use 'New' to create a new folder. Click 'OK' when the correct folder is selected. When finished creating the filter, click 'OK'.

Creating a Filter from a Message

Select the message on which to base the filter. Right-click and select 'Create Rule From Message'. Select the filter option desired. This opens the filter creation dialog with the correct criteria already selected. Add additional criteria if desired. Select the appropriate filter action. Click 'OK' when finished.

Applying Filters

Filters are applied in the order listed in the dialog under 'Tools' → 'Filters'. Change the order by highlighting a filter and clicking 'Up' or 'Down'. Click 'OK' to close the filter dialog when finished.

Filters are applied to all new mail messages. They will not be applied to mail already in your folders. To apply filters to messages already received, highlight the desired messages then select 'Actions' → 'Apply Filters'.

VFolders

Evolution offers unique VFolders. A VFolder is a virtual folder that displays messages based on search or filter criteria. Rather than moving the messages into a folder, messages shown in a virtual folder remain in their original folder. Actions taken occur to the message in the original folder.

VFolders are a useful means of reading new mail in one place after it has been sorted into a number of different directories with filters. For example, a VFolder could be created to search all your folders for unread mail.

To create a new VFolder, select 'Tools' → 'Virtual Folder Editor...'. In the dialog, click 'Add'. VFolders can also be created from a message as with filters. Right-click, select 'Create Rule from Message', then select the correct VFolder criteria.

Enter a 'Rule Name'. For the new mail example mentioned above, set the criterion to 'Status' 'is not' 'Read'. Set the sources as desired. Other VFolder searches can be set similarly. Click 'OK' when finished. This returns to the virtual folder list. The order can be changed if desired. Click 'OK' to close it.

The new VFolder will be shown in the folder list under 'VFolders'. You can read, answer, and delete mail with the VFolder. However, deleting the message deletes it from the real folder in which it is stored, not just the VFolder.

Calendar

Adding Appointments

To add a new appointment to your calendar, click 'New Appointment'. Under the 'Appointment' tab, enter the details for the appointment. Select a category, if desired, to ease searching and sorting later. Optionally set for Evolution to provide a reminder before your appointment under the 'Reminder' tab. If the appointment occurs regularly, set that under 'Recurrence'. Click 'Save and Close' after all settings are made. The new appointment will be shown in your calendar.

Scheduling a Meeting

To schedule a meeting with other people, click 'New Appointment' then select 'Actions' → 'Schedule Meeting'. Enter information like for an appointment. Under 'Meeting', add attendees. For those in your 'Contacts', click 'Invite Others...' and select attendees from the dialog. When finished, click 'Save and Close'. The attendees will be sent an e-mail about the scheduled meeting.

This system can also be used to schedule a time that fits all attendees or to reserve resources. For more information about using the scheduling functions, refer to the internal help.

Adding Tasks

Evolution can be used to keep track of a list of things to do. To add a new task to your list, click 'New Task'. Enter summary information, your due and start dates, and a description. Enter task status and other information under 'Details'. Click 'Save and Close' to add the task to your list. Double-click the task to reopen the dialog and make changes or mark it completed.

Contacts

Adding Contacts

Along with the name and e-mail address, Evolution can store other address and contact information about a person. To quickly add the name and e-mail address of someone who has sent you an e-mail, right-click the underlined address in the message preview. Select 'Add to Contacts'. To enter more information, click 'Edit Full'. Otherwise, click 'OK'. If you have selected 'Edit Full', click 'Save and Close' when finished.

To enter a completely new contact, click 'New Contact' in the 'Contacts' view. Enter all desired contact information. Click 'Save and Close' when finished.

Making a List

If you frequently send messages to the same group of people, make this easier by creating a list. Click 'New List' when in 'Contacts' view. Enter a name for the list. Add addresses by typing the address in the box then clicking 'Add' or by dragging contacts from the Evolution Contacts view and dropping them in the box. Toggle 'Hide addresses' to select whether or not the recipients can see who else has recieved the mail. Click 'Save and Close' when finished. The list is now one of your contacts and will appear in the composition window after the first few letters are typed.

Sharing Contacts

To send contact information from your address book to another Evolution user, right-click the contact to forward. Select 'Forward Contact'. This sends the contact "card" as an attachment in an e-mail. Compose and send this message as usual.

To add a contact you have been sent, view the contact inline. Click 'Save in addressbook' to add the complete contact card to your address book.

Using the Address Book in Evolution

By means of the LDAP protocol, Evolution can access public address books, such as those used by SuSE Linux Openexchange Server or Microsoft Exchange. Evolution offers full access to these address books. It can read them and add new entries.

Configuring the LDAP Access

In the left menu window, click 'Contacts' or select the folder with this name from 'Local Folders'. From the menu bar, select 'Tools' → 'Addressbook Sources ...'. A new window opens, displaying the address books already configured.

To add a new source or a new server, select 'Add'. To edit or delete an existing link, select 'Edit' or 'Delete'. Then click 'Add' to open a new dialog for entering the data required for configuring the address book.

The following fields must be filled to access, for example, a SuSE Linux Openexchange Server address book:

'Basic' Enter a name under 'Account Name' and enter the host name or the IP address of the SuSE Linux Openexchange Server or LDAP server under 'Server Name'. In the case of SuSE Linux Openexchange Server, you can only use the address book after you have logged in to the server. For this purpose, the respective option must be activated. Check if 'Distinguished name (DN)' is marked under 'Authenticate with server using'. Enter the DN values in the respective field. For example, the values required for SuSE Linux Openexchange Server are as follows for the user `hili` who works in Switzerland for a company called 'Penguinlovers' (LDAP server: mail.penguinlovers.ch):

```
uid=hili,dc=penguinlovers,dc=ch
```

'Advanced' Setting the port: usually the default value 389 can be used. Enter your base node under 'Search base'. Get the needed values from your system administrator.

After clicking 'Apply' or 'OK', the data of the address book is displayed in the 'Contacts' folder. The configuration is similar for a Microsoft Exchange Server. You may leave the option 'Authenticate with server using:' unchecked if you only want to read (and not write to) the address book in question.

For More Information

Evolution includes extensive internal help. Use the 'Help' menu to access this information. For more information about Evolution, refer to Ximian's web site at `http://www.ximian.com`.

ISDN Telecommunication

In the times of Internet and e-mail, traditional communication forms, like the telephone and fax, have virtually no significance. The new communication package CAPISuite offers an ISDN-based solution for a computer-supported answering machine and fax handler.

The following chapter intends to explain the workings of CAPISuite in more detail. This is followed by a description of its installation with YaST and a short introduction to the usage of the system.

CAPISuite Basics

CAPISuite is a daemon (a program that runs in the background) that provides basic telecommunication functions. The current version especially offers functions for telephone and fax connections.

This means that the system supports, for instance, the initiation and termination of incoming and outgoing fax and voice connections. Fax and audio files can then be sent and received over these connections. Some special functions, like the switching of a phone connection to a fax connections and the processing of DTMF (Dual Tone Multi Frequency — common touch tone phone tones), are supported.

The system, however, does not constitute a complete application suite for the completion of certain tasks, like an answering machine application. The actual application is written in the Python scripting language (a language especially well suited for beginners) and can thus be freely adjusted to the current requirements. CAPISuite merely processes the provided scripts and executes the commands listed. This allows the creation of flexible solutions from a simple answering machine up to a small call center (for which the system is still lacking a few basic features).

The CAPISuite package provides some predefined scripts that offer a multiuser answering machine and a fax solution. The following pages refer to the usage of these scripts. Information in more detail about the system and instructions on writing custom scripts can be found in `/usr/share/doc/packages/capisuite/manual/index.html` after installation and on the web site of the project (http://www.capisuite.de/).

Configuration

Capisuite accesses the CAPI programming interface for ISDN hardware. Because this has only been recently made available for Linux, suitable drivers are not yet available for all common ISDN adapters. They are however available for the very common ISDN adapters of the manufacturer AVM and can comfortably be installed and configured with YaST.

A simple test for the operational status of the CAPI drivers is the execution of the `capiinfo` command as the `root` user.The driver is installed correctly if the command returns detailed information about capability of the ISDN adapter. CAPISuite can then be installed and used.

The capisuite package must be installed with the YaST software installation module to be able to configure CAPISuite. More information on installing software is provided in the respective section of the YaST chapter.

Caution

It was not yet determined by print deadline whether CAPISuite could be included in the Personal Edition. This package is, in any case, available for download on the SuSE Internet servers. A corresponding installation instruction is published if needed on the web site of the CAPISuite project at http://www.capisuite.de/.

Caution

After installation, YaST offers two modules for the configuration of the fax and answering machine functionality.

Configuring Fax Services

The YaST module 'Fax' from the 'Network Devices' group contains a form with a user list and buttons for the processing of list entries. The list contains all the users already configured for the fax system. The CAPISuite scripts used here are multiuser-capable and allow each user to send and receive faxes individually. The target number of an incoming call determines which user receives the fax. The list of this module is, of course, empty when it is started for the first time.

If various users want to receive faxes with CAPISuite, it must be ensured that the associated phone numbers are all different and that all these numbers are also associated with the line to which the ISDN adapter is connected. This is of importance if you concurrently use an ISDN PBX.

Tip

Use exclusively the answering machine module if you intend to recieve both faxes and normal calls, because this offers an integrated recognition and reception module for faxes. See *Configuring the Answering Machine* on page 237.

Tip

Existing entries can be edited or deleted and new entries can be created with the assistance of the icons grouped below the list. A dialog box appears for entering the following data when creating a new entry or modifying an existing one:

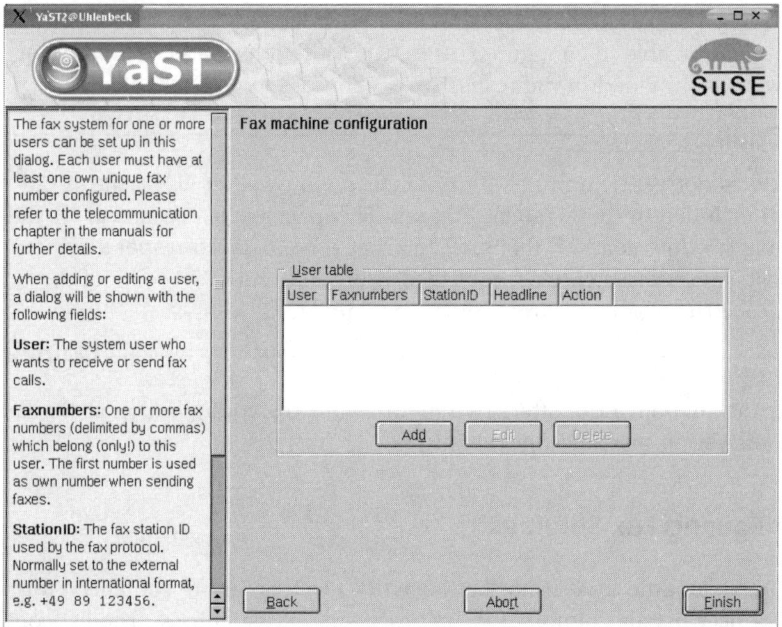

Figure 15.1: YaST Module for the Configuration of the Fax Function

'User' Select the user of the system for which the fax functionality should be activated. This user account then receives incoming faxes and status reports.

'Fax Numbers' This field must contain at least one phone number associated with the user for fax reception. The input of various numbers separated by commas is also possible. All faxes sent to those numbers are sent to the user as e-mails. The first number in the list is used for the identification of outgoing faxes.

'StationID' The fax protocol uses an ID transmitted during handshaking for identification, which should normally contain the external phone number of the fax device in international notation. An example for a valid StationID is `+49 89 123456` for the fax number 123456 in Munich in Germany. The maximum length of this entry is twenty digits. Valid characters are numerical digits, spaces, and the + symbol as prefix to the international country code.

'Header' This field can contain an arbitrary text to use as a header for sent

Figure 15.2: *Fax Functionality: User Preferences*

faxes. Whether and how this text is featured on the sent document depends on the respective ISDN driver.

'Action' An incoming fax is saved in the system and sent to the user as an e-mail in the default configuration `MailAndSave`. The `SaveOnly` option ensures that the fax will only be saved to hard disk. This option is only recommended for expert users.

Click 'OK' to accept the changes. Click 'Cancel' to drop the changes and close the form.

Configuring the Answering Machine

The provided standard scripts also offer a comfortable multiuser answering machine. This can be be configured with the YaST 'Answering Machine' module in the 'Network Devices' group.

Similar to the fax configuration, there is a list with the already configured users (which is empty at first start). The recorded incoming call is sent to the user associated with the phone number. This shows the importance of assigning unique phone numbers to the users. The individual user welcome message cannot be set at this point. The recording will be made later with the remote access function of the configured answering machine.

The answering machine has an automatic silence recognition routine that terminates the recording session after five seconds without noises.

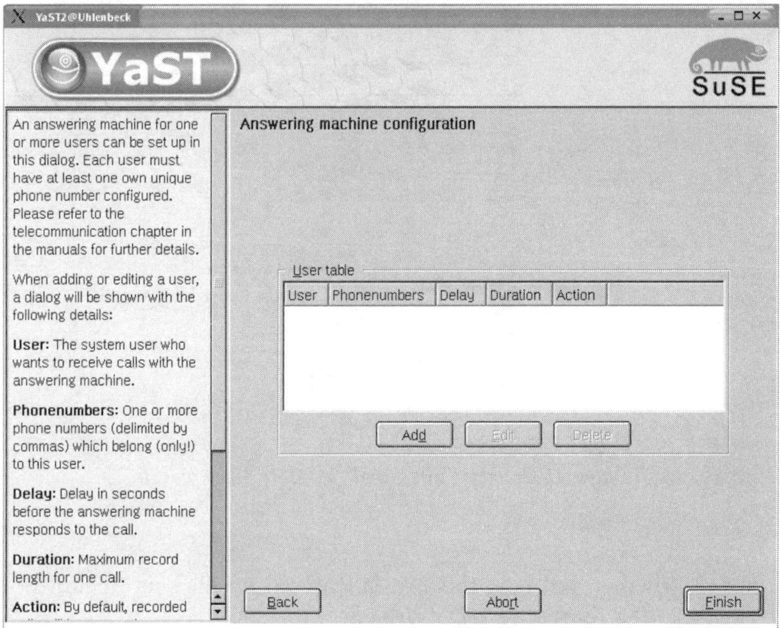

Figure 15.3: YaST Module for the Configuration of the Answering Machine

Tip

Incoming fax calls are also automatically recognized and received in most cases. This automatic routine can, however, fail with older fax machines, which is why a separate fax number is to preferred wherever possible.

Tip

Use 'Add', 'Edit', and 'Delete' to administer the entries. The entry form for creating a new entry or for modifying an existing one contains the following fields:

'User' Select the system user for whom the answering machine should be configured. One or more fax numbers are assigned to each registered user. Incoming calls to these numbers are then sent to the user as e-mails.

'Phone Numbers' Set the phone numbers for which messages should be recorded for the user. Faxes can also be sent to the declared phone

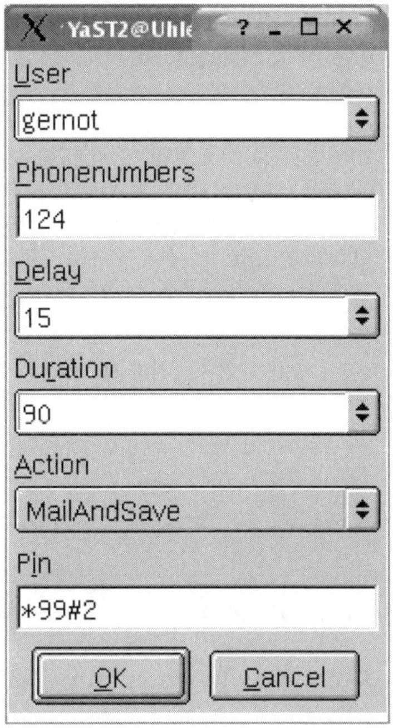

Figure 15.4: Answering Machine: User Preferences

numbers as the answering machine has an automatic fax recognition feature. Separate multiple numbers with commas.

'Response Time' This value defined in seconds determines after how much time the answering machine should answer an incoming call. A value can be selected from the list or entered.

'Duration' Determines the maximum recording time for the answering machine — the maximum duration of a recorded incoming call in seconds. This value is usually of secondary importance because recording is usually terminated by the caller hanging up. It is advisable to set this value to a sensible amount of time, such as two minutes (120 seconds).

'Action' The answering machine features various different processing options for incoming messages. The default setting `MailAndSave` records a message, saves it in the system, and delivers it to the user as an e-mail. The `SaveOnly` option can be chosen if the reception of e-mails is not desired. It merely saves the message to hard disk. This option is only recommended for expert users. The None option completely deactivates the recording of messages. It only play the welcome message then hangs up.

'PIN' Enter a personal identification number (PIN) for remote access. A numerical code of arbitrary length can be entered here. If it is entered during playback of the welcome message, the user is taken to the remote access menu. The remote access feature is disabled if the field is left empty.

'OK' accepts the changes. 'Cancel' closes the dialog box without applying any changes.

Usage

General Notes about Reception

The development of CAPISuite heavily relied on using already existing capabilities of Linux. This is why the delivery of incoming faxes and voice messages is handled by the internal Linux mail system instead of proprietary applications and protocols.

This requires the configuration of a mail client for receiving local messages for each user of CAPISuite. For details, read the respective chapters about the mail program or the documentation provided with the application.

Fax Operation

No further instructions are necessary here for the reception of faxes. As soon as a fax is received for a number assigned to a user, the document is stored in the system and delivered to the user as an e-mail with a PDF attachment. PDF is a common exchange format for documents and can be read in virtually any operating system with the Adobe Acrobat Reader. The user can then open, read, and print the document as needed.

Each received document is also stored on the hard disk in `/var/spool/capisuite/users/<username>/received/`. This directory can be accessed if anything goes wrong during e-mail delivery of if an e-mail was accidentally deleted. More information can be found in the CAPISuite documentation in `/usr/share/doc/packages/capisuite/manual/index.html`.

The command line tool `capisuitefax` is available for the sending of faxes. It accepts one or more target fax numbers and one or more documents in the PostScript format. This format is generated by virtually all Linux applications when printing to a file.

`capisuitefax` accepts the following parameters:

`-h` or `--help` Returns a short summary of valid parameters.

`-d <number>` or `--dialstring=<number>` This parameter declares the target number to which the fax should be sent.

`-q` or `--quiet` `capisuitefax` usually generates a few informative messages. This option suppresses this and only allows the display of possible error messages.

The following command would send the two documents `document1.ps` and `document2.ps` to the target number 089123456:

```
capisuitefax -d 089123456 document1.ps document2.ps
```

`capisuitefax` converts the documents into the correct format and stores them with a description file in a special folder from which they are then fetched and sent by CAPISuite. This is why there could be a short delay between running the command and the actual sending. The user receives an e-mail once the fax has been successfully sent or when a set number of attempts have failed.

Faxes can even be comfortably sent from any KDE application with the assistance of the KDEPrintFax utility. KDEPrintFax should be configured in the following way for this:

- Start KDEPrintFax. This can be done, for instance, by pressing (Alt) + (F2) and entering `kdeprintfax`.
- Select 'Settings' → 'Configure KDEPrintFax'.
- Click the 'System' icon in the left pane.
- Because `capisuitefax` is predominantly compatible with the HylaFAX suite, select 'Use HylaFAX system' here.
- Alter the command line entry to the following: `/usr/bin/capisuitefax -d %number %files`.

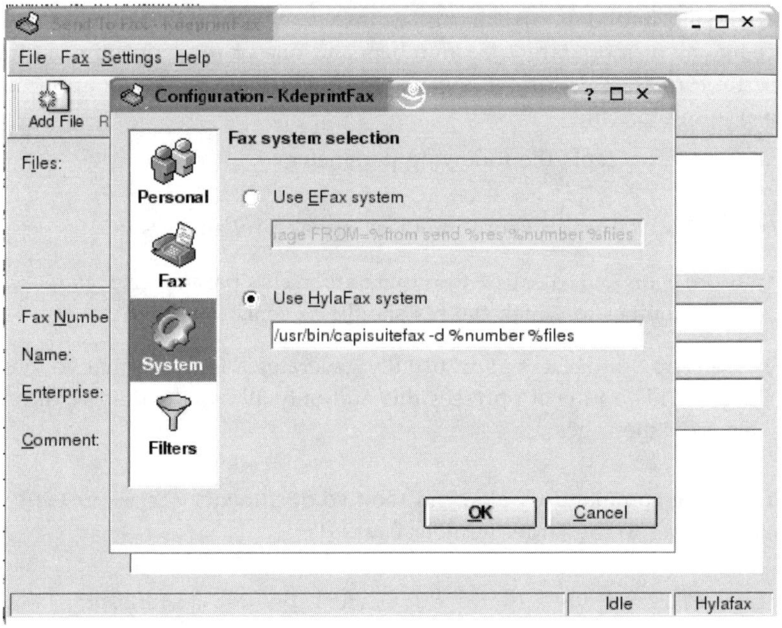

Figure 15.5: Configuring CAPISuite in KDEPrintFax

- Finish the configuration by clicking 'OK' and closing KDEPrintFax.

The option 'Send to Fax' is then available in the 'Print' menu of any KDE application. Selecting it starts KDEPrintFax, which requests the target phone number and sends the fax.

Non-KDE applications can also use this function if they allow the manual setting of the printing command. The commonly used `lpr` should then be replaced with `kprinter`, which makes the KDE printing menu appear along with its faxing capability.

Caution

`capisuitefax` does not yet support the complete set of HylaFAX features. This means that advanced features, like the resolution setting, are currently silently ignored.

Caution

Operation of the Answering Machine

If e-mail dispatching has not been turned off, voice messages left on the answering machine are sent as an e-mail to the recipient associated with the incoming phone number. This means that the operation of the answering machine does not require any additional description. All incoming messages can be comfortably received and opened with the e-mail client. The incoming messages are additionally stored in `/var/spool/capisuite/users/<username>/received/` for backup reasons.

The recording of the personal welcome message is performed directly over the remote access feature of the answering machine.

To access your answering machine remotely, call your associated number from any telephone. Enter the previously-defined PIN during the welcome message playback. Wait a few seconds if you mistype your PIN then try again after the beep. Shortly after having correctly entered the PIN, the answering machine gives the number of stored messages. You then have the choice of either recording a new welcome message or listening to your stored messages. Follow the instructions given.

The following table provides a brief overview of the menu items for the remote accessing of messages. It is recommended to carry a copy of it if you use the remote access frequently. The commands can be entered at any time during the playback of the messages. This means that an excessively long voice message can be skipped easily.

Key	Function
1	delete current message
4	skip to the next message
5	skip to the previous message
6	replay current message

Table 15.1: *Commands for Message Playback*

Multimedia Applications in Linux

Linux offers a wide range of sound applications in various states of development. Because of the variety of applications and their unusual names, it can be difficult both to determine what an application does and to find the application that suits a particular purpose. The following is an overview of the vast range of applications for the various tasks in multimedia. Some of the more powerful applications included in the SuSE Linux distribution are described in more detail here.

Many of these applications are not included in the default installation. Use YaST to install the corresponding packages.

> **Note**
>
> Unless otherwise specified, applications can be started from the 'SuSE Menus' under 'Multimedia' → 'Sound'.
>
> **Note**

Mixers

Mixers are a convenient way of controlling the volume and balance of the computer's sound output and input. The main differences in the various mixers are the interfaces. Select one that meets your needs with which you are comfortable working. Other mixers are available. Most programs in the 'Multimedia' → 'Sound' menu with "mix" in the name are mixer applications.

> **Tip**
>
> Generally, it is advisable to open a mixer application prior to opening other sound applications. Use the mixer to test and adjust the control settings for the input and output of the sound card. Some sound cards may not allow simultaneous access from multiple applications. If a sound application freezes, this may be the cause.
>
> **Tip**

gamix

If you have multiple sound cards, gamix provides a set of controllers for each card. Slide the control sliders to set the levels as desired.

alsamixer

alsamixer can be run from the command line without the X environment. The application is operated with the cursor keys. Q, W, E, Y, X, and C can be used to set different levels for the left and right channels.

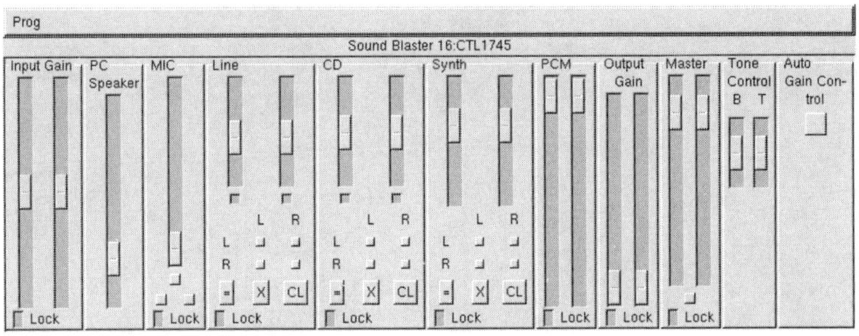

Figure 16.1: The gamix Mixer

Note

The look and feel of alsamixer depends on the type of sound card used. The following description refers to the commonplace AC97 standard for mixer functionality. Expect some deviations from it, if your sound card does not comply with this standard. The mixer Envy24 should be used for sound cards equipped with the Envy24 (ice1712) chip.

Note

The basic sliders for sound output are 'Master', 'PCM', and 'CD'. 'Master' sets the general volume. 'PCM' and 'CD' control the balance of the PCM and audio CD channels.

(M) mutes single channels. 'MM' appears above the muted controller in this case.

Determine the recording source by pressing (Space). The 'capture' controller regulates the input amplifier. The 'Line' controller and the 'MIC' controller are used depending on the recording source.

Close alsamixer by pressing the (Esc). Get more information with `man alsamixer`.

alsamixergui is a mouse-operated variation of alsamixer with a graphical interface. See Figure 16.2 on the following page.

KMix

KMix is the KDE mixer. It provides a convenient and familiar interface for KDE users. It can also be integrated into the KDE panel.

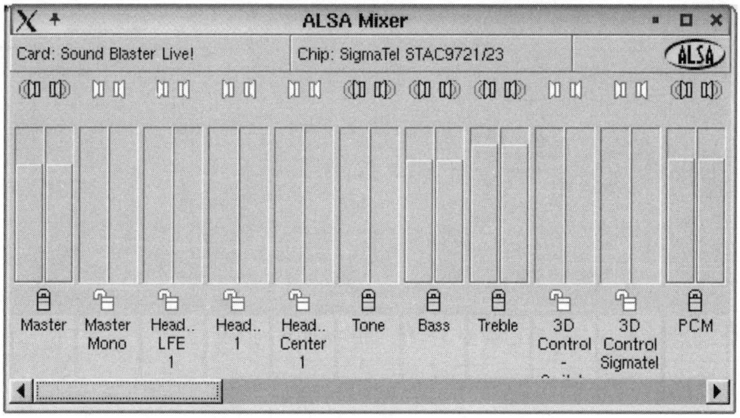

Figure 16.2: The alsamixergui Mixer

GNOME Mixer Applet

If you use GNOME, this applet provides a convenient volume control that can be integrated in a panel. To add it to a panel, right-click then select 'Panel' → 'Add to Panel' → 'Applet' → 'Multimedia' → 'Mixer'.

Players

Linux offers a variety of programs for playing audio CDs and the various music formats available, including MP3, OGG, and WAV files. Where possible, the supported formats of the players are listed.

kscd — Audio CD Player

kscd is an easy-to-use audio CD player. It can be accessed from the 'SuSE menu' under 'Multimedia' → 'Multimedia' → 'CD' → 'KsCD'. Access the configuration menu by clicking the tool icon. kscd can be configured to search an online CDDB server for the name and track names of a CD.

The WorkMan Audio CD Player

WorkMan offers a simple, handy, user interface with an abundance of functions. It is ideal for anyone who prefers to run a CD player without the KDE

Figure 16.3: The kscd User Interface

look and feel.

GNOME CD Player Applet

This is a simple applet that can be added to a GNOME panel. It can be added by right-clicking the panel and selecting 'Panel' → 'Add to Panel' → 'Applet' → 'Multimedia' → 'CD Player'.

XMMS — An MP3, WAV, OGG, and Stream Player

XMMS is a full-blown audio player with robust jitter resistance. The application is easy to use. The button for displaying the options menu is somewhat hard to find — it is located in the upper left corner or the program window.

Select the output plug-in module with 'Options' → 'Preferences' → 'Audio I/O Plugins'. The aRts sound server can be configured here if the `xmms-kde` package is installed.

Note

XMMS redirects its output automatically to the 'Disk Writer Plugin' when it does not find a configured sound card. The played files are written to the hard disk as WAV files in this case. The time display then runs faster than when playing the output through a sound card.

Note

Various visualization plug-ins can be started through 'Options' → 'Preferences' → 'Visualization Plugins'.

There are five buttons with different letters on them. Find them below the menu button. These buttons allow quick access to additional menus, dialog boxes, and configurations. The Playlist can be opened with the 'PL' button and the equalizer is activated with the 'EQ' button.

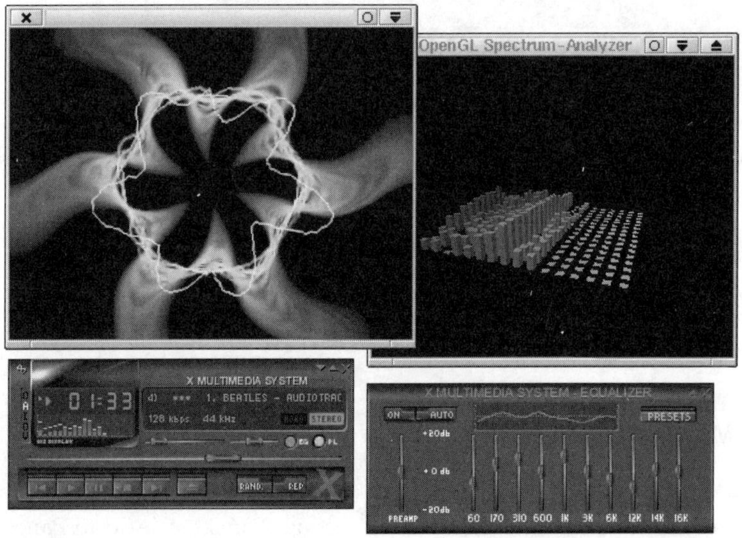

Figure 16.4: XMMS with Equalizer, OpenGL Spectrum Analyzer, and Infinity Plug-Ins

FreeAmp — MP3, OGG, and Stream Player

FreeAmp is another popular player, available for several platforms. Use 'MyMusic' to arrange your collection and create playlists. FreeAmp offers a number of themes that can be used to completely change the appearance of the player.

Composition and Scores

Although graphical composition programs are not as advanced or capable as might be desired, it is still possible to use Linux to create and edit musical scores.

NoteEdit

NoteEdit is probably the most complete score editing software with a graphical interface for Linux. With it, it is possible to create scores with a full range of musical symbols. Notes are entered by right-clicking and rests by middle-clicking. Internal documentation is available in the 'Help' menu. After creating the score here, it can be exported in LilyPond format for printing.

Start the application with `noteedit`. A few examples can be found in `/usr/share/doc/packages/noteedit/examples/`, which can be opened with 'File' → 'Open'. Use 'TSE3' → 'TSE3 Midi In' to import Midi files. These are loaded into the editor with 'TSE3' → 'Score'. Various options for the conversion can be set in the 'Filter' dialog box.

'Midi' → 'Devices' allows selecting one of the ALSA Midi devices configured in the system. This one is then used for playback as well as for recording. The instrument, the MIDI channel, and many other parameters, such as the stereo panorama, can be set under 'Staff' → 'Staff Properties'.

The notes can simply be entered with the mouse. The length of the note and any required accidental are selected in the toolbar. Middle-click to insert a note. Right-click to insert a rest. The 'Insert' menu provides objects like clef, meter, and key. These objects can also be inserted by middle-clicking.

The menu entry 'Edit' → 'General Properties' → 'allow insertion from keyboard' configures the keyboard for note input. The pitch can be determined with the cursor keys and the playing length can be determined with the numeric keypad with (NumLock) locked. (Return) then inserts a note and (Space) inserts a rest.

More information about noteedit can be found in the directory `/usr/share/doc/packages/noteedit/`.

Reading Audio CDs

Konqueror can easily convert audio CDs to audio files just like the other, usually console-based tools. Insert a CD into the drive and enter `audiocd:/` in the URL window. After a few seconds, the contents of this CD is displayed. If you receive an error message, check to make sure you are a member of the group `disk` (use `id`). Add yourself to this group with YaST if needed. Log out of KDE, log back in, and try again.

If you have an open Internet connection, even the title of the audio CD is shown. This is automatically queried from a CDDB server. Entries are made there by many different users. It is quite likely that your CD title can be found. Copying audio tracks from the CD to your hard disk is also possible. Even convert them to ogg-vorbis (a nonpatented music format similar to MP3).

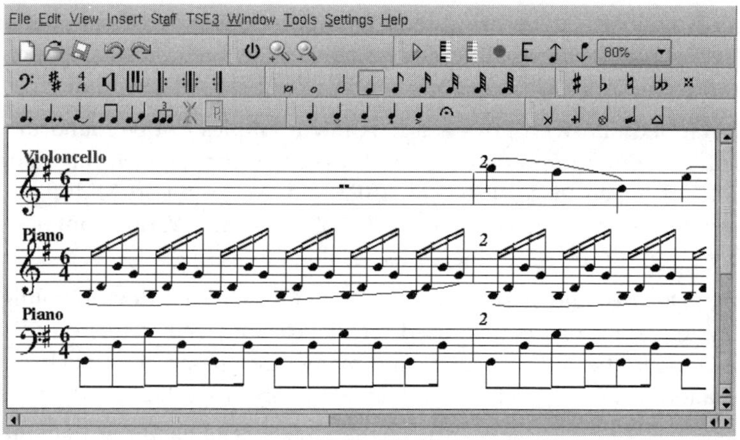

Figure 16.5: The Composition Editor noteedit

TV, Video, Radio, and Webcam

The configuration of TV cards is integrated in the configuration tool YaST. If your card has been correctly identified, it can be automatically configured. Otherwise, enter the card settings manually.

The following sections focus on the motv application, created by the author of the BTTV driver. Another TV application is KWinTV. If you prefer KWinTV, it should be easy to use after reading this chapter.

Watching TV with motv

motv is an improved successor to xawtv. It incorporates all essential functions into the user interface. Start the application with 'SuSE' → 'Multimedia' → 'Video'. Start it at the command line with `motv`. Initially, only a TV window appears after the application starts. Open a menu window by right-clicking it.

Video Source and Network Search

In 'Settings' → 'Input', select the video source. If you select 'Television' here, set up the broadcasting network before starting the application. This automatically takes place with the network search, also found under the 'Settings' menu. If you click 'Save settings', the network found is entered into

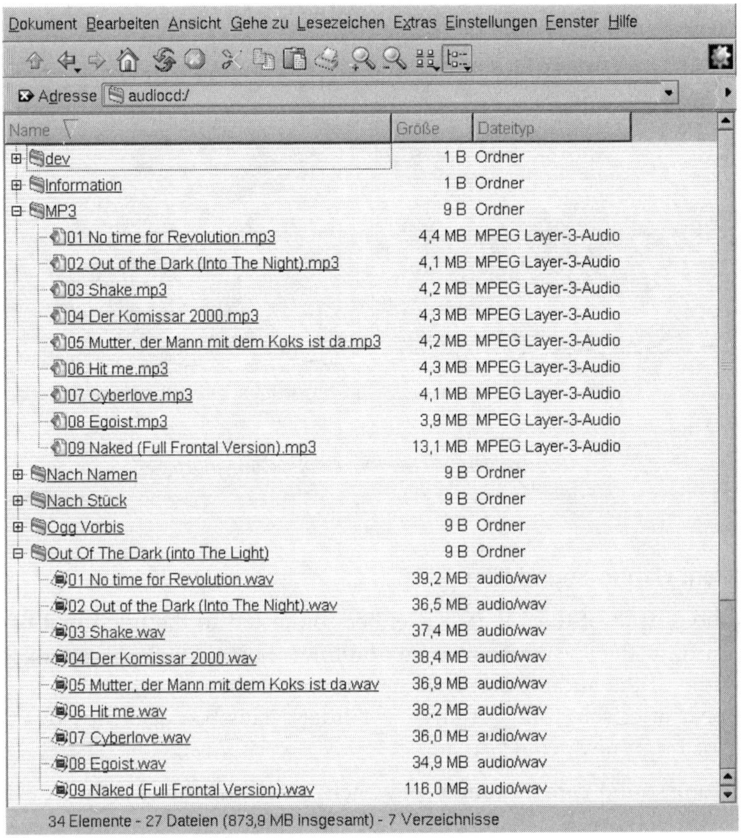

Figure 16.6: Copying CDs with konqueror

the `.xawtv` file in your home directory and will be available the next time you start the application.

Tip

If you do not want to browse for all available channels, find the next channel with Ctrl + ↑. If needed, subsequently adjust the broadcast frequency with ← or →.

Tip

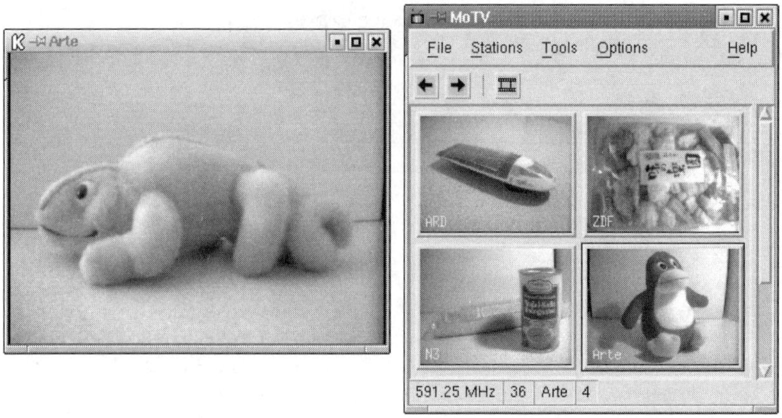

Figure 16.7: The TV Application motv

From Silent Film to Sound Film

The audio output of the TV card is either connected to the line input of your sound card, to the speakers, or to an amplifier. Some TV cards can change the volume of the audio output. The volume can then be set with the sliders that appear after selecting 'Settings' → 'Slider'. This box also provides the sliders for brightness, contrast, and color.

To use your sound card for audio playback, check the mixer settings using gamix, described in *Mixers* on page 246. For sound cards meeting the AC97 specifications, set 'Input-MUX' to 'Line'. The volume can then be adjusted with the 'Master' and 'Line' sliders.

Screen Proportions and Full-Screen Mode

Most television images have a height and width ratio of 4:3. These proportions can be set with 'Tools' → 'Screen Dimensions'. If '4:3' is selected here (this is the default setting), the screen dimensions are retained automatically, even when the display size is changed.

With Ⓕ or 'Tools' → 'Fullscreen', switch to full-screen mode. If the TV image in full-screen mode is not scaled to the full monitor size, some fine-tuning is required. Many graphics cards can scale the full-screen mode television image to the full monitor size without changing the graphical mode. If your card does not support this function, the graphics mode needs to be switched to 640x480 pixels for the full-screen mode. Create the related configuration in

'Settings' → 'Configuration'. After restarting motv, the monitor mode is also changed if you have switched to full-screen mode.

Tip

The `.xawtv` file is created automatically and updated by clicking 'Settings' → 'Save settings'. Here, the broadcasters are saved along with the configuration. More information pertaining to the configuration file can be found in the man page for `xawtvrc`.

Tip

The Launcher Menu

Use the launcher menu to start other applications to use with motv. Start the audio mixer gamix and the video text application alevt, for example, using a keyboard shortcut.

Applications to launch from motv must be entered in the `.xawtv` file. The entries should look like this:

The shortcut then the command used to start the application should follow the application name itself. Start the applications entered under [launch] via the 'Tool' menu.

Video Text with alevt

Use alevt to browse video text pages. Either start the application via 'SuSE' → 'Multimedia' → 'Video' → 'alevt' or at the command line with `alevt`.

The application saves all the pages of the selected station just activated with motv. Pages can be browsed by either entering the desired page number or by clicking a page number. Move forward or backward through the pages by clicking '<<' or '>>', located in the lower window margin.

Webcams and motv

If your webcam is already supported by Linux, access it with motv. Find a summary of the supported USB devices at `http://www.linux-usb.org`. If you have already used motv to access the TV card prior to accessing the webcam, the bttv driver is loaded. The webcam driver is loaded automatically when your webcam is connected to the USB. Start motv at the command line with the parameter `-c /dev/video1` to access the webcam. Access the TV card with `motv -c /dev/video0`.

When connecting the webcam to the USB before the bttv driver has been automatically loaded (this normally occurs when you call up a TV application), /dev/video0 is reserved for the webcam. In this case, if you start motv with the -c /dev/video1 parameter to access the TV card, you might get an error message, because the bttv driver will not be automatically loaded. Deal with this problem by loading the driver separately with modprobe bttv as the user root. An overview of the configurable video devices on your system can be viewed with motv -hwscan.

Listening to the Radio with kradio

The kradio application can be found in the 'SuSE' → 'Multimedia' menu. To start the channel search, click the buttons with the double arrows. Use the buttons with the single arrows to change the frequency in 50 kHz intervals. Engage the six broadcasting network buttons by right-clicking them then enter the name of the network. This will be saved, along with the frequency just set, to the ~/.kde2/share/config/kradiorc file.

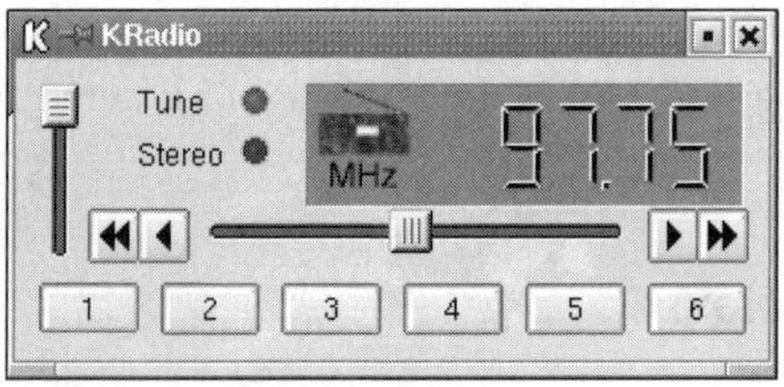

Figure 16.8: The Radio Application kradio

The volume cannot be changed for every TV card. If you have connected the TV card's audio output with the line in of your sound card, set your volume with the mixer gamix.

nxtvepg — The TV Magazine for Your PC

From some broadcasters, an EPG signal (Electronic Program Guide) is transmitted along with the video text signal. Easily view this electronic guide using the program nxtvepg. To do this, however, you must have a TV card supported by the bttv driver and be able to receive one of the channels broadcast with an EPG.

With nxtvepg, the broadcasts are sorted according to channel and topic, such as 'movie' and 'sport', and filtered according to criteria, such as "Live",

"Stereo", or "Subtitle". Either start the application via the 'SuSE' → 'Multimedia' → 'Video' menu or at the command line with `nxtvepg`.

Importing the EPG Database

To set up and update the program database via the EPG signal, set the tuner of your TV card to a station that broadcasts EPG. This can be done using a TV application, such as motv or nxtvepg. Only one application at a time can access the tuner.

If you set an EPG broadcaster in motv, nxtvepg will immediately begin importing the current list of TV programs. The progress will be displayed.

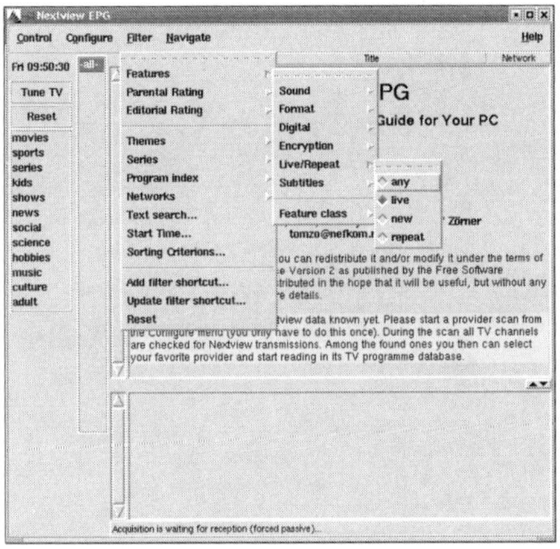

Figure 16.9: The Electronic TV Magazine nxtvepg

If you have not started a TV application, let nxtvepg search for EPG broadcasters. To do this, use 'Configure' → 'Provider scan'. The check box 'Use .xatv' is activated by default. This indicates that nxtvepg is accessing the broadcasters saved in this file.

Tip

If there are problems, check to see if the proper video source has been chosen under 'TV card input'.

Tip

The EPG providers found can be selected in the 'Configure' → 'Select Provider' menu. 'Configure' → 'Merge Providers' even creates flexible associations between the various provider databases.

Sorting the Programs

nxtvepg provides a convenient filter function for managing even the most extensive program offerings. Activate a network selection list with 'Configure' → 'Show networks'. The 'Filter' menu offers plenty of filter functions.

Of particular interest is the 'Navigate' menu. This is built directly from the EPG data. It will appear in the language provided by the network.

Right-click the program list to open a special filter menu in which to activate contextual filter functions.

K3b — The KDE Burning Application

K3b is a very comprehensive program for writing data and audio CDs. Along with the usual features, the program offers some additional options that facilitate work, especially in the field of multimedia. Access the program under 'Multimedia' → 'CD' in the KDE or SuSE menu. The following section describes the main program functions.

The First Launch

Following the first program launch, the K3b setup assistant appears. Root permission is required to set up the program, so enter the `root` password.

Follow the procedure of the setup assistant, which usually makes all settings automatically. In the fourth point of the setup assistant, you can manually assign the mount point and the entries in the file `/etc/fstab`. If you do not know anything about this file, do not modify anything. In step five, define the users authorized to create their own CDs. Enter at least one user. Step six completes the setup. The program is now ready for use.

Creating a Data CD

Creating a data CD is easy. Select 'File' → 'New Project' → 'New Data project'. As shown in Figure 17.1, a tab displaying a folder for your new data project appears at the bottom left side. Drag and drop the desired directories or individual files to the project folder. Select 'Burn' from the toolbar. A dialog with four tabs offering various options for writing the CD is displayed. See Figure 17.2 on page 262.

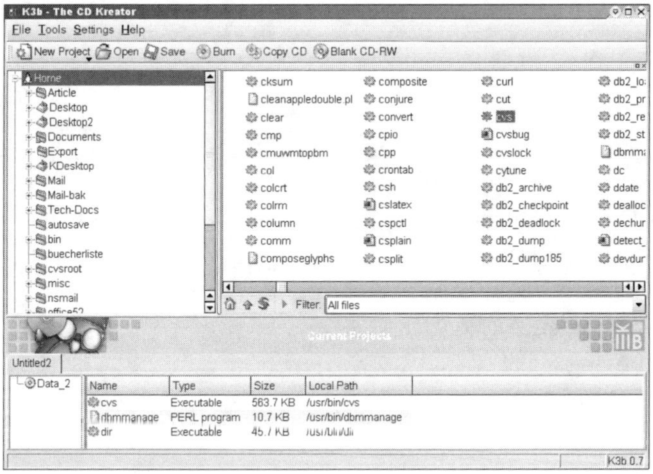

Figure 17.1: Creating a New Data CD

Burning CDs

The detected writer is displayed under 'Device' in the burning dialog. Set the burning speed in 'Burning Speed'.

The following options are offered here:

- 'Simulate writing' — This function can be used to check if your system is able to keep pace with the requirements of the current writing speed. The writing is performed with the laser deactivated to test the system.
- 'Writing on the fly' — Burns the desired data without first creating an image file. Do not use this function if the system performance of your computer is limited.

> **Note**
>
> An image file — also known as ISO image — is a file containing the entire CD contents that is subsequently written to the CD exactly as it is.
>
> **Note**

- 'Only create image' — Creates only an image file. Write it to a CD later. For this purpose, use 'Tools' → 'Write Iso Image'.
- 'Delete image' — Delete the image file after the CD is written.
- 'Disc at once' — The CD is burned without interruption. This is recommended for audio CDs (see below).
- Use BURN-PROOF — If your writer supports this function, activate it to prevent interruption of the data flow. The button is deactivated if this function is not supported.

Under the 'Settings' tab, enter information about the CD, such as a name. This is optional.

'Multisession' displays several options required for writing CDs with multiple data or audio tracks.

The 'Advanced' tab is used for the file name conventions. To achieve a high level of compatibility, make sure 'Generate Joliet entries' is marked.

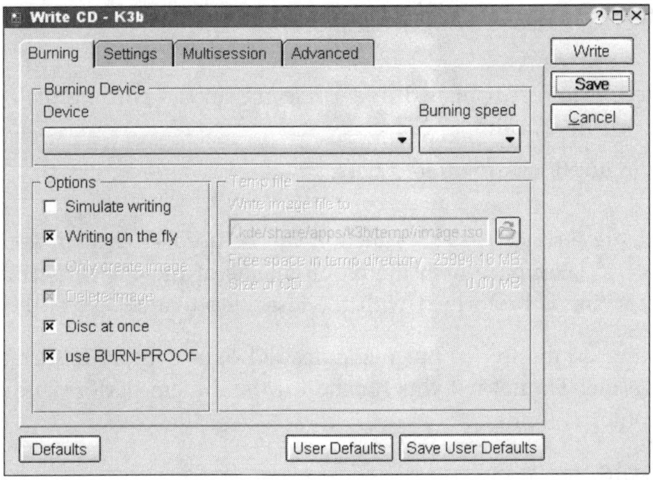

Figure 17.2: Burning CDs with K3b

Creating an Audio CD

Basically, there are no significant differences between creating an audio CD and creating a data CD. Select 'File' → 'New Audio Project'. Copy the individual audio tracks to the project folder with drag and drop. The audio data must be in MP3, WAV, or Ogg Vorbis format.

Set the sequence of the tracks in the project folder by shifting them with drag and drop.

The dialog for burning an audio CD is not very different from the dialog for burning a data CD. However, the option 'DiscAtOnce' and the 'TrackAtOnce' mode bear greater importance. The 'TrackAtOnce' modes inserts a silent break of two seconds after each track.

Copying a CD

Select 'Copy CD' from the toolbar. In the following dialog, specify settings for the reading and writing device (Figure 17.3 on the facing page). The options introduced above are also available here. An additional function enables you to create several copies of the CD.

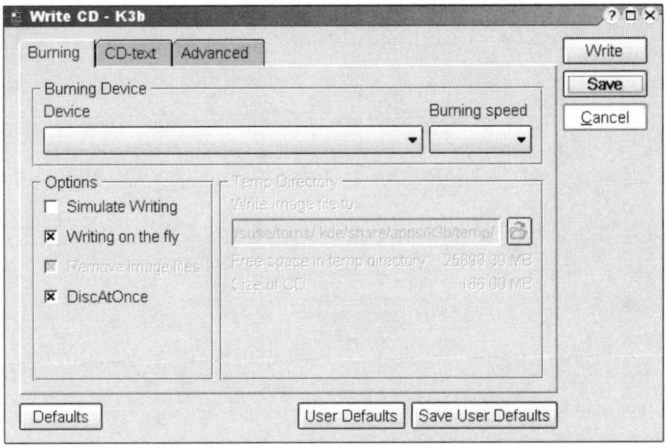

Figure 17.3: The CD Copying Dialog of K3b

For More Information

Apart from the two main functions described above, K3b offers other functions that are not described here. This includes the creation of DVD copies, reading audio data in WAV format, rewriting CDs, or the integrated audio player. A detailed description of all available program features is available at `http://k3b.sourceforge.net`.

Digital Cameras and Linux

A wide range of digital cameras can currently be used with Linux. One of the best programs supporting these devices is gphoto2. gPhoto 2.0 is a command line program, called a "back-end library". It is compatible with several graphical interfaces (the "front-ends"), including gtKam, Konqueror, Kamera, and GnoCam. The use of gtKam and Konqueror is discussed in this chapter.

Tip

A full list of supported cameras is available at `http://www.gphoto.org/cameras.html`. If gphoto2 is installed, obtain the list with the command `gphoto2 --list-cameras`.

`gphoto2 --help` provides information about the available commands in the command-line interface.

Tip

Connecting to the Camera

The fastest and most convenient connection between the digital camera and the computer is USB. This requires USB support both in the camera and in the computer. The default SuSE kernel provides this support, provided your computer has a USB port. An appropriate connecting cable is also required.

Note

Using the USB connection can quickly drain your camera's batteries. Consider using a power adapter.

Note

To use it, simply connect the camera to the USB port. Turn the camera on.

Installation and Preparation

Use YaST to install the gtkam package. The other required packages will be selected automatically. For more information on installing packages with YaST, refer to *Install and Remove Software* on page 47.

Using Konqueror

For KDE users, accessing a digital camera through Konqueror provides a familiar interface and easy access. Connect your camera to the USB port. A camera icon should appear on the desktop. Double-click this icon to open the camera in Konqueror. The camera can also be accessed by entering the URL `camera:/` in Konqueror. Navigate through the camera's directory structure until the files are shown. Use the usual Konqueror file management features to copy the files as desired. More information about using Konqueror is available in *Konqueror — The KDE File Manager and Web Browser* on page 191.

Using gtKam

gtKam is compatible with all window managers. It is a fast and simple graphical interface for downloading and deleting pictures from the digital camera. To adjust or edit your pictures, use The GIMP as described in *Graphics with The GIMP* on page 281.

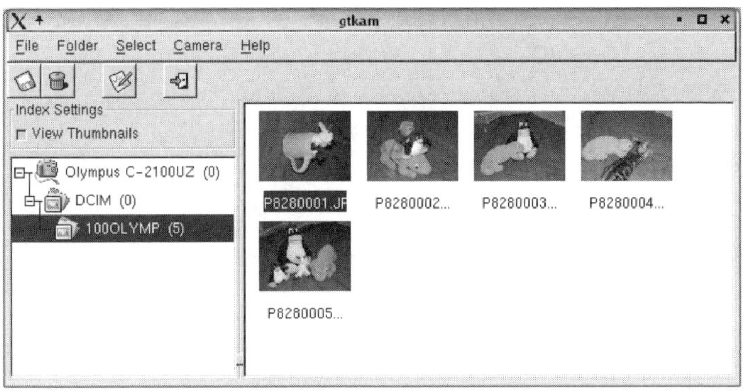

Figure 18.1: *The Main Window of gtKam*

Connect your camera to the appropriate port and turn it on. Start gtKam with the command `gtkam &`. From the menus, select 'Camera' → 'Select Camera...'. In the dialog, select the camera model or use 'Detect'. Select the appropriate port if not detected.

The main gtKam window is divided into three sections the menu and toolbars, the left pane with index settings and camera and directory selection, and the right pane for displaying an index listing with or without thumbnails. The icons in the toolbar provide the main functions needed. The disk icon saves the selected images. The trash icon deletes them. The icon with the arrows reloads the image index displayed in the right pane. The icon with the paper and pencil opens the camera configuration options. The door icon exits the program.

Your camera should be listed in the left pane. Use the plus sign ('+') to the left to expand the tree display of the directory structure. Your exact directory stucture depends on the camera make and model. Continue expanding until you reach the entries that cannot be expanded. Those are the index listings of the actual pictures. Click an item to select it. If 'View Thumbnails' is activated, the picture names and thumbnails will be displayed in the right window pane. Otherwise, the names and an icon are displayed.

Images in the right pane can be selected or deselected by clicking them. Select all images with 'Select' → 'All' or ⇑ Shift + A. Use the disk icon in the toolbar, 'File' → 'Save Selected Photos...', or Ctrl + S to save the selected images. The 'Save' dialog, shown in Figure 18.2 on the facing page, has a number of options. Under 'What to Save', select whether to save the thumbnails, the images, or both. With 'Open image(s) with:', you can both save the image and open it in another program. To open the images in The GIMP immediately, enter `gimp`. Using the file names provided by the camera is recommended.

For More Information

For more information about using digital cameras with Linux, refer to the following web sites.

- http://www.gphoto.org Information about gPhoto, gPhoto2, and gPhoto2-compatible GUIs
- http://www.thekompany.com/projects/gphoto/ Information about Kamera, a KDE front-end for gPhoto2
- `http://www.stud.uni-karlsruhe.de/\char126{}urc8/GnoCam/` GnoCam information

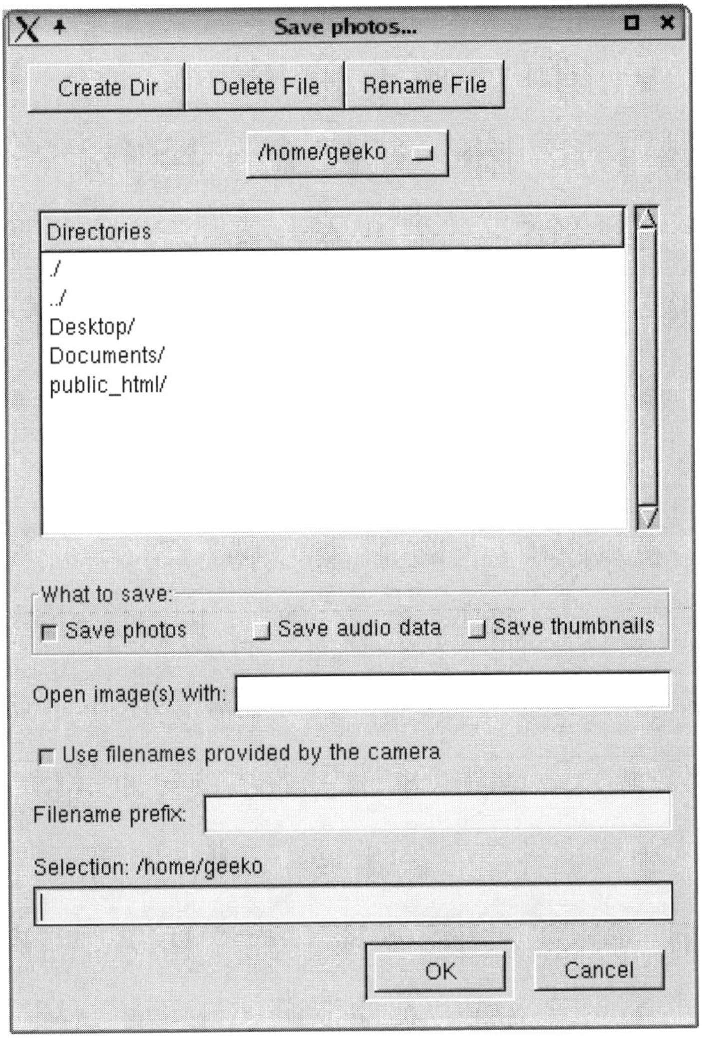

Figure 18.2: Saving Images

Kooka — The Scanning Application

Kooka is a graphical scanning application combining the simplicity of operating xscanimage with the functional breadth of XSane, incorporating the easy and user-friendly operation common in KDE applications. Kooka is a KDE application with integrated SANE system libraries. The SANE package must be installed to use Kooka. This chapter consists of two parts. The first part includes a short description of the Kooka application. The second part outlines some general scanning tips.

Refer to `http://www.mostang.com/sane` for information about which scanners are supported and the status of driver development. Check this before purchasing a scanner, if possible.

Start Window

Start Kooka from a console with the command `kooka`. If desired, create a link to the application on your KDE desktop. When Kooka starts, it first opens a two-frame window with a menu bar and a toolbar. Optionally, include an additional window with a thumbnail view of an image directory. Use the mouse to enlarge or reduce the windows as needed. If desired, separate an individual window entirely from the Kooka window and move it to a location of your choice on the desktop. To move the windows, click the thin double line above the respective window and drag it with the mouse. Rearrange windows as desired. If a window is placed centrally over another window, both windows have the same size, are superimposed, and can be selected with tabs.

Use tabs to toggle between the preview window and the gallery view. The latter is a small file browser that assists in easily saving scanned images. For more information about the tabs 'Gallery' and 'Preview', see *Save* on page 276.

Use the scanner-dependent part of your window to modify certain scanner-specific settings. At the bottom, see the two buttons for generating a preview and for starting the final scan. The scanned image appears in the large window to the right ('Image'), which is the only window that cannot be moved. The last window is for thumbnail display of the respective directory of the gallery.

For the sake of better understanding, these sections assume the gallery and the preview window are located at the top left and the scanner settings at the bottom left. The image viewer and thumbnail view are to the right.

The Preview

Figure 19.1 on the facing page diplays the preview window at the top left and the size and orientation settings next to it. By pressing 'Preview Scan' (bottom left), the image in the scanner is test scanned and appears in the preview window. This preview scan does not generate a file. 'Final Scan' activates the actual scanning process to create a file, but only use it after making the appropriate settings.

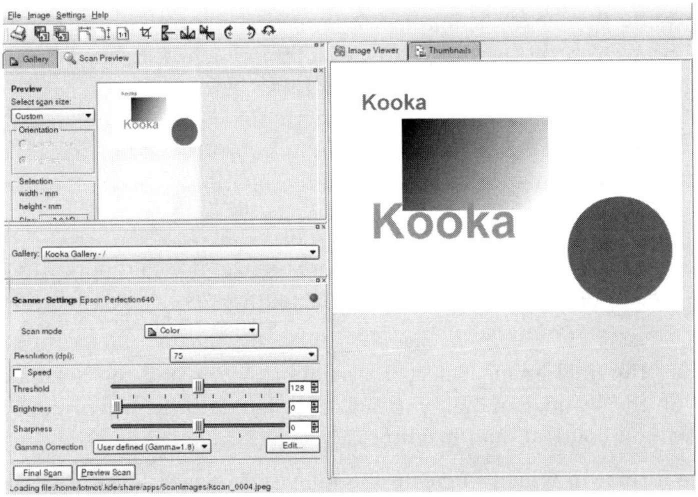

Figure 19.1: The Kooka Control Window

Find information regarding the size and memory requirements of your image in the upper left section under the document's size and orientation information. Use the preview window to define the scanning range and for adjusting the gamma value, brightness, and contrast. Do not assume that the printout will look exactly like the preview display. Correctly adjusting the monitor, scanner, and printer is a difficult procedure.

Scanning the Preview

Before scanning a preview, set the mode for generating the preview in the window containing the scanner settings (bottom left in our example). 'Color' and 'Gray' are self-explanatory. 'Binary' means that only black and white are used, without any gray tones. This option only makes sense for the preview if only pure text or black-and-white graphics are involved. It is required to perform a final scan of an image or text for text recognition purposes (see *The Final Scan*). The resolution and other settings in the window below especially affect the final scan.

Scan size and orientation can also be defined in the upper left section, if 'Preview' is selected. The size is given below in both `mm` and `KB` or `MB`. If you select 'User defined' as your scan size, you cannot choose the orientation. Mark the display window after the preview scan to define the area to scan.

This is usually the most sensible mode. After all settings are adjusted, press 'Preview Scan' to scan the image preview. Subsequently, a small version of the image will appear in the preview window.

The Final Scan

If you selected 'User defined' for the scanning size, use the mouse to highlight the rectangular area to scan. The selected area is marked with dotted borders.

To generate the final image, select the scanning mode and the resolution. Depending on the scanner model, you will be offered additional options such as gamma values, contrast, and brightness.

Select the format in which to create the image. To generate future scans in the same format without confirmation, mark 'Don't ask again' then click 'OK'. Reconfigure this under 'Settings' → 'Configure Kooka' → 'Image Saving'.

The image appears in full size in the image window to the right. The size shown varies depending on the scanning area and resolution selected. If you selected a higher resolution, you will probably only see part of the image displayed to the right. In the right-hand window, scale the displayed area to your preferences.

The Menus

The toolbar functions can be found under the 'File' and 'Image' menus. Modify Kooka settings under 'Settings' → 'Configure Kooka'. Under 'Tool Views', display or hide the individual windows.

Under 'File', find 'Print...', which opens a print assistant, and 'Quit'. The option 'Open image in graphic application' is located under 'Image'. A description of these menu items follows.

Open image in graphic application
: Select an application for viewing the scanned image using a file browser or a command line. The GIMP is very useful for this purpose, but it is not included in the default package selection.

Character Recognition (OCR) image...
Opens the window for optical character recognition (OCR). If you have gocr installed, the path `/usr/bin/gocr` should be specified in the path line. This application then allows you to start the character recognition for the preview image or for the selection highlighted in the preview image.

OCR on selection...
Opens the character recognition window for the area marked in the final scan. See *Character Recognition with gocr*.

Scale to Width
Use this option to scale the image in the main image display to fit the width of the window.

Scale to Height
Scales the image to the full height of the image display.

Original Size
Resets the image in the display to its original scanned size.

> **Note**
>
> Access more possibilities for scaling the image display by right-clicking the image. The options include the three options previously mentioned along with options for enlarging it to your own specifications. You can also do the same in the preview window.
>
> **Note**

Create from selection
If you did not accurately select the area for the image in the small preview window, use this tool to crop your image permanently by marking a selection in the large image display to the right then clicking this tool. See the results to the right.

Mirror image vertically
Flips the image vertically.

Mirror image horizontally
Flips the image horizontally.

Mirror image both directions
Flips the image vertically and horizontally at the same time.

Rotate image clockwise
Rotates the image clockwise by 90°.

Rotate image counterclockwise:
Rotates the image counterclockwise by 90°.

Rotate 180 degrees
Rotates the image by 180°

Save

Saving images in Kooka is somewhat different from methods to which you may be accustomed. Clicking the 'Gallery' tab in the upper left window shows a small file browser depicting the gallery. It shows the content of the directory `~/.kde/share/apps/ScanImages/`.

This is where all scanned images are initially saved as files. `ScanImages` is the only directory that exists when you first start Kooka. Subfolders can be created by right-clicking this main folder. The selected folder (highlighted in blue) is the first location to which scanned images are saved. The images will be named in the format `kscan_0001`, `kscan_0002`, etc., and be assigned consecutive numbers.

To save the image, click the name. Now, give it a new name and assign the correct file ending — the format in which the image was scanned. If you specify the wrong ending, receive an error message notifying you that the ending does not correspond to the format in which the image was scanned. Currently Kooka does not support "on-the-fly" conversion.

If you do not want to manage your images under `~/.kde/share/apps/ScanImages/`, save your images to another location. To do this, right-click the name of image and select 'Save'. Then enter the path. You can also close or permanently delete the image here. External images you have not scanned yourself can be added to the gallery using Konqueror's drag and drop feature. Start Konqueror (the earth symbol in your KDE bar), go to the directory containing the images to add to your gallery, then simply drag them with the mouse and drop them in the Kooka gallery directory.

Character Recognition with gocr

As mentioned above, you need to install gocr. Once this is done, scan a preview of your document using either gray or color mode. You can also scan in binary mode.

In the preview window, mark the area of the text to recognize. Choose binary mode for the final scan then scan with 'Final Scan'.

Click the second icon from the left inside the toolbar, 'Character recognition image...', or select this menu item from the 'Image' menu. For the first try, do not modify the default settings in the OCR window that opens (Figure 19.2). These settings suit most users' needs. Now click 'Start character recognition'. A window like that in Figure 19.3 on the following page shows the results of the character recognition. The quality largely depends on that of the document itself.

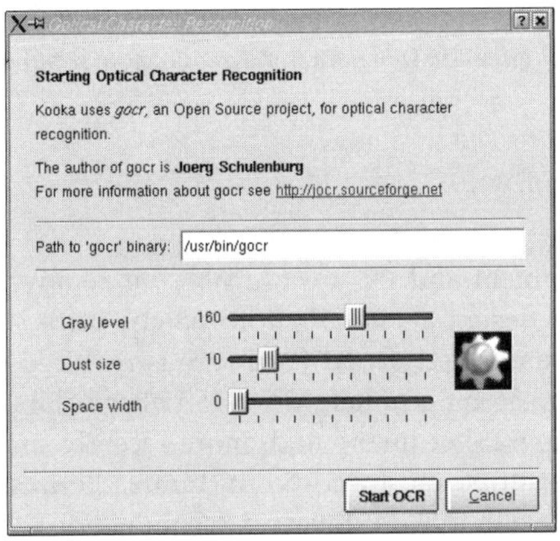

Figure 19.2: The gocr Window

If you only want to submit part of the text or image after the final scan in binary mode, mark your selection in the image display to the right. Then click the third button from the right in the toolbar or select 'Image' → 'Character recognition on selection'. Proceed as described in the previous paragraph.

Some Scanning Tips

Although Kooka is very easy to use, scanning can be very tricky, especially with scanners featuring numerous setting options or when trying to scan low-quality documents. As a beginner, expect to do some experimenting until the results meet your satisfaction. A perfect color printout of your favorite picture requires time and practice.

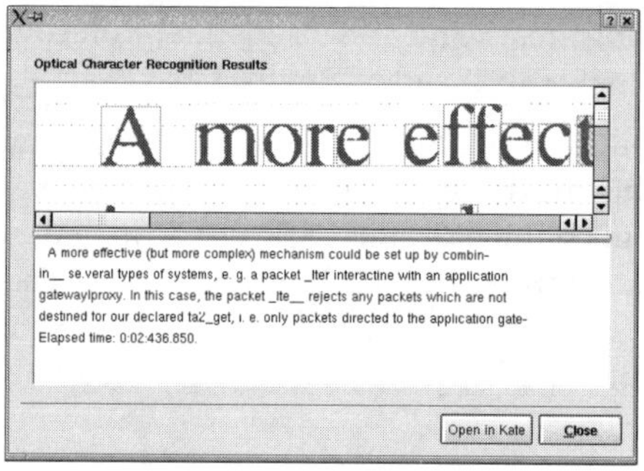

Figure 19.3: *Character Recognition Results*

Hardware

Your scanning equipment and PC are probably far removed from those of a professional graphic design agency. Unfortunately, price is also a factor in the performance of these devices. Good hardware is required for successful and convenient scanning. 36-bit scanners provide richer colors and gray scales than 24-bit scanners. SCSI scanners and, more recently, an increasing number of USB scanners are supported by SANE in Linux. Because of their overall better quality, purchasing a SCSI device is recommended. The configuration of a USB scanner with YaST2 has become really simple.

Some companies offer Linux drivers for parallel port scanners. However, the functionality and quality is currently unknown. If using a SCSI scanner, you need a controller for it. Most SCSI scanners are sold together with a simple controller card of minimal functionality. Refer to the web pages of the SANE project before buying a scanner to check the development status of the available drivers.

Large images — manipulated or in their original format — may, under certain circumstances, require extensive memory space. Therefore, your computer should have at least 64 MB RAM, preferably 128 MB or more. The faster the CPU, the quicker your data can be processed. However, you do not need a high-end device. A middle-of-the-road one should do for household use. For an adequate display of the images on your desktop, you will also need a graphics card capable of depicting the right color depth in high resolutions.

Resolutions

A scanner resolution of 75 to 100 ppi is sufficient for scanning a simple photograph and viewing it on your screen. Screens usually have a default resolution of 75 dpi. A higher ppi value for scanning only uses more storage space without enhancing the screen display.

If you are not yet sure how you want to use your image later or if you simply want to create an image file, scan with a resolution of 150 ppi. A higher resolution most often leads to immense memory consumption. There may be times when you would want to scan a section of an image with a higher resolution, but this is not needed for normal photographs. Most graphics applications can save an image with lower resolution if needed.

To scan an image at a ratio of 1:1 for a printout, it is generally recommended to set the scanning resolution to 1.6–2 times the printer resolution is generally recommended. A normal laser printer usually produces 75 lpi. If you have a printer of this type, you should set 120 to 150 ppi for scanning according to this multiplication factor. To generate images for display on the Internet, the default resolution of 75 dpi is sufficient.

To use your printer to enlarge pictures, you will need an extremely high dpi setting. When making the enlargement, the scanner resolution should be multiplied by the magnification factor. Doing this, you will quickly approach the interpolated resolution range. Using the example above, a five-fold magnification would require ppi settings of 750 or more. As scanners usually cannot reach such high physical dpi values, the values are calculated by the software.

Note

The printer resolution is usually stated in dpi ("dots per inch"), the halftone resolution of the printer in lpi ("lines per inch"), and the scanner resolution in ppi ("pixels per inch").

Note

Adjusting Brightness and Contrast

The desktop display does not necessarily reflect the actual print results. It is only an approximation. It is generally recommended to set slightly higher brightness and contrast values for a black-and-white or color printout. You do not have to specify these values when scanning unless you want to print the scanned image directly. Otherwise, wait to make these settings later in The GIMP.

Strange Patterns in the Image

When scanning documents from print (books, magazines, newspapers), the individual pixels that comprise the image may produce a "Moiré pattern". Kooka cannot remove this pattern. In The GIMP, find a filter for removing the Moiré pattern under 'Filter' → 'Enhance' → 'Despeckle'. It works at the cost of a certain degree of clarity.

Tip

If your scan produces in a repeating pattern, try rotating the document five to ten degrees and scanning it again. Later, reset the image to its original orientation in The GIMP. Often, this gives better results than using the enhancement filter to despeckle.

Tip

Graphics with The GIMP

GIMP (*G*NU *I*mage *M*anipulation *P*rogram) is a very powerful program for the processing of pixel graphics. GIMP is the first choice for retouching or modifying photographs and other image files. Once you are familiar enough with the program, you will even be able to create entire images from scratch. An average user, however, will not need all of the powerful functions of GIMP. It can even be used for free-style painting. All tools, such as brush, pencil, or airbrush, are available (see Figure 20.1 on the next page). Frequent users of these features should definitely consider acquiring a graphics tablet.

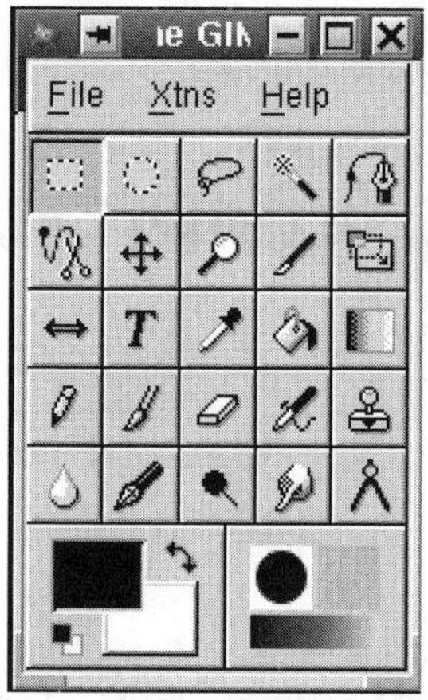

Figure 20.1: The GIMP Toolbox: The Default Window

Taking into account the power and performance of GIMP and the prices for commercial 'professional' graphics programs, it soon becomes evident that the GNU Image Manipulation Program is a phenomenal gift to the Linux community. As with so many Linux programs, GIMP is under constant development.

This introduction cannot cover the whole range of features. The "official GIMP manual" has 924 pages and is available on the Internet at http://manual.gimp.org. Unfortunately, some of its descriptions and illustrations are outdated, because GIMP has undergone extensive development since the manual was written. The internal help system, still under development, also provides valuable assistance to the new user.

Note

The version included in this distribution and discussed in this manual is the most recent release of the stable 1.2 series. The unstable GIMP 1.3 series is not intended for regular users. It is only intended for those involved in developing GIMP itself.

Note

Image Processing and Graphics Formats

Pixel Images

GIMP has been designed for processing pixel graphics. These images consist of small blocks of color that together create the entire image. A full-screen image on a monitor of 800×600 resolution has exactly that number of pixels. It contains 480,000 individual pixels. Considering this, it is not surprising that image files are generally quite bulky. In addition to the coordinates of each pixel, the color information is stored. With an image of 800×600 pixels, it is easy to get more than one MB of data. From the outset, therefore, much time and energy has been invested in developing compression procedures that squeeze the amount of information together. Some well-known graphics file formats for pixel images include:

XCF The native GIMP format. It supports the layer technique discussed later and other specific GIMP functions. If you have created an image using the GIMP-specific settings and save it in a different file format, information is lost.

BMP A format without compression used by Microsoft Windows. An advantage of this format is that graphics can be loaded and saved very quickly, but this positive aspect is outweighed by the file size.

GIF The "*G*raphics *I*nterchange *F*ormat" has been specially developed for data transfer on the Internet and has special features to support this. For licensing reasons, many programs are no longer able to support this format. One special feature of GIF is the animated Gif, a GIF file in which several images are stored. In an Internet browser, these individual images are displayed so quickly one after the other that the impression of a moving image is created. GIF, despite its limitations, is popular predominantly because it allows transparency.

PNG The "*P*ortable *N*etwork *G*raphics" is a popular replacement for the GIF format. It can generate the same quality of compressed files without loss of information and is freely available. It allows a better form of transparency, but is not yet fully supported by all Internet browsers.

PSD This format is used by the professional Adobe Photoshop application and supports the multilayer technique.

TIFF The " *T*agged *I*mage *F*ile *F*ormat" is yet another method of saving files in the professional arena. It is particularly popular in the printing business.

JPEG The compression method of the "*J*oint *P*hotographic *E*xperts *G*roup" allows a highly efficient reduction of image files. Depending on the compression factor, image information is lost. Nevertheless, it is an ideal file format for images on the Internet.

Tip

Always save an XCF version of images you create. This makes future modifications much easier.

Tip

Vector Graphics

Unlike pixel graphics, vector graphics do not store information on all individual pixels. Instead they store information on how image points, lines, or areas are grouped together. A line that runs horizontally across the screen, representing a total of 800 pixels, only needs four information units: the coordinates of the starting point, the coordinates of the end point, the information that these two points are connected by a line, and, possibly, the color of the line. With four coordinates and four lines connecting them, you can easily create a rectangle. The fact that this rectangle is filled with a specific color basically requires just one more information unit. In this way, even complex images can be represented with relatively little basic information. The drawing application of OpenOffice.org, for example, uses this format.

Using The GIMP

Starting The GIMP

By default, GIMP is included in the standard installation of SuSE Linux. Start GIMP with 'SuSE' → 'Multimedia' → 'Graphics' → 'GIMP' or by typing `gimp` in a command line. When GIMP is newly installed, some postinstallation procedures are conducted when it is first started for a user. The left button in the bottom part of dialog box that opens is the 'Install' button. Click this button then, in the following dialog box, click 'Continue'. GIMP is then correctly installed and set up.

Since many files need to be loaded when it first starts, GIMP takes some time to load. By default, a window is displayed after each start showing the 'Tip of the Day'. If desired, deactivate it by unchecking the 'Show tip next time' box on the left.

The Toolbox

Initially, GIMP appears on screen in a rather unspectacular way. It opens a relatively small window containing the toolbox. The buttons of this window are the main functions needed for powerful image manipulation. The following is a description of the icons and their functions.

GIMP toolbox window can be subdivided into three parts: the menu bar with the 'File', 'Xtns' (Extensions), and 'Help' menus; the tool icons; the color, pattern, and brush selection icons.

The Menu Bar

The menu bar can be been in Figure 20.1 on page 282. Use 'File' for creating a new graphics file, loading an existing image with the file manager, creating screenshots (screenshots are images of sections of your screen), setting basic options, and accessing the most recently processed files. The main items under the 'Xtns' menu are Modules, Plug-ins additional programs linked into GIMP that implement a specific graphical functionality, Scripts, and GIMP web pages. The 'Help' menu contains various ways of accessing help information.

The Tool Icons

Each graphic in the toolbox represents a specific function. The toolbox can be resized both in width and height. Overall, a distinction can be made between three or four function areas.

Selection Tools
In image processing, you will want to process either the whole image or only a specific section of it. GIMP needs know to which area the following actions should be applied. Several selection tools will help define a specific area. Once a selection has been made, it can be processed without affecting other parts of the image. Selection areas can also be increased or decreased in size with the aid of ⇑ Shift (additive selection) and Ctrl (subtractive selection). The cursor changes to show a plus or a minus sign.

Transform Tools
These functions are used to modify selections. Many functions are available, including crop, flip, and transform.

Paint Tools

The paint tools represent pencil, paintbrush, airbrush, pen, and finger (smudge) and try to emulate their real-world properties on the PC.

A fourth functional area to be classed with these three areas might include the color, fill, and brush options, which specify the paint color or the tip of the painting tool.

Tip

One click on a tool icon activates the tool. A double-click opens an additional window with the option settings for the specific tool.

Tip

The Selection Tools

Rectangular select is the simplest selection tool. By keeping the left mouse button pressed and dragging the mouse at the same time, a rectangular area is marked. When you release the mouse button, a frame indicates the selected area. If you press (⇧ Shift) after you begin drawing the selection, only perfect squares can be selected.

This tool works like rectangular select, except it selects a circular or elliptical area. It is used in the same way, except pressing (⇧ Shift) after you begin selecting limits the selection to perfect circles.

This is the first usable selection tool for photographs. The lasso allows a free-hand selection of an irregular shape. Press the left mouse button and follow the shape as required. When you release the mouse button, the start point and end point are joined with a straight line. An accurate selection is difficult, so working with an enlarged image is recommended.

The magic wand fuzzy selection tool selects an image area through color similarity of adjacent pixels. If the default settings are not suitable, either change the threshold value in the option box or combine several selections using (⇧ Shift). The magic wand is ideal for selecting irregular areas of similar color.

With a bit of effort, the Bezier Curves tool allows you to capture specific areas or objects of an image. With the aid of anchor points set with mouse clicks, draw clean, curved lines. One advantage of this technique is that you can change the selection with the aid of control points. Once you have marked the area required, just click inside it and it will be selected. This tool requires some practice to master, but is invaluable for more advanced work. Selections made with this tool can also be saved and manipulated with the 'Paths' tab of the Layers, Channels, and Paths dialog.

As you click, Intelligent Scissors tries to draw a selection along color or brightness edges. Sometimes it works quite well. Modify the settings in the option box.

Transformation Tools

When Move is activated, grab and move your selection with the mouse.

The magnifier is not a true transformation tool because it only zooms the screen representation in or out. The image itself is not changed. To use the zoom out function, which reduces the image on the screen by a certain percentage, press and hold (Ctrl) while clicking with the mouse.

For a true enlargement of your image, open the context menu with a right-click in your image and select 'Image' → 'Scale Image'. In the dialog box that opens, change the height and width of the image by percentages or by pixel values.

Crop and resize your image. For an aesthetically pleasant impression for landscape photographs, for example, it is recommended to assign the sky one-third and the landscape two-thirds of the image height. Using the mouse, click and drag to open a rectangle. A click inside this rectangle crops the surrounding area. You can always undo this immediately by (Ctrl) + (Z). Take your time to experiment with this tool. You can also change the size of this rectangle. Resize the section by grabbing and moving the top left or bottom right corners. The whole rectangle can be moved by grabbing and moving the bottom left or top right corners.

This icon hides a multitude of functionalities that might confuse a beginner. Either process the whole image by clicking the tool icon first then the image or a portion by first making a selection then clicking the tool icon.

Four functions are available: rotate the image or the selection around an arbitrary rotation point, enlarge or reduce (Scaling), convert a rectangle into a trapezoid (Shearing), or distort the perspective of an area. The default setting is Rotation. Other functions can be specified in the option box opened by double-clicking the tool icon.

A simple tool that flips (mirrors) the selected area horizontally or vertically.

Once you have modified your whole image or a selection with the aid of a transformation tool, reconnect this floating selection to the image. Prior to this integration, you can still modify the result of your transformations. There are several possibilities for integrating the changes into the image. Use the anchor layer keyboard shortcut (Ctrl + H), click in the image somewhere outside the selection, or choose a different selection tool and apply it.

Paint Tools

The first few tools in the following list are somewhat different from the other paint tools. They are included in this section, however, because they are used to add colors or text rather than modify it. The main paint tools provided by GIMP have particular properties in the real world that are emulated by the program. Set the appropriate options to simulate various pencils or to adjust the paintbrush to your personal requirements. In the option boxes of the paint tools, find the slider 'Opacity'. This is used to set the opacity of the color employed. With the 'Mode' drop-down box, specify how painted lines or surfaces should be integrated into the image. Depending on the tool, the different modes have different effects.

The T stands for text input. In GIMP, text input is done in two ways and many options are available. Double-click the tool to open the option box. By activating or deactivating the 'Use Dynamic Text' button, select multiline text input with alignment or single line text input. A click in the image with the T tool activated opens the corresponding dialog box in which to enter text and select font, size, and other parameters.

Caution

If you do not save the text in a separate layer, you will later be unable to modify it because it is integrated into your image in pixel form. See Section *Layers* on page 295 for more information.

Caution

GIMP provides a relatively simple text tool. Many text effects, such as shadows or gradients, must theoretically be input by hand. In practice, however, 'Script-Fu' and the 'Filters' submenu provide many automatic modification procedures, which have, in part, been specifically designed for use with text.

The color picker allows a controlled selection of a color from your image and transfers it to the color selection box. When you click a specific color in the image with the color picker tool, this color is selected. With it, quickly find, for example, a specific skin tone needed to retouch a photograph.

With the paint bucket, fill a selected area with color. Instead of a color, it can also fill with a pattern. Prior to the filling action, activate 'Pattern Fill'. Everything in the selection is then painted over with the selected settings.

The icon represents a color or grayscale gradient. GIMP has several predefined gradients to use to fill the selected area. This tool is relatively complicated and requires some practice, especially if you want to overlay an image with transparent color gradients.

The pencil is a painting tool with which every user is familiar. With the virtual pencil as with a real pencil draw free-hand lines. The type of line the width and shape of the pencil point is selected with the brush dialog. Either double-click the brush icon in the bottom right corner of the toolbox or select 'File' → 'Dialogs' → 'Brushes'. Pencil points are available that do not actually exist in the real world. Make your pencil point extra-fine or extra-thick or select one of the special shapes.

The paintbrush draws with a softer, more liquid effect than the pencil. In the appropriate option box, set a fade out (the color intensity slowly diminishes while painting) or a gradient (selection via the gradient setting options). When the fade out option is activated, release the paintbrush and begin again to apply more color.

The eraser erases. It also unerases. The brush selection also sets the shape of the eraser.

The airbrush allows you to work in the same way as with a real airbrush. Change the 'Pressure' and use the many different brush settings.

This tool is ideal for use with a pressure-sensitive graphics tablet.

The clone tool (the icon represents a rubber stamp) is the ultimate instrument for photo retouching. It can be used to specify parts of images that are then cloned. In practice, this means that you specify very precisely which part of the image to copy where and in what form. This has relatively little to do with the 'Cut' and 'Paste' functions. It uses the paint functionality, allowing you to set shape and opacity of your imaginary rubber stamp.

Things become interesting, for example, if you have an old photograph with white stains. Activate the Clone tool and, if needed, its option box. Keep ⇑ Shift held down and click the image area to use for the copy. Then release the mouse button and place the cursor on the damaged image area. If you now press the left mouse button and move the mouse, the image area marked in the first step of the procedure is inserted. When you move the mouse upwards, the area being copied moves upwards, too. The point is marked by a crosshair. Depending on the brush settings, a small or a large radius is copied and, depending on the tool settings, copying is carried out in a translucent or opaque manner. You will need this quite frequently to retouch photographs. You can, for example, eliminate unwanted text from scanned images or even skin blemishes from portraits.

The Convolver tool (the icon shows a drop of water) is used for precise manual blurring or sharpening of image parts. Which of the two actions is active is set in the option box. The brush selection determines size and borders of the manipulation area. Blurring lays a kind of haze over the image or, as when using a drop of water on a water color painting, blurs the "painted" areas. Sharpening is the opposite. Here the program attempts to increase the contrast and make a neater separation of edges. Sharpening works very well if you later look at your image from a distance. It also means a loss of information, however. Seen from very close up, the images look extremely pixellated.

The pen can be used not only for drawing, but also for calligraphy. Writing well, however, can only be achieved with the aid of a graphics tablet. In the tool settings, adapt the shape of the pen to your own requirements.

The tool icon that looks like a pin is, in reality, a thin wooden stick with a glued-on opaque cardboard circle. Such an instrument is needed in a photographic laboratory for the perfect exposure of a manual paper copy. Since only a small part of the negatives (or positives) is exposed perfectly, this instrument is moved over the areas that would otherwise become too dark while the paper is being exposed. Thus, the exposure of specific problem areas can be adjusted individually. The opposite is a piece of cardboard with a little hole in it for postexposure. Both functions are fulfilled by this GIMP tool. Dodge (make lighter) individual image areas or burn (make darker) them. To create soft transitional borders, use a diffuse brush shape.

The finger shown in this tool icon moves over the color just applied to the paper and smudges it. This can be used to create very interesting effects.

With the calipers, measure distances and angles. In the associated option box, activate the 'Use Info Window' button.

Color, Brush, Pattern, and Gradient Selection

The selected colors, brush, pattern, and gradient are shown in your toolbox. The color selection functions are on the left. On the right are the currently active brush shape , the active pattern , and the active gradient . A click on each of these opens a dialog window for individual configuration.

Working with The GIMP

Opening Images

You have, for example, stored a scanned image or an image from the Internet on your hard disk and want to work on it with GIMP. Click 'File' → 'Open' or Ctrl + O to open GIMP file manager dialog, shown in Figure 20.2 on the following page).

On the left-hand side, change to a different directory by double-clicking. On the right-hand side, the files are listed. The file list is sorted alphabetically. Individual sorting by file type or date is not possible. A handy feature is the small integrated preview window. If GIMP recognizes the file format, see a thumbnail picture of the currently selected file. Double-click the file name or click 'OK' to open the image.

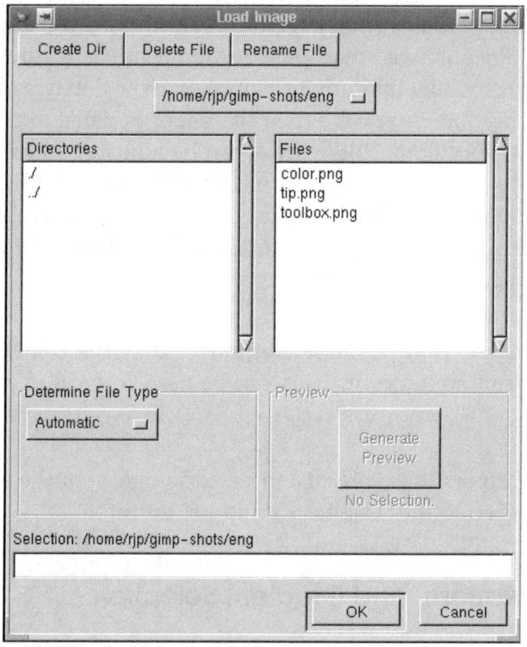

Figure 20.2: Load Images

For convenience, GIMP works with an image in a separate image window completely independent from the window containing the tool icons. You can move the image window around on your screen and, if needed, change its size and zoom settings independently.

Creating a New Image

To create a new image, select 'File' → 'New' or press Ctrl + N. A dialog box opens in which to specify several image attributes (see Figure 20.3 on the next page). The most important ones are width and height, usually represented in pixels, image type, and fill type. If you specify a width of 800 and a height of 600 pixels and your screen resolution has the same value, you can use your painted image later as a full-size background image. In the 'Fill Type' selection area, select the type of fill to use in the new image: the current foreground or background color, white, or transparent. By default, transparent areas are rendered with gray checks.

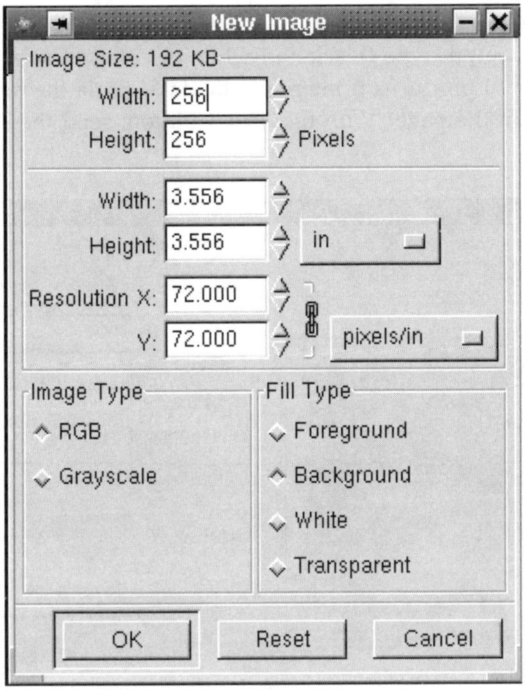

Figure 20.3: Creating a New Image

Saving Images

Save with the mouse or Ctrl + S. When using the mouse, right-click inside the image to open the context menu of the image. To save your image, activate 'File' → 'Save'. If you have already assigned a name to the image, it is saved under that name. If not, GIMP file manager opens and lets you specify the required file name and path. With 'Determine file type', specify which image format GIMP should use for saving. Use a correct file extension. In theory, it is no problem to save a GIF file with a `.TIF` extension. If the file type is set to 'By Extension', GIMP saves in the file type identified by the file extension in the file name.

Printing Images

To print your images, open the context menu with the right mouse button. With 'File' → 'Print', open the print dialog. Select the correct print queue (printer), media size (default setting "Letter"), orientation (auto, portrait, landscape), and output type (black-and-white or color). Use a `raw` queue because GIMP-Print produces printer-specific data. Scale the image and specify its position on the page. With the 'Print' button, send the print job to the printer.

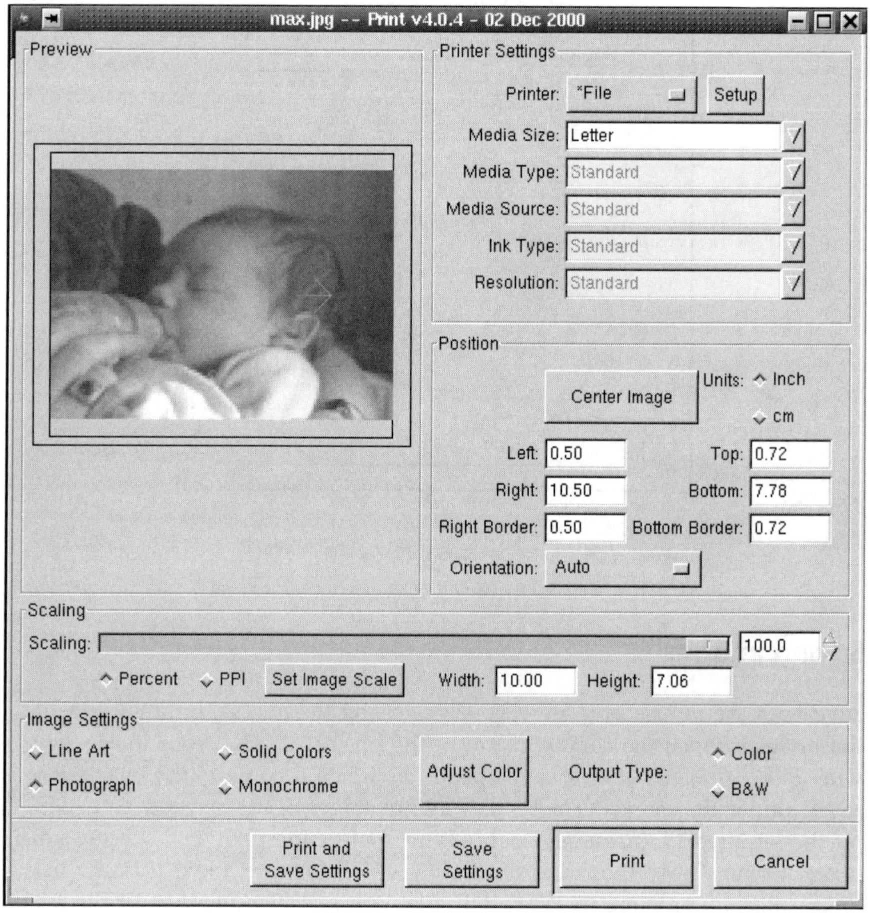

Figure 20.4: *Printing Dialog in GIMP*

Configuring The GIMP

GIMP provides some simple setting options for fast and efficient work. Explore 'File' → 'Preferences' to see the range of options available. Once you are more familiar with GIMP, experiment with the various settings. Refer to the internal help system for advice.

An important setting is the multilevel Undo, used to undo your last actions. To use it, select 'Edit' → 'Undo' in the context menu or press Ctrl + Z. It is important to set how many levels of changes GIMP should save. Set this in the 'Environment' category of the 'Preferences' dialog mentioned previously.

If you memorize the keyboard shortcuts, GIMP is much easier to work with. Change the shortcuts to your individual requirements. Right-click the required menu item and keep the mouse button pressed. Then type the required key combination it is immediately assigned. Avoid repeating shortcuts, as that is possible and will confuse the program.

Tip

Many functions or tool settings have their own windows that you can open and close as needed. On a larger screen, leave frequently needed dialog windows open without any problem.

Tip

Tear-off menus are another outstanding feature of GIMP. Whenever a menu shows a dotted line on top, click this line, detaching the menu from the larger context menu. The menu is then displayed on your desktop in its own window.

Layers

Layers are crucial to using GIMP effectively. They allow you to arrange image contents and more easily edit and modify your image. To store layer information when saving a file, save in GIMP's native format, .XCF. As well as preserving layer information, it also saves GIMP features such as the location of guides.

To understand how layers work, imagine an image created from a stack of transparent sheets. Different parts of the image are drawn on different sheets. The stack can be rearranged, changing which pieces are on top. Individual or groups of layers can shift position, moving sections of the image to other locations. New sheets can be added and others set aside. This is very much how the layers work in GIMP.

By drawing parts of your image on separate layers, you can manipulate, change, or delete those parts without damaging the other parts of the image. Using separate layers for text is the most common usage, but the possibilities are much more extensive.

GIMP includes a layer manager. Access it via 'Layers' → 'Layers, Channels & Paths ' in the context menu then under the 'Layers' tab in the dialog that opens (see Figure 20.5). Here you can create, copy, and delete layers or anchor a layer in the background image. In addition, the eye icon in the layer manager can be used to make layers invisible without losing their information. The icon with four arrows indicates linked layers. Layers showing this icon will be moved as a group.

Under the 'Channels' tab, view the three color channels red, green, and blue individually or in any combination. The 'Paths' tab provides information about paths which have been drawn with the Bezier selection tool.

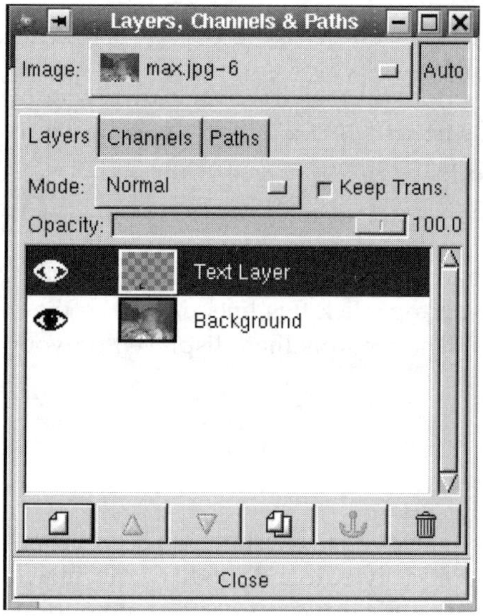

Figure 20.5: Layers, Channels, and Paths Dialog

Image Modes

GIMP has three basic image modes RGB, grayscale, and indexed. RGB is the main color mode usually used in GIMP. Grayscale is for black, white, and gray images. Indexed is used almost exclusively for converting images to the GIF file format. There are a few things to remember when working with image modes:

- Only RGB mode has all the filters available. Most, however, are available in grayscale mode. To run filters on an indexed image, convert to RGB first.
- Convert to indexed only right before saving to image formats that require it, such as GIF. Never work with an image in indexed mode.
- Regardless of any color used on a grayscale image, the color will be desaturated and applied in a shade of gray.
- Study the internal help system for more information about image modes.

Introduction to Image Manipulation

The following sections provide tips for working with your own images. This only introduces a small part of the things possible in GIMP.

Preparing Photographs for Printing

You have, for example, an image of your kids and want to produce a perfect printout on your color printer. Unfortunately, the first printout was not what you expected. The colors were quite bleak and there is a point in the image which is quite dark.

There is a fundamental problem when printing color images. Color and contrast of the image as seen on screen do not correspond to what comes out of your printer. The images on screen are often richer in contrast and more brilliant. Only in professional systems are all components adjusted in such a way that screen representation and future print output match to a high degree. To improve an image, the following manipulations are recommended.

Before you start, create a backup copy of your image. Once you have saved your manipulation, you can no longer recreate the original state. Although these corrections can be made using 'Image' → 'Colors' → 'Brightness-Contrast', better results are obtained through the Levels dialog found in the context menu under 'Image' → 'Colors' → 'Levels'.

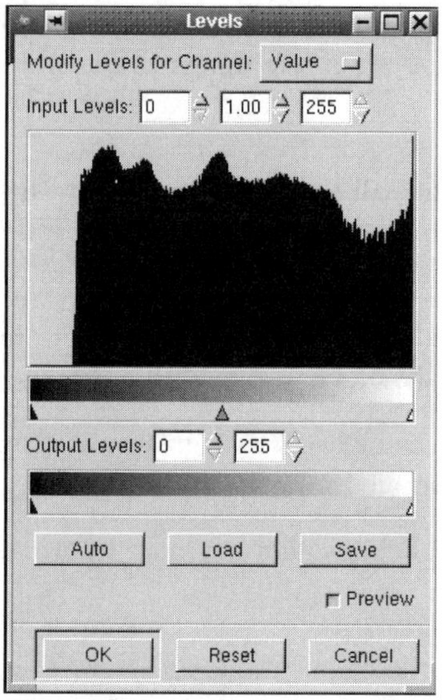

Figure 20.6: *The Levels Dialog*

The Levels Dialog shows how the color values and colors are spread throughout the image (see Figure 20.6). By adjusting the end sliders to where the black areas begin and end, you redistribute them over the entire range of values. This means that somewhere in the image will become completely black, somewhere will be completely white, and the rest of the range will be spread accordingly. Usually, clicking 'Auto' gives acceptable results, but sometimes manual adjustment is needed. To adjust manually, drag the end sliders to where the black area in the graph begins and ends. Do this in each of the channels (select from the drop-down box showing Value as default). This should correct both brightness and contrast problems.

Occasionally, you may need to to sharpen the whole image to obtain a good quality printout. During sharpening, edges and color transitions are emphasized. Right-click and, in the context menu, select 'Filters' → 'Enhance' → 'Sharpen'. Watch the effect in the small preview window and even undo it with (Ctrl) + (Z).

To make individual image areas brighter or darker, use the 'Dodge or Burn' tool from the toolbox. For the best results, select a brush tip with a diffuse border in the brush selection dialog.

Finally, cut the image to size with the 'Crop or resize' tool and print it out.

Special Effects

In the context menu, many different manipulation tools are available under 'Filter' or 'Script-Fu'. These include some easy-to-apply effects. Usually, clicking the filter in the menu opens an option box with which to control the effects of such filters. Refer to the internal help system for descriptions of the filters.

Inserting Text

You can easily integrate text into your images with GIMP. First determine the text color with the aid of the color selection icon in the toolbox. Then activate text input with the T icon and click the image. A dialog box as in Figure 20.7 opens in which to specify your text and the font settings. Depending on which fonts are available on your system, specify a font family in the first selection column. The second column determines style and weight (medium, bold, or italic) and the third column sets the type size. Click 'OK' to add the text to your image. As long as dotted lines surround your lettering, you can move the text. However, once the text is anchored in your image, you can only remove it with 'Undo' as long as you have not saved the image. Put text on its own layer for easy modifications later.

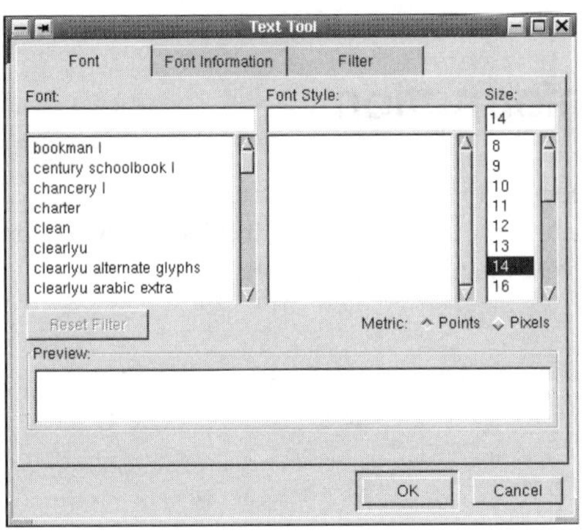

Figure 20.7: Entering Text

In the option box of the text tool, select between a single line of text and a text window with several lines and text alignment. When you activate the

'Use Dynamic Text' button, a click inside the image opens an option box in which to enter and align multiline text.

Retouching Images

The most suitable tool for this purpose is the clone tool. It is represented by a rubber stamp in the tool window. Since we have already explained earlier how this tool functions, some brief hints are sufficient here:

- Set the brush to a medium size with a diffuse border area.
- Work on an enlarged representation of your image.
- Open a second view of the image with 'View' → 'New View' and zoom to 1:1 to see how the changes look.
- Save your work from time to time under a different file name. If you do not like one of your modifications, revert to a previous stage.

Retouching may take some time because you often need to change brushes and redefine the image section to copy. Working with the clone tool requires some experience.

For More Information

There is a very good GIMP web site at `http://www.gimp.org`. There, find and download documentation, plug-ins, and more. Also, 'Important Links' offers an impressive collection of links for GIMP.

Working with the Shell

Graphical user interfaces are increasingly becoming important for Linux, but using the mouse is not always the best way to perform daily tasks. The command line readily provides high flexibility and efficiency. The first part of this chapter provides an introduction to the Bash shell. It is followed by an explanation of the user permissions concept in Linux and a list of the most important commands. The chapter closes with a description of the vi text editor.

Introduction

Text-based applications are especially important for controlling older Linux computers that do not have the resources for demanding display systems. Virtual consoles are used in this case. Six of them are available in text mode. Press (Alt) + (F1) through (Alt) + (F6). The seventh console is reserved for X.

Introduction to Bash

In the KDE taskbar, there is an icon depicting a monitor with a seashell. When you click this icon with the mouse, a console window opens in which to enter commands. The console will normally run Bash (which stands for "Bourne again shell"), a program developed as part of the GNU project. It is by far the most widely used derivative of the Bourne shell (sh). Once you have opened the shell, you will see the prompt on the first line, which usually consists of the user and the host name along with the current path. However, the prompt can also be configured individually. When the cursor is behind this prompt, you can send commands directly to your computer system.

```
newbie@earth:~ >
```

Commands

A command consists of several elements. The first element is always the actual command, followed by parameters or options. Commands are executed when you press (↵). Before doing so, easily edit the command line, add options, or correct typing errors. One of the most frequently used commands is `ls`, which can be used with or without arguments. Entering the plain `ls` command in the console shows the contents of the current directory. Options are prefixed with a hyphen. The command `ls -l`, for instance, shows the contents of the same directory in full detail. Next to each file name, see the date when the file was created, the file size in bytes, and further details discussed below. One very important option that exists for many commands is the `--help` option. By entering `ls --help`, all the options for the `ls` command are displayed.

Also use the `ls` command to view the contents of other directories. To do so, the directory must be specified as a parameter. For example, to see the contents of `Desktop`, enter `ls -l Desktop`.

Files and Directories

To use the shell efficiently, it is really useful to have some knowledge about the file and directory structures of a Linux system. You can think of directories as electronic folders where files, programs, and subdirectories are stored. The top level directory in the hierarchy is the root directory, referred to as /. This is the place from which all other directories can be accessed.

The /home directory contains the home directories of the individual users, where they can put their personal files. Figure 21.1 shows the standard directory tree in Linux, with the home directories of the example users xyz, linux, and tux. The directory tree of a Linux system has a functional structure that follows the "File System Standard". Table 21.1 on the following page provides a brief description of the standard directories in Linux.

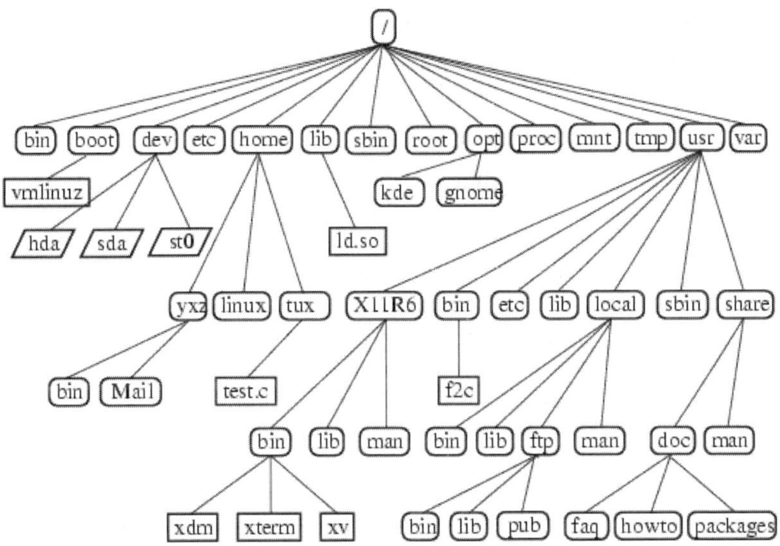

Figure 21.1: Excerpt from a Standard Directory Tree

Directory	Description
/	root directory, starting point of the directory tree
/home	(private) directories of users
/dev	device files that represent hardware components
/etc	important files for system configuration
/etc/init.d	boot scripts
/usr/bin	generally accessible programs
/bin	programs needed early in the boot process
/usr/sbin	programs reserved for the system administrator
/sbin	programs reserved for the system administrator and needed for booting
/usr/include	header files for the C compiler
/usr/include/g++	header files for the C++ compiler
/usr/share/doc	various documentation files
/usr/share/man	system manual pages (man pages)
/usr/src	source code of system software
/usr/src/linux	kernel source code
/tmp	temporary files
/var/tmp	large temporary files
/usr	contains all application programs
/var	configuration files (e.g., those linked from `/usr`)
/var/log	system log files
/var/adm	system administration data
/lib	shared libraries (for dynamically linked programs)
/proc	process file system
/usr/local	local, distribution-independent extensions
/opt	optional software, larger add-on program packages (such as KDE, GNOME, Netscape)

Table 21.1: *Overview of Important Directories*

Bash Functions

There are two important functions of the shell that can make your work a lot easier:

- The history function — To repeat a command that has been entered before, press ⇧ until the previous command appears at the prompt. Move forward through the list of previously entered commands by pressing ⇩. To edit the command line, just move the cursor to the desired position using the arrow keys and start typing. Use Ctrl + R to search in the history.

- The expansion function — Expand a file name to its full length after typing its first letters until it can be uniquely identified. To do so, type the first letters then hit Tab. If there are several file names starting with the same letters, obtain a list of them by hitting Tab twice.

First Example: Managing Files

Now that you know what a command looks like, which directories exist in SuSE Linux, and how to speed up things when using Bash, put this knowledge into practice with a small exercise.

1. Open a console from the KDE desktop by clicking the shell icon.
2. Enter the `ls` command to see the contents of your home directory.
3. Use the command `mkdir` (which stands for "make directory") to create a new subdirectory called `test` by entering `mkdir test`.
4. Now launch the KEdit editor by pressing Alt + F2 and entering "kedit" in the input field. Type a few letters in the editor then save the file as `Testfile` in your home directory. Linux distinguishes between uppercase and lowercase. For this example, use an uppercase T.
5. View the contents of your home directory again. Instead of typing `ls` again, just press ⇧ twice and the `ls` command should reappear at the prompt. To execute the command, hit ↵. The newly created directory `test` should appear in blue letters and `Testfile` in black. This is how directories and files can be distinguished in a console.
6. Move `Testfile` into the subdirectory `test` with the command `mv`. To speed this up, use the expansion function: just enter `mv T` and press the tab key;. As long as there is no other file beginning with this letter in the directory, the shell expands the file name and adds the string "estfile". Otherwise, add a letter or two yourself and test the tab key; each time whether the shell can now expand the name. Finally, type a space then `test` after the expanded file name and press ↵ to execute the command.

7. At this point, Testfile should no longer be in the directory. Check this by entering ls again.

8. To see whether the file has been successfully moved, change into the directory test with the command cd test. Now enter ls again. You should see Testfile in the listing. Change back to your home directory at any point by entering only cd (which stands for "change directory").

9. To make a copy of a file, use cp. For instance, enter cp Testfile Testbackup to copy Testfile to Testbackup. Once again, the command ls can be used to see whether both files are in the directory.

Specifying Paths

When working with files or directories, it is important specify the correct path. However, you do not need to enter the entire (absolute) path to the corresponding file. Rather, you can start from the current directory. A ~ represents your home directory. Accordingly, there are several ways to list the file Testfile in the directory test: either by entering the relative path with ls test/* or by specifying the absolute path with ls ~/test/*. To list the contents of home directories of other users, enter ls ~ username. In the above-mentioned directory tree, one of the sample users is tux. Thus, the command ls ~tux lists the contents of the home directory of tux.

The current directory can always be referred to by putting a dot. The next higher level in the tree is represented by two dots. By entering ls .., see the contents of the parent directory of the current directory. The command ls ../.. shows the contents of the directory two levels higher in the hierarchy.

Second Example: Working with Paths

Here is another example to illustrate how you can move around in the directories of your SuSE Linux system.

- Change into your home directory with the command cd. Then create a directory in it with the name test2 by entering mkdir test2.

- Change into the new directory with cd test2 and create a subdirectory in it with the name subdirectory. To change into it, you can use the expansion function: enter cd su then press (Tab). The shell will expand the rest of the directory name.

- Now try to move the previously created file Testbackup into the current directory (which is subdirectory) without changing the directory again. To achieve this, specify the relative path to that file: mv ../../test/Testbackup .. The dot at the end of this command is required to tell the shell that the current directory is the destination to which the file will be moved. Two dots (..), on the other hand, take you one level up in the directory tree. In our example, ../../ refers to your home directory.

Wild Cards

Another convenience offered by the shell is wild cards. There are four different types of these in Bash:

? Matches exactly one arbitrary character

***** Matches an arbitrary number of characters

[set] Matches one of the characters from the group specified inside the square brackets, which is represented here by the string "set"

[!set] Matches one character other than those identified by "set"

Assuming that your test directory contains the files Testfile, Testfile1, Testfile2, and datafile, the command ls Testfile? lists the files Testfile1 and Testfile2. With ls Test*, the list also includes Testfile. The command ls *fil* shows *all* the sample files mentioned above. Finally, use the set wild card to address all files whose last character is a number: ls Testfile[1-9].

Among the four types of wild cards, the most inclusive one is the asterisk. It could be used to copy all files contained in one directory to another one or to delete all files with one command. The command rm *fil*, for instance, would delete all files in your test directory whose name includes the string "fil".

More or Less

Linux includes two small programs that enable you to view text files directly in the shell. Rather than starting an editor to read a file like Readme.txt, for example, simply enter less Readme.txt and the text is shown in the console window. With (Space), scroll down one page. You can also use

(Page ↑) and (Page ↓) to move forward or backward in the text. To exit from less, press (Q). The program less can also be used to view the output of commands in a more convenient way. To see how this works, read *Redirection* on the current page.

Apart from less, you can also use the older program more. However, it is less convenient because it does not allow you to scroll backwards. One could say you get more with less.

Redirection

Normally, the standard output of the shell is your monitor or — to be more precise — the console window. The standard input device is your keyboard. To redirect the output of a command to a program like less, use a "pipe". To view the list of files in `test`, try the command `ls test | less`. On your console, now view the contents of the directory `test`, as displayed by less. In general, this only makes sense if the output of `ls` is longer than one screen page. For instance, if you try to list the contents of `/dev` with a simple `ls /dev`, only a small part of the list fits into the window. With `ls /dev | less`, on the other hand, scroll through the entire list of files without any problem. The shell also allows you to save the output of a command to a file. As a variation of the above sample command, enter `ls test > listing`. This creates a new file with the name `listing` that contains a list of files and directories in `test`. The command `less listing` lets you view the contents of this file. Conversely, you can take a file and use it as the input of a command. For example, to sort the lines in the previously created test file in alphabetical order, enter `sort < Testfile`. The command `sort` sends its output to the screen — you are shown the contents of that file with the lines sorted according to first letter.

A command like this may come in very handy to arrange the entries of a name list or similar data. To create a file containing the sorted list, the output of the `sort` command needs to be redirected into a file. To try this yourself, create an unsorted list of names in an editor and save it under the name `unsortedlist` in the `test` directory. Then change into `test` and enter the command `sort < unsortedlist > sortedlist`. Finally, view the sorted list with `less`.

Just like the standard output, the standard error output is sent to the console as well. However, to redirect the standard error output to a file named `errors`, you need to append `2> errors` to the corresponding command. On the other hand, both standard output and standard error are saved to one file named `alloutput` if you append `>& alloutput`. Finally, to append the output of a command to an already existing file, the command must be followed by >> instead of a single >.

Archives and Data Compression

Now that you have already created a number of files and directories, consider the subject of archives and data compression. Suppose you want to have the entire `test` directory packed in one file that you can save on a floppy disk as a backup copy or send by e-mail. To do so, use the command `tar` (for "tape archiver"). With `tar --help`, view all the options for the `tar` command. The most important of these options are explained here:

-c (for create) Create a new archive

-t (for table) Display the contents of an archive

-x (for extract) Unpack the archive

-v (for verbose) Show all files on screen while creating the archive

-f (for file) Allows you to choose a file name for the archive file. When creating an archive, this option must always be given as the last one.

To pack the `test` directory with all its files and subdirectories into an archive named `testarchive.tar`, you definitely need the options `-c` and `-f`. For the testing purposes of this example, also add `-v` to follow the progress of the archiving, although this option is not mandatory. After using `cd` to change to your home directory where the `test` directory is located, enter `tar -cvf testarchive.tar test`. After that, view the contents of the archive file with `tar -tf testarchive.tar`. The `test` directory with all its files and directories has remained unchanged on your hard disk. To unpack the archive, enter `tar -xvf testarchive.tar`, but do not try this yet.

For file compression, the obvious choice on Linux is the popular gzip program. Just enter `gzip testarchive.tar`. With `ls`, now see that the file `testarchive.tar` is no longer there and that the file `testarchive.tar.gz` has been created instead. This file is much smaller and therefore much better suited for transfer via e-mail or storage on a floppy.

Now, unpack this file in the `test2` directory created earlier. To do so, enter `cp testarchive.tar.gz test2` to copy the file to that directory. Change to the directory with `cd test2`. A compressed archive with the .tar.gz extension can be "unzipped" with the `gunzip` command. So just enter `gunzip testarchive.tar.gz` , which will result in the file `testarchive.tar`, which then needs to be extracted or "untarred" with `tar -xvf testarchive.tar`. You can also "unzip" and extract a compressed archive in one step by adding the -z option. The complete command would be `tar -xvzf testarchive.tar.gz`. With `ls`, you can see that a new `test` directory has been created with the same contents as your `test` directory in your home directory.

mtools

`mtools` are a set of commands you can use to work with MS-DOS file systems. This is useful, especially when dealing with floppy disks. The commands included in `mtools` allow you to address the first floppy drive as a:, just like under MS-DOS, and the commands are like MS-DOS commands except they are prefixed with an :

`mdir a:` displays the contents of the floppy disk in drive `a:`

`mcopy Testfile a:` copies the file `Testfile` to the floppy disk.

`mdel a:Testfile` deletes `Testfile` in `a:`

`mformat a:` formats the floppy disk in MS-DOS format (using the `fdformat` command).

`mcd a:` makes `a:` your current directory

`mmd a:test` creates the subdirectory `test` on the floppy disk

`mrd a:test` deletes the subdirectory `test` from the floppy disk

Cleaning Up

After this crash course, you should be familiar with the basics of the Linux shell or command line. You may want to clean up your home directory by deleting the various test files and directories using the `rm` and `rmdir` commands.

At the end of this chapter, find a list of the most important commands and a brief description of their functions.

Users and Access Permissions

Since its inception in the early 1990s, Linux has been developed as a multiuser system. Any number of users can work on it simultaneously. This resulted in some notable distinctions from the Microsoft end-user Windows operating systems.

The most important distinguishing feature is the necessity for users to log in to the system before starting a session at their workstation. Each user has a user name with corresponding password. This differentiation of users guarantees that unauthorized users cannot see files for which they have no permission. Larger changes to the system, such as installing new programs, are also usually impossible or restricted for normal users. Only the ☞*root* user, or "superuser", has the unrestricted capacity to make changes to the system and has unlimited access to all files. Those who use this concept wisely, only logging in with full `root` access when necessary, can cut back the risk of unintentional loss of data. Because under normal circumstances only the super user can delete system files or format hard disks, the threat from the "Trojan horse effect" or from accidentally entering destructive commands can be significantly reduced.

File System Permissions

Basically, every file in a Linux file system belongs to a user and a group. Both of these proprietary groups and all others can be authorized to write, read, or execute these files.

A group, in this case, can be defined as a set of connected users with certain collective rights. For example, call a group working on a certain project `project3`. Every user in a Linux system is a member of at least one proprietary group, normally `users`. There can be as many groups in a system as needed, but only `root` is able to add groups. Every user can find out, with the command `groups`, of which groups he is a member.

File Access

Look at how permissions are organized. Initially, concentrate on files only. Permission information can be displayed with the command `ls -l`. The output could read like this:

```
-rw-r----- 1 tux project3 14197 Jun 21 15:03 Roadmap
```

***Output 1:** Sample Output Showing File Permissions*

As shown in the third column, this file belongs to user tux. It is assigned to the group project3. To discover the user permissions of the Roadmap file, the first column must be examined more closely.

This column is comprised of one leading character followed by nine characters grouped in threes. The first of the ten letters stands for the type of listed file system components. The dash (-) shows that this is a file. A directory (d), a link (l), a block device (b), or a character device could also be indicated.

The next three blocks follow a standard pattern. The first three characters refer to whether the file is readable (r) or not (-). A w in the middle portion symbolizes that the corresponding object can be edited and a dash (-) means it is not possible to write to the file. An x in the third position denotes that the object can be executed. Because the file in this example is a text file and not one that is executable, executable access for this particular file is not needed.

In our example, tux has, as owner of the file Roadmap, read (r) and write access (w) to it, but cannot execute it (x). The members of the group project3 can read the file, but they cannot modify it or execute it. Other users do not have any access to this file. Other permissions can be assigned by means of ACLs (Access Control Lists). See *Access Control Lists* on page 316 for details and refer to the chapter *Access Control Lists in Linux* of the *Administration Guide* for further background information.

Directory Permissions

The permissions of directories, which are identified by the d as the first character in the list, use the permissions somewhat differently than described so far. Consider this example:

```
drwxrwxr-x 1 tux project3 35 Jun 21 15:15
       ProjectData
```

Output 2: *Sample Output Showing Directory Permissions*

Here, the owner (tux) and the owner group (project3) of the directory ProjectData is easy to recognize. In contrast to the file access permissions from *File System Permissions* on the current page, the set reading permissions (r) means that the contents of the directory can be shown. The write permission (w) means new files can be created. The executable permission (x) means the user can change to this directory. In the above example, this consequently means that the user tux as well as the members of the group project3 can change to the ProjectData directory (x), view the contents (r) and add new files to it (w). The rest of the users, on the other hand, are given less access. They may enter the directory (x) and browse through it (r), but not insert any new files (w).

Modifying File Permissions

Changing Access Permissions

The permissions of a file or directory can be changed by the owner (and of course by root) with the command chmod, which must be entered together with the parameters specifying the changes to perform and the names of the files in question.

Both parameters are comprised of

1. the categories concerned
   - u (*user*) — owner of the file
   - g (*group*) — group that owns the file
   - o (*others*) — additional users (if no parameter is given, the changes apply to all categories)
2. a character for deletion (-), setting (=), or insertion (+)
3. the abbreviations
   - r —*read*
   - w —*write*
   - x —*execute*

file name or names separated by spaces

If, for example, the user tux in the example 2 on the facing page also wants to grant other users write (w) access to the directory ProjectData, he can do this using the command:

If, however, he wants to deny all users other than himself write permissions, he can do this by entering the command

To prohibit all users from adding a new file to the folder ProjectData, enter

```
newbie@earth:~ >  chmod -w Projektdaten
```

Now, not even the owner can write to the file without first reestablishing write permissions.

Changing Ownership Permissions

Other important commands to control the ownership and permissions of the file system's components are chown (change owner) and chgrp (change group). The command chown can be used to transfer ownership of a file to another user. However, only root is permitted to perform this change.

Suppose that the file Roadmap from the example 2 on page 312 should no longer belong to tux, but to the user geeko. The command root should enter is:

chgrp is also fairly self-explanatory — it changes the group ownership of the file. However, the owner of the file must be a member of the new group. In this way, the user tux from Output 1 on page 311 can switch the group owning the file ProjectData to project4, as long as he is a member of this new group, by entering

```
newbie@earth:~ >  chgrp project4 ProjectData
```

The Setuid Bit

In certain situations, the access permissions may be too restrictive. Therefore, Linux has additional settings that enable the temporary change of the current user and group identity for a specific action.

For example, the cdrecord program normally requires root permissions to access the writer for writing CDs (or DVDSs). Thus, a normal user would not be able to create CDs, as it would be too dangerous to grant all users direct access to all devices.

A possible solution to this problem is the "setuid mechanism". setuid (set user ID) is a special file attribute that instructs the system to execute programs marked accordingly under a specific user ID. Consider the cdrecord command:

Set the setuid bit with the command chmod:

The following command assigns the cdrecord program to the group users:

The following access permissions are granted:

By means of the setuid bit, all users belonging to the group users will be able to use the program. In effect, this means that the program is executed as root.

> **Caution**
>
> Setting the setuid bit for a program makes your computer more vulnerable to attacks. Only do this in exceptional cases when you know the program well and are aware of the potential risks.
>
> **Caution**

The Setgid Bit

The setuid attribute applies to users. However, there is also an equivalent property for groups – the setgid attribute. A program for which this attribute was set will run under the group ID under which it was saved, no matter which user starts it.

Therefore, in a directory with the setgid bit, all newly created files and subdirectories will be assigned to the group to which the directory belongs.

To set the setgid bit, use the command:

```
earth:~ #  chmod g+s /test
```

Subsequently, the access permissions appear as follows:

```
earth:~ #  ls -ld /test
drwxrwsr-- 2 root archive 48 Nov 19 17:12 backup
```

The Sticky Bit

Apart from the setuid and setgid bits, there is the "sticky bit". It makes a difference whether it belongs to an executable program or a directory. If it belongs to a program, a file marked in this way will be loaded to the RAM to avoid having to get it from the hard disk each time it is used. Nowadays, this attribute is used rarely, as modern hard disks are fast enough.

If this attribute is assigned to a directory, it will prevent users from deleting each other's files. Typical examples include the `/tmp` and `/var/tmp` directories:

```
earth:~ #  ls -dl /tmp
drwxrwxrwt 2 root root 1160 2002-11-19 17:15 /tmp
```

Access Control Lists

The traditional permission concept for Linux file system objects, such as files or directories, can be expanded by means of ACLs (Access Control Lists). They allow the assignment of permissions to individual users or groups other than the original owner or owning group of a file system object.

Files or directories bearing extended access permissions reveal themselves after the execution of a simple `ls -l` command:

```
earth:~ #  ls -l

-rw-r--r--+ 1 tux projekt3 517 2003-01-08 18:12 Roadmap
```

The output of `ls` does not reveal much of a change compared to an `ls` on a file without an ACL. `Roadmap` is owned by `tux` who belongs to the group `projekt3`. `tux` holds both write and read access to this file and his group as well as all other users have read access. The only difference that discerns this file from a file without an ACL is the additional + in the first column holding the permission bits.

Get details about the ACL is revealed by executing `getfacl Roadmap`:

```
earth:~ #  getfacl Roadmap


\# file: Roadmap
# owner: tux
# group: projekt3
user::rw-
user:jane:rw-        # effective: r--
group::r--
group:djungle:rw-    # effective: r--
mask::r--
other::---
```

The first three lines of the output do not hold any information not available with `ls -l`. These lines only state file name, owner, and owning group. Lines 4 to 9 hold the ACL entries. Conventional access permissions represent a subset of those possible when using ACLs. Our example ACL grants read and write access to the owner of the file as well as to a user `jane` (lines 4 and 5). The conventional concept has been expanded allowing access to an extra user. The same applies to the handling of group access. The owning group holds read permissions (line 6) and the group `djungle` holds read and write permissions. The mask entry in line 8 reduces the effective permissions for the user jane and the group djungle to read access. Other users and groups do not get any kind of access to the file (line 9).

Further background information about ACLs can be found in *Access Control Lists in Linux* in the *Administration Guide*.

The Most Important Linux Commands

This section gives insight into the most important commands of your SuSE Linux system. Along with the individual commands, parameters are listed and, where appropriate, a typical sample application is introduced.

To learn more about the various commands, it is usually possibleto get additional information with the man program followed by the name of the command, for example, man ls.

In these ☞*manual pages*, move up and down with PgUp and PgDn and move between the beginning and the end of a document with Home and End. End this viewing mode by pressing Q. Learn more about the man command itself with man.

There are many more commands than listed in this chapter. For information about other commands or more detailed information, we recommend the O'Reilly publication *Linux in a Nutshell*. In the following overview, the individual command elements are written in different typefaces.

- The actual command is always printed as command. Without this, nothing can function.
- Options without which the respective program cannot function are printed in *italics*.
- Further details, like file names, which must be passed to a command for correct functioning, are written in the *Courier* font.
- Specifications or parameters that are not required are placed in [brackets].

Adjust possible specifications to your needs. It makes no sense to write ls file(s), if no file named file(s) actually exists. You can usually combine several parameters simply by writing ls -la instead of ls -l -a.

File Commands

File Administration

`ls [option(s)] [file(s)]`

If you run `ls` in its bare form — without any arguments — the program will list the contents of the current working directory in short form.

Options:

`-l` detailed list

`-a` displays hidden files

`cp [option(s)]` *`sourcefile targetfile`*

Copies `sourcefile` to `targetfile`.

Options:

`-i` Waits for confirmation, if necessary, before an existing `targetfile` is overwritten

`-r` Copies recursively (includes subdirectories)

`mv [option(s)]` *`sourcefile targetfile`*

Copies `sourcefile` to `targetfile` then deletes the original `sourcefile`.

Options:

`-b` Creates a backup copy of the `sourcefile` before moving

`-i` Waits for confirmation, if necessary, before an existing *targetfile* is overwritten

`rm [option(s)]` *`file(s)`*

Removes the specified *file(s)* from the file system. Directories are not removed by `rm`, except when the `-r` option is specified to force this behavior.

Options:

`-r` Also delete existing subdirectories

`-i` Waits for confirmation before deleting each file

`ln [option(s)]` *`sourcefile targetfile`*

Creates an internal ☞*"link"* from the `sourcefile` to the `targetfile`, under a different name. Normally such a link points directly to the sourcefile on one and the same file system. However, if ln is executed with the -s option, it creates a symbolic link that only points to the directory where the sourcefile is located, which makes it possible to link across file systems.

Options:

-s Creates a symbolic link

cd [options(s)] [directory]
: Changes the current (working) directory. A bare cd (with no arguments) changes to the home directory.

mkdir [option(s)] *directoryname*
: Creates a new directory.

rmdir [option(s)] directoryname
: Deletes the specified directory, provided that no files remain in it.

chown [option(s)] username.group file(s)
: Transfers the ownership of a file to the user with the specified username.

Options:

-R Changes files and directories in all subdirectories.

chgrp [option(s)] groupname file(s)
: Transfers the group ownership of a given file to the group with the specified groupname. The file owner can only change group ownership if he is a member of both the existing and the new group.

chmod [options] *mode file(s)*
: Changes file permissions.

The mode parameter has three parts: group, access, and access type. group accepts the following characters:

Options:

u user

g group

o others

For access, access is granted by the + symbol and denied by the

- symbol.

The `access type` is controlled by the following options:

Options:

- `r` read
- `w` write
- `x` eXecute — for executing files or changing to the directory
- `s` Set uid bit — the application or program is started as if it were being started by the owner of the file.

`gzip [parameters] file(s)`

This program compresses the contents of files, using complex mathematical algorithms. Files compressed in this way are given the extension `.gz` and normally need to be uncompressed before they can be used again. To compress several files at once, or even entire directories, you can use the `tar` command.

Options:

- `-d` decompresses the packed gzip files so they return to their original size and can be processed normally (like the command `gunzip`).

`tar` *`options archive file(s)`*

The `tar` puts one file or (usually) several files into one archive, which may optionally be compressed.

`tar` is a quite complex command with a number of options available. The most frequently used options are:

Options:

- `-f` Writes the output to a file and not to the screen as is usually the case
- `-c` Creates a new tar archive
- `-r` Adds files to an existing archive
- `-t` Outputs the contents of an archive
- `-u` Adds files, but only if they are newer than the files already contained in the archive
- `-x` Unpacks files from an archive ("extraction")
- `-z` Packs the resulting archive with `gzip`
- `-j` Compress the resulting archive with `bzip2`

-v List files processed

The archive files created by tar end with .tar. If the tar archive was also compressed using gzip, the ending is .tgz or .tar.gz. If it was compressed using bzip2, .tar.bz2.

Application examples can be found in *Archives and Data Compression* on page 309.

locate *pattern(s)*
: The locate command allows you to find out where a specific file is located. You can also use ☞*wild cards* to specify file names. The program works very quickly because it uses a database specifically created for the purpose (rather than searching through the whole file system). This very fact, however, also results in a major drawback: locate is unable to find any files created after the latest update of its database.

The database can be generated by root with updatedb.

updatedb [options(s)]
: This command performs an update of the database used by locate. To include files in all existing directories, run the program as root. It also makes sense to place it in the background by appending an ampersand (&), so you can immediately continue working on the same command line (updatedb &).

find [option(s)]
: The find command allows you to search for a file in a given directory. The first argument specifies the directory in which to start the search. The option -name must be followed by a search string to match a file name. The string may be specified using ☞*wild cards*. Unlike locate, which uses a precompiled database, find scans the actual directory contents as exist on the disk.

Commands to Access File Contents

cat [option(s)] file(s)
: The cat command displays the contents of a file, printing the entire contents on the screen without stopping.

Options:

-n Numbers the output on the left margin

less [option(s)] file(s)
: This command can be used to browse the contents of the speci-

fied file. It allows you to scroll the text half a screen page up or down with (PgUp) and (PgDn), respectively. Alternatively, scroll a full screen page down with (Space). You can also jump to the beginning or the end of a document using (Home) and (End). Pressing (Q) exits the program.

`grep [option(s)] searchstring filenames`

The grep command makes it possible to find a certain `searchword` in the `file(s)` as specified. If the search string is matched, the command displays the line in which the `searchword` has been found, along with the name of the corresponding file.

Options:

- `-i` Ignores case
- `-l` Only displays the names of the respective files, but not the text lines
- `-n` Additionally displays the numbers of the lines in which it found a hit
- `-l` Only lists the files in which *searchword* does *not* occur

`diff [option(s)] file1file2`

The `diff` command compares the contents of any two files. The output produced by the program lists all lines where the files differ from each other.

This is frequently used by programmers who need only send their program alterations and not the entire source code.

Options:

- `-q` Only reports *whether* the two given files differ

File Systems

`mount [option(s)] [<device>] mountpoint`

This command mounts any available data media (volumes) to integrate them into the overall Linux file system structure. After mounting a hard disk, a CD-ROM drive, or other drives or partitions, they can be accessed under a specific directory.

Options:

- `-r` mount read-only

`-t filesystem` Specifies the file system. The most common are `ext2` for Linux hard disks, `msdos` for MS-DOS media, `vfat` for the Windows file system, and `iso9660` for CDs.

For hard disks not defined in the file `/etc/fstab`, the device type must also be specified. In this case, only `root` can mount. If the file system should also be mounted by other users, enter the option `user` in the appropriate line in the `/etc/fstab` file (separated by commas) and save this change. Further information is available in the man page for (`man`).

`umount [option(s)] mountpoint`
This command detaches (unmounts) a mounted drive from the file system. It must be run before taking out a removable data medium from its drive. Otherwise there is a risk of losing data. Normally, only `root` is allowed to run the commands `mount` and `umount`. To circumvent this, edit the `/etc/fstab` file to include `user` as one of the options for the corresponding drive.

System Commands

System Information

`df [option(s)] [directory]`
The `df` (disk free) command, when used without any options, displays information about the total disk space, the disk space currently in use, and the free space on all the mounted drives. However, if a directory is given as an argument, the information is limited to the drive on which that directory is located.

Options:

`-H` shows the number of occupied blocks in gigabytes, megabytes, or kilobytes — in "human readable" format

`-t` Type of file system (ext2, nfs, etc.)

`du [option(s)] [path]`
This command, when executed without any arguments, shows the total disk space as used by files and subdirectories in the current directory.

Options:

`-a` Displays the size of each individual file

`-h` Output in human-readable form

`-s` Displays only the calculated total size

`free [option(s)]`

The `free` displays information about RAM and swap space usage, showing the total and the used amount in both categories.

Options:

`-b` Output in bytes

`-k` Output in kilobytes

`-m` Output in megabytes

`date [option(s)]`

This simple program displays the current system time. If run as `root`, it can also be used to change the system time. Details about the program are available in the corresponding ☞*man page* (the man page for (`man`)).

Processes

`top [options(s)]`

With top, get a quick overview of the currently running ☞*processes*. Pressing Ⓗ from within top shows a list that briefly explains the main options to customize the process table.

`ps [option(s)] [process ID]`

If run without any arguments, this command displays a table of all "your own"programs or processes — those started by yourself. Most options for this command do not need to be preceded by a dash.

Options:

`aux` Displays a detailed list of all processes, independent of the owner.

`kill [option(s)]` *`process ID`*

Unfortunately, sometimes a program cannot be terminated in the normal way. However, in most cases you should still be able to stop such a runaway program by executing the `kill` command, specifying the process ID (see `top` and `ps`) of the problem program as an argument.

It sends a "TERM" signal, which instructs the program to shut itself down. If this does not help, the following parameter can be useful.

Options:

- `-9` Sends a "KILL" signal instead of a "TERM" signal, with which the process really is "annihilated" by the operating system. This brings the specific processes to an end in almost all cases.

`killall [option(s)] processname`
This command is similar to `kill`, but is able to take a process name (instead of a process ID) as an argument, which causes all processes with that name to be killed.

Network

`ping [option(s)]` *`host name|IP address`*
The ping command is typically used to test whether a TCP/IP network link is up. It sends a small data packet to a destination host, requesting an immediate reply. If this works, ping displays a message to that effect, which indicates that network link is basically functioning.

Options:

- `-c number` Determines the total number of packages to send and ends after they have been dispatched. By default, there is no limitation set.
- `-f` "flood ping": sends as many data packages as possible. A popular means, reserved to `root`, to test networks.
- `-i value` Specifies the interval between two data packages in seconds. Default: one second

`nslookup`
This command is related to the Domain Name System, which has the purpose of translating (resolving) domain names into IP addresses. With `nslookup`, send queries to the corresponding information servers (DNS servers).

`telnet [option(s)] host name or IP address`
Telnet is actually an Internet protocol that enables you to work on remote hosts across a network.

telnet is also the name of a Linux program that uses this protocol to enable operations on remote computers.

Caution

Do not use telnet over a network on which third parties can "eavesdrop." Particularly on the Internet, use encrypted transfer methods, such as `ssh`, to avoid the risk of malicious misuse of a password (see the man page for `ssh`).

Caution

Miscellaneous

`passwd [option(s)] [username]`
: Users may change their own passwords at any time using this command. Furthermore, the administrator `root` can use the command to change the password of any user on the system.

`su [option(s)] [username]`
: The `su` command makes it possible to log in under a different user name from a running session. When using the command without specifying a user name, you will be prompted for the `root` password. Otherwise, supply the specified user's password and you may then work in that user's environment. However, if you do the latter as ☞*`root`*, you will not have to supply any password: `root` can assume the identity of any user.

`halt [option(s)]`
: Always use this command to shut down your system in an orderly way to avoid loss of data.

`reboot [option(s)]`
: Does the same as the `halt` command, with the difference that the system performs an immediate reboot.

`clear`
: This command cleans up the visible area of the console. It has no options.

The vi Editor

Operating the `vi` editor takes some practice. For many, it is the preferred editor, partly because it is available on any UNIX-like operating system and is included in default Linux installations. Also, if nothing else works, vi will. The short instructions that follow should enable you to edit various configuration files and other types of files with vi.

vi recognizes three operating modes:

- Command mode:

  Keys are interpreted as command elements.

- Insert mode:

  Key are interpreted as text entries.

- Last line mode:

  Used for more complex commands, which are edited in the last line.

The most important commands in command mode are:

i	Changes to insert mode (characters will appear at the current cursor position).
a	Changes to insert mode (characters will appear *after* the current cursor position).
A	Changes to insert mode (characters will be added at the end of the line).
R	Changes to command mode (overwrites the old text).
r	Changes to insert mode and overwrites *each* character.
s	Changes to insert mode (the character where the cursor is positioned will be replaced by the next entry you make).
C	Changes to insert mode (the rest of the line is replaced by the new text).
o	Changes to insert mode (a new line is inserted *following* the current one).
O	Changes to insert mode (a new line is inserted *preceding* the current one).
x	Deletes the current character.
dd	Deletes the current line.
dw	Deletes up to the end of the current word.
cw	Changes to insert mode (the rest of the current word is overwritten by the next entries you make).
u	Undoes the last command.
J	Joins the following line with the current one.

***Table 21.2:** continued overleaf...*

.	Repeats the last command.
:	Changes to last line mode.

Table 21.2: *Simple Commands of the vi Editor*

Each command can be preceded by a number specifying on how many objects the following command should operate. Three words can be deleted in one go by entering `'3dw'`. The command `'10x'` deletes ten characters after the cursor position and `'20dd'` deletes twenty lines.

The most important commands in last line mode are:

`:q!`	exits vi without saving any changes
`:w` ⟨*filename*⟩	saves as ⟨*filename*⟩
`:x`	saves the modified file and exits the editor
`:e` ⟨*filename*⟩	edits (loads) ⟨*filename*⟩
`:u`	undoes the last edit command

Table 21.3: *Complex Commands of the vi Editor*

Switch to command mode by pressing (Esc).

Help and Documentation

Installation Support

SuSE will gladly assist you if you encounter problems during the installation. SuSE Installation Support is available as a free service if you experience difficulties of this kind. All details are listed in the separate support flyer in your SuSE box.

There are many questions and issues for which we have already found a solution. This information is available around the clock in our online Support Database, which contains several hundred articles, at `http://sdb.suse.de/en/sdb/html`.

SuSE Help

SuSE Help can be started by selecting the lifesaver icon (the one with the Geeko) on KDE's desktop panel or the 'SuSE Help' menu item from the K menu or the SuSE menu. Also see Figure 22.1 on the following page.

The SuSE Help system is also available if KDE is not installed. In this case, use any web browser to access the help documents. However, the `apache` package is required for this. See Section *Install and Remove Software* on page 47 for more information.

Start the SuSE Help by entering `hilfe` in a console or by entering the URL `http://localhost/help/index.html.en` in a web browser. It can also be started from the KDE menu.

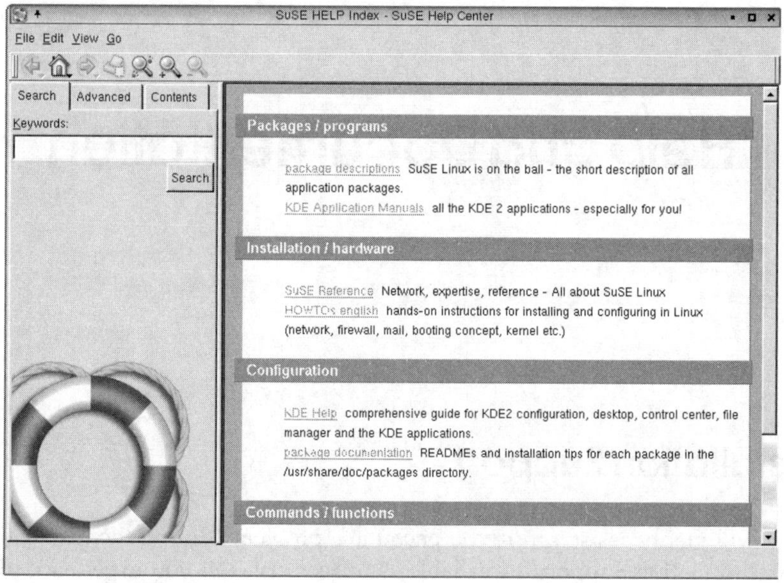

Figure 22.1: The SuSE Help Home Page

Note

To make SuSE Help available in HTML format through a documentation server, the `inf2htm` package must be installed. Instructions for configuring the help system on an intranet documentation server can be found in `/usr/share/doc/packages/susehelp/README`.

Note

Support Database

SuSE has already found a solution for many problems and questions. This information is available around the clock in our online Support Database at `http://sdb.suse.de/en/sdb/html`. Many articles from the Support Database are also included in SuSE Linux on CD in package `sdb_en`. They can be viewed with any web browser.

Tip

Enter the command sdb: then a keyword in Konqueror's location field to start the Support Database and search quickly.

Tip

Manual Pages

Manual pages are the traditional way to access descriptions of application usage and commands (such as C functions) in UNIX. All parameters and options for the command are included.

Man pages are divided into the following sections, given when accessing them:

1 User commands

2 System commands

3 C functions

4 File formats, device files

5 Configuration files

6 Games

7 Miscellaneous

8 System administration

9 Kernels

n New commands

Access man pages in the following ways:

Console In text mode, display man pages with a command in the syntax `man <section-number> <command-name>`. To list the man pages of related commands in all sections, use the "-k" option, as in `man -k <command-name>`.

Konqueror Using the location field, the syntax to view manual pages is `man:/<command-name>(<section-number>)`

SuSE Help SuSE Help allows you to browse all man pages according to section and to search them for keywords. Man pages can be accessed by opening the category 'Commands and Functions' then selecting 'Man Pages'.

Info Pages

Info pages have become standard for more complex commands. They not only describe options and parameters, but also offer a more in-depth explanation of how the commands are used and applied. These explanations are mostly accompanied by related examples.

Console You have three basic options:

- `info` shows a list of the available info pages
- `info apropos <command-name>` shows info pages related to "command-name".
- `info <command-name>` displays the info page of the corresponding command.

Konqueror In the location field, enter: `info:/<command-name>`. Navigate with the mouse as usual in the info page.

SuSE Help Using SuSE Help (see *SuSE Help*), find them in the 'Commands and Functions' category under *Info Pages*. The corresponding summary page lists all available info pages, which are displayed by the browser in HTML format.

HOWTOs

HOWTOs are detailed, practical installation and configuration guides and hints on several Linux-related topics; they are found in the directory `/usr/share/doc/howto/`. To read them in HTML format, install the `howtoenh` package.

In the `docu/howto` directory of the first CD, find the current versions of the most important HOWTO files as of the CD release. These files are not compressed and can already be easily viewed, even prior to installation.

Console View the HOWTO text in a console with the `less` command, even if the text is compressed. To view the HOWTO text regarding Linux installation, for example, enter the following:

```
less /usr/share/doc/howto/en/Installation-HOWTO.txt.gz
```

SuSE Help Read the HOWTO texts in a more user-friendly environment via SuSE Help. It is also possible to perform searches.

Kernel Documentation

For problems with the kernel itself, the `/usr/src/linux/Documentation` directory is an extensive information source. It is only available if the kernel sources (packages `linux` and `kernel-source`) have been installed. Also find several valuable tips in the individual subdirectories of the kernel sources and in the kernel sources themselves.

Free Books

The `books` package contains some books in PostScript format that can be viewed and printed with gv. Before printing a book, consider that it may actually be more economical to purchase it.

The SuSE Linux FAQ

Here, we answer the most *Frequently Asked Questions.*

1. *I am the only person using my computer. Why do I always need to log in?*

   Linux is a multiuser system. Giving a user name and a password is necessary so Linux knows who is working with it. Only log in as `root` to make changes to your system (installing software or changing configuration). For everyday use, create a regular user. This prevents accidental damage to the installation.

2. *Where can I get more information about SuSE Linux?*

   Find information mainly in the included manuals, as far as the installation and any SuSE Linux–specific matters are concerned. You can also install the package `suselinux-adminguide_en` to read the *Administration Guide* as a PDF document (see `/usr/share/doc/packages/suselinux-adminguide_en`). Documentation for individual programs can be found in `/usr/share/doc/packages`. Instructions on a variety of topics are provided by the HOWTOs, which are found in `/usr/share/doc/howto/en`. To read a HOWTO, use a command like:

3. *Where can I get special tips or help?*

   Enter the path `/usr/share/doc/sdb/en/html/index.html` in Konqueror. There, view the SuSE Support Database, which includes numerous tips and help entries. If the path does not yet exist, first install the packages *sdb* and *sdb_en*. On the Internet, find the most recent version at `http://sdb.suse.de/sdb/en/html/`.

4. *How can I enter commands in KDE?*

Click 'K' → 'Tools' → 'Terminal'. Alternatively, press (Alt) + (F2) then enter `xterm` to open a terminal window in which to enter commands. In KDE, you can also click the icon with the screen and the seashell in the desktop panel, which opens a konsole, a more sophisticated terminal (as compared to xterm).

5. *I cannot find many programs in KDE.*

   You can start all programs from a terminal window, such as `xterm` (see above), by entering the program name and pressing (↵).

6. *What is a mirror? Why should I not get these things from `ftp.suse.com`?*

   Because there are many users who need to retrieve things from the server at the same time, it would be overburdened quickly if everyone used the same server. There are a number of other FTP servers that contain a duplicate of the SuSE server. A server such as this is called a "mirror". Access a mirror geographically near you — in the same country or a nearby area — so it is quicker to download. Find a list of mirrors at `http://www.suse.de/en/support/download/index.html`.

7. *I cannot find any `.exe` files. Where are all the applications?*

   In Linux, executable files normally do not have file extensions. Most programs are located in `/usr/bin` and `/usr/X11R6/bin`.

8. *How can I recognize executable files?*

   Using the command `ls -l`, see all the executable files in the directory in red. Also recognize them by the `'x'` in the first column.

```
-rwxr-xr-x   1 root   root    64412 Jul 23 15:23 /usr/bin/ftp
```

9. *I want to remove Linux. How does this work?*

   With `fdisk`, the Linux partitions are deleted. You might need to run `fdisk` in Linux. Afterwards, boot from the MS-DOS disk and run `fdisk /MBR` in DOS or Windows.

10. *I need firewall, masquerading, mail, and a web server. Will your installation support help me with this?*

    No, the installation support will assist you in getting Linux up and running. For concerns extending beyond this, there are good books available at your local book store and excellent documentation in `/usr/share/doc/packages`, `/usr/share/doc/`

howto/en/NET-3-HOWTO.gz, and /usr/share/doc/howto/en/NET3-4-HOWTO.gz.

Furthermore, you can make use of our Advanced Support. For details, visit http://support.suse.de/en/.

11. *How can I access my CD?*

    You must first mount the CD with the mount command. Information about this command can be found in *File Commands* on page 323

12. *I cannot get my CD out of the drive. What should I do now?*

    First, unmount the CD. This is done with the umount command. More information about this can be found in *File Commands* on page 323. In KDE, just right-click the CD-ROM icon and select 'Unmount Drive'. If YaST is running on your computer, exit it.

13. *How can I find out how much space is available in Linux?*

    With the df -hT command. See *System Commands* on page 323.

14. *Can I copy and paste in Linux?*

    Yes, this is possible. To copy and paste in the text mode, you must have gpm running. In the X Window System and in the text mode, highlight the text block by clicking and dragging with the left mouse button then insert by clicking with the middle mouse button. The right mouse button has a special function in most programs and applications.

15. *Do I need to be afraid of a virus in Linux?*

    In Linux, there have been no serious viruses found. Also, viruses cannot cause any serious damage if they are *not* activated by root. The only virus scanners available in Linux serve to search e-mails for Windows viruses (if Linux is being used as a router or server).

16. *Do I need to compile a kernel myself?*

    No, this is usually unnecessary. The kernel has become so large that there are about eight hundred options to consider during the configuration. Because it is almost impossible to master all possible configurations and their effects, it is strongly discouraged for inexperienced users to recompile the kernel. Do so only at your own risk. In cases of custom compiled kernels, SuSE cannot provide any installation support.

17. *Where can I see the system messages?* In a terminal window, enter the following command as root: tail -f /var/log/messages

Additional interesting programs relating to this one are `top`, `procinfo`, and `xosview`.

Use the command

to view the boot messages.

18. *I cannot log in to my computer with* `telnet`. *I always get the answer "Login incorrect".*

    You are probably trying to log in as `root`. For security reasons, this is not possible via telnet by default.

    With YaST2, set up a normal user account. Log in with this user name. Then change to the user `root` with `su`. It is much better and safer, however, to use the program ssh instead of telnet. The ssh program uses encoded, secure connections.

19. *How do I connect to the Internet in Linux?*

    KInternet — Connecting to the Internet on page 121 provides information about this.

20. *I found a bug in SuSE Linux. Where should I report it?*

    First, ascertain whether it is actually a bug in the program or just an error in operation or faulty configuration settings. Also read the documentation in `/usr/share/doc/packages` and `/usr/share/doc/howto`. The bug may have already been discovered. Check in the support database at `http://sdb.suse.de/sdb/en/html/`. Enter a keyword or work your way forward or backward via the "History" link. If it really is a bug, send a description of it by e-mail to `feedback@suse.de`.

21. *How can I install applications?*

    Applications included in the SuSE Linux CDs are best installed with YaST2.

22. *I "only" have an application in source code. How can I install it?*

    Some know-how is required with some applications. Find more information in a good Linux book.

    Briefly, decompress the archive with `tar xvzf name.tar.gz`, read the `INSTALL` or `README` files, and follow the instructions. Usually, the following command sequence needs to be executed: `./configure;make;make install`. We cannot offer any installation support for the phases of compilation or for self-compiled programs.

23. *Is my hardware supported?*

    It is best to refer to the component database at `http://hardwaredb.suse.de` or `http://cdb.suse.de`. `less /usr/share/doc/howto/en/Hardware-HOWTO.gz` can also provide some information.

24. *How can I defragment my hard disk?*

    Linux has an intelligent file system. This file system makes defragmentation superfluous, because it prevents fragments from occurring. Your partitions should not be more than ninety percent used. Use `df -h` to view information about used and available hard disk space.

25. *What is meant by partitioning?*

    Partitioning means dividing the hard disk into individual sections. Windows and MacOS are also located in their own partitions. For the default configuration, SuSE Linux requires at least two partitions (one for Linux itself and one swap partition for the virtual main memory).

26. *How much space do I need for Linux?*

    This depends on how many and which packages you want to install. A standard installation with office applications requires about 1 GB. 2 GB is recommended if you want space for your own data as well. To install just about everything, you need 3 GB to 6 GB, depending on the version.

27. *I need more space for Linux. How can I add another hard disk?*

    To make more space available, integrate a new hard disk or parts of it (i.e., partitions) into your Linux system at any time. For example, if it turns out that you need more space in `/opt`, mount an additional hard disk partition to this directory. To do so, follow this procedure:

    (a) Install your hard disk following the instructions of the manufacturer then start Linux.

    (b) Log in as user `root`.

    (c) Partition the new hard disk with `fdisk`. For further information refer to the manual page of fdisk with `man fdisk`.

    (d) Format the partition with `mke2fs /dev/hdb1`.

    (e) Enter the following commands:

    Check thoroughly to see whether all the data has been copied. Afterwards, you can move the old directory and add a new one — an empty mount point:

Use an editor to add the new partitions in `/etc/fstab`. This could resemble that in File 2.

```
/dev/hdb1          /opt       ext2        defaults    1    2
```

***File 2:** Sample Line in /etc/fstab for an Additional Partition*

Now, shut down the computer and reboot.

(f) After rebooting, check that `/dev/hdb1` has actually been mounted to `/opt` using the command `mount`. If everything is working as desired, remove the old data in `/opt.old`:

28. *My computer crashed. Can I just press the reset button without risking anything?*

    If your computer no longer reacts to your mouse or keyboard, this does not necessarily mean that your whole system has crashed. Possibly one program is blocking the mouse or the keyboard, but all other programs are still running. If your machine can be accessed remotely (serial terminal, network), log in elsewhere and abort the respective program with `killall` ⟨*programname*⟩. If this does not work, try `killall -9` ⟨*programname*⟩.

    If this is not possible, try switching to another console using Ctrl + Alt + F2 to kill the faulty process from there. If the computer does not respond to any of the keys and network intervention is not possible, wait at least ten seconds before pressing reset to make sure there is no hard disk activity.

29. *How can I switch from a virtual text console to the graphical user interface?*

    By default, there are six virtual text consoles that can be accessed with Ctrl + Alt + F1 to F6. Press Alt + F7 to go to the graphical user interface.

Glossary

account
See ☞*access permissions*.

access permissions
The account is defined by the user name or login name and the password. The access permissions are generally set by the ☞*system administrator*. The access permissions define to which user group the new user is assigned and the resulting permissions.

ADSL (Asymmetric Digital Subscriber Line)
Transmission procedure that transmits data about one hundred times faster than ISDN in the telephone network.

AGP (Accelerated Graphics Port)
A high-speed slot for graphics cards based on PCI, but offering a larger ☞*bandwidth*. Furthermore, AGP graphics cards can revert directly (without routing around the processor) to the ☞*Random Access Memory* and ☞*main memory*, in contrast to PCI models, to swap graphics data there.

ATAPI (Advanced Technology Attachment Packet Interface)
ATAPI is a type of CD-ROM drive that is connected to an (E)IDE controller. Apart from ATAPI drives, there are SCSI CD-ROM drives, handled by a SCSI controller, and proprietary CD-ROM drives that use their own controller or are connected to a sound card.

backup
A backup is a duplicate of data used to restore data that has been damaged or lost. Backups should be done regularly, especially the important files.

bandwidth
Maximum load capacity of a data channel.

BIOS

Small component responsible for the initialization of important hardware processes. This essential procedure is complete when the boot menu appears on the screen.

bookmark

A mostly personal collection of interesting web page or file references directly accessible in the browser.

booting

The sequence of computer operations from power-up until the system is ready for use.

browser

Program that searches and displays contents. Today it is mostly used for programs that graphically display contents of ☞*World Wide Web* pages.

cache

In relation to the ☞*main memory*, it is rather small, but still a fast memory buffer. For example, open files are saved to the cache to spare the hard disk next time the file is loaded.

client

Workstation in a computer network operated by a ☞*server*.

command line

Text-based mode of operating where commands are entered at a prompt. A command line can be accessed from within a graphical environment as well as from virtual consoles.

console

Formerly synonymous with ☞*terminal*. In Linux, there are several*virtual consoles* that allows the screen to be used for several independent, parallel work sessions.

CPU (Central Processing Unit)

☞*Processor*.

cursor

The cursor is normally a block character that marks the place for input on a computer screen. This term also often refers to the symbol representing the location of the mouse in graphical interfaces.

B

Glossary

daemon

A daemon D*isk* a*nd* e*xecution* mon*itor* is a program that monitors in the background and comes into action when required. Such daemons answer FTP or HTTP requests, for example, or control activity in the PCMCIA slots.

DDC (Direct Display Channel)

Communication standard between the monitor and the graphics card, which transmits various parameters, such as monitor name or resolution, to the graphics card.

directory

Directories make up the structure of a ☞*file system*. A directory lists file and directory names.

DNS (Domain Name System)

A system that converts name-based addresses to ☞*TCP/IP* addresses and vice versa.

driver

A program between the operating system and the hardware that "translates" the communication between these two layers.

e-mail (electronic mail)

The means of transporting mail electronically between registered users via a network. As with "normal" mail (often referred to as "snail mail"), the address must be entered. In e-mail, it is in the form "sender@sender's-domain" to "recipient@recipient's-domain". E-mail not only lets you send text, but also sound files or pictures. It has many advantages: it is inexpensive and mail usually reaches its destination within minutes.

environment

A ☞*shell* usually provides an environment in which the user can perform temporary settings. These settings include path specifications for programs, the user name, the current path, and the appearance of prompts. The data is saved in an ☞*environment variable*. The assignment of the environment variables is possible, for example, by means of the configuration files of the shell.

environment variable

A position in the ☞*environment* of the ☞*shell*. Every environment variable has a name that is usually capitalized. The variables are assigned values, such as path names.

EIDE (Enhanced Integrated Drive Electronics)
Improved ☞*IDE* standard that allows hard disks with a size over 512 MB.

ethernet
Popular standard for less expansive computer networks.

EXT2 (Second Extended File System)
EXT2 is the default file system used by Linux.

FAQ (Frequently Asked Questions)
Common reference to documents answering typical questions.

file system
A file system is a system for structuring files. There are many file systems available, which differ (sometimes quite extremely) in performance and power.

firewall
Protects a local network or host from unauthorized access from the Internet using various security measures.

free software
See ☞*GNU*.

FTP (file transfer protocol)
A ☞*protocol* based on ☞*TCP/IP* for transferring files.

GNU (GNU is Not Unix)
GNU is a project of the Free Software Foundation (FSF). Closely linked to the "GNU Project" is the name of Richard Stallman (RMS). The aim of the "GNU Project" is to create a "free" Unix-compatible operating system — "free" not so much in the sense of *free of cost*, but in the sense of *freedom*: having the right to obtain, modify, and change the software. To guarantee the freedom of the source code (the actual program code), every change of the original code must be free as well, so modifications of or additions to the original software cannot compromise this freedom in any way. The now classic GNU Manifesto (`http://www.gnu.org/gnu/manifesto.html`) explains many aspects of this thinking. In legal terms, GNU software is protected by the GNU General Public License, or "GPL" (`http://www.gnu.org/copyleft/gpl.html`), and by the GNU Lesser General Public License, or "LGPL" (`http://www.gnu.org/copyleft/lgpl.html`).

In connection with the GNU Project, all Unix tools and utilities are being redeveloped and, in part, provided with more or enhanced functionalities. Even complex software systems, such as Emacs or glibc, are integral components of the "Project".

The ☞*Linux* kernel, subject to the GPL, profits from this "Project" (especially from the tools), but should not be seen as the same thing.

GPL (GNU GENERAL PUBLIC LICENSE)
See ☞*GNU*.

home directory
Your own private directory in the Linux file system. This belongs to a specific user (usually in `/home/<username>`). Except the superuser ☞ *root*, only the user has full access rights in his home directory.

host name
Name of a machine in Linux, usually the name by which it can be reached on the network.

HTML (Hypertext Markup Language)
The most important language used in the ☞*World Wide Web* for designing the contents. The layout commands made available by HTML define how a document looks and how it is displayed in a ☞*browser*.

HTTP (Hypertext Transfer Protocol)
A protocol used between the ☞*browsers* and Internet servers to transmit ☞*HTML* pages over the ☞*World Wide Web*.

IDE (Integrated Drive Electronics)
A widely-used hard disk standard in low-grade and middle-grade PCs.

Internet
World-wide computer network based on ☞*TCP/IP*, which is used by a very large population.

IP address
A numerical 32-bit Internet address, appearing in four decimal series separated by periods (for example, 192.168.10.1), which is uniquely assigned to a machine connected to ☞*TCP/IP* networks.

IRQ (Interrupt Request)
A request to the ☞*operating system* carried out by a hardware component or a program to assign it processor capacity.

ISDN (Integrated Services Digital Network)
A popular digital standard for high-speed data transferral over the telephone network.

KDE (K Desktop Environment)
A popular desktop environment for Linux. KDE with its corresponding window manager is the default graphical interface in SuSE Linux.

kernel
The kernel is the central core of the Linux operating system. It manages memory, contains the drivers that enable communication with the hardware, and handles processes and tasks. Applications run on top of the kernel.

LAN (local area network)
A LAN is a local ☞*network* and is usually rather small.

LILO (Linux Loader)
Small program installed in the boot sector of the hard disk that not only can be started by Linux, but by other operating systems as well.

link
A link is a pointer to a file, just as widely used in the Internet as in the Linux file system. In Linux, there is a distinction made between "hard" and "symbolic" links. While "hard" links refer to the exact position in the file system, the symbolic link only points to the respective name.

Linux
High performance UNIX-like operating system core distributed freely under the GPL (☞*GNU*). The name is an acronym ("Linus's uniX") and refers to its creator, Linus Torvalds. Although the name, in a strict sense, only refers to the kernel itself, the popular understanding of the term "Linux" usually entails the entire system.

login
Authentication of a user by user name and password to gain access to a computer system or network.

logout
The procedure of closing down an interactive Linux session and get ting back to the ☞*login* prompt where you enter your user name and password.

main memory
Physical memory of limited capacity that can be accessed rather quickly. This is often referred to as RAM, Random Access Memory.

man pages
: Traditional documentation for Unix systems, which can be read using the command `man`.

MBR (master boot record)
: The first physical sector of the hard disk from which the content is loaded to the main memory and executed by the ☞*BIOS*. This code then loads either the operating system from a hard disk partition or a more sophisticated boot loader, such as ☞*LILO*.

mounting
: This describes the "insertion" of file systems into the directory tree of the system.

MP3
: Very efficient compression procedure for audio files that reduces the size by a factor of ten in contrast to an uncompressed audio file.

multitasking
: Operating systems that can invoke more than one program simultaneously are called multitasking systems.

multiuser
: Enables more than one user to work simultaneously on the same system.

network
: The interconnection of several computers, accomplished normally using ☞*servers* and ☞*clients*.

NFS (Network File System)
: A ☞*protocol* for accessing a ☞*file system* shared over a network.

NIS (Network Information Service)
: A centralized data administration system in networks. User names and passwords can be simultaneously managed network-wide by the NIS.

operating system
: Program that permanently runs in the background on a computer and enables basic system operations.

partition
: Logically-independent section of a hard disk, each possibly containing different file systems. In Windows, also known as "drives".

path

Unique description of a file's position in a file system.

plug and play

Automatic hardware component configuration technology. Resources, such as IRQ and DMA, are configured and managed separately from the system.

process

In Linux, started programs or executable files run as processes, often referred to as tasks. Processes can be controlled by commands like `top` entered in the ☞*shell*.

processor

The processor is the "brain" of every computer, working through and performing commands given by a user or a program in machine language. The processor has control over the entire system and is responsible for the actual performance of the computer.

prompt

See ☞*command line*.

protocol

Standard specifically defined for regulating communication for hardware, software, or networks. There is a multitude of these standards. The most common examples are ☞*HTTP* and ☞*FTP*.

proxy

Most commonly used cache implemented by Internet providers that stores frequently requested contents in a database to allow other machines requesting those pages to load them directly from it. This process not only reduces the time it takes to download this information, but also conserves the available bandwidth.

RAM (Random Access Memory)

See ☞*main memory*.

root

The user undertaking the configuration and maintenance of a complex computer system, such as a network. This system administrator is usu ally the only person who has access to all parts of the system (root permissions).

root directory
The base directory of the ☞*file system* that does not have any parent directory (all other directories have a parent directory). In UNIX, the root directory is represented as a '/'.

SCSI (Small Computer Systems Interface)
Hard disk standard implemented in servers and other high-level machines because of its high-speed performance. See ☞*server*.

server
A server is usually a rather powerful computer that offers services, such as HTTP, DNS, and FTP, or data to other machines connected via a network. There are also programs called servers, like the ☞*X server*.

shell
An especially flexible command line often equipped with its own specific programming language. Examples of shells are Bash, sh, and tcsh.

SMTP (Simple Mail Transfer Protocol)
☞*Protocol* for transferring ☞*e-mails*.

SSL (Secure Socket Layer)
Encryption procedure for transferring ☞*HTTP* data.

superuser
See ☞*root*.

system administrator
See ☞*root*

task
See ☞*process*.

TCP/IP
Internet communication protocol finding increased use in local networks, known as "intranets".

telnet
Telnet is the ☞*protocol* and command for communicating with other hosts. Normally, the user only sees telnet as a means for logging into a remote system.

terminal
Previously, a keyboard and monitor combination connected to a central computer. This combination, when connected to a multiuser machine,

does not have its own computing power. This term is also used to describe programs that emulate an actual terminal.

UNIX
UNIX is an operating system that is widely distributed, above all on workstations in networks. Since the beginning of the 1990s, there has been a freely available version for PCs: Linux.

URL (Uniform Resource Locator)
Unique Internet address that contains the type (e.g., `http://`) and the name of the host (e.g., `www.suse.de`).

user account
See ☞*access permissions.*

user directory
See ☞*home directory.*

VESA (Video Electronics Standard Association)
Industrial consortium that defines, among other things, important video standards.

wild cards
Placeholder for one (symbol: `'?'`) or more (symbol: `'*'`) unknown characters, most often used in commands (especially search commands).

window manager
A window manager is the layer that interacts between the ☞*X Window System* and the user. It is responsible, among other things, for your desktop display. There is a wide variety of window managers available, one of the more popular ones being kwm for ☞*KDE.*

WWW (World Wide Web)
Based on the ☞*HTTP* protocol, this is a hyperlinked collection of documents, files, and images that can be viewed with a web browser.

X11
See ☞*X Window System.*

X Window System
The X Window System is the standard for graphical interfaces in Linux. It is simply the middle layer between the hardware and the ☞*window manager*, such as KDE or GNOME.

YP
See ☞*NIS.*

Index

D